Teaching Shakespeare Today

Teaching Shakespeare Today

Practical Approaches and Productive Strategies

Edited by

James E. Davis
Ohio University

Ronald E. Salomone
Ohio University–Chillicothe

National Council of Teachers of English
1111 W. Kenyon Road, Urbana, Illinois 61801-1096

We wish to express our gratitude to Hazel and Ann, whose assistance and support made this book possible. And we especially wish to thank our research assistant, Jacquelyn S. Johnson, for her exceptional work through-out the entire project.

NCTE Editorial Board: Keith Gilyard, Ronald Jobe, Joyce Kinkead, Louise W. Phelps, Charles Suhor, chair, *ex officio*, Michael Spooner, *ex officio*

Manuscript Editor: Michael E. Himick

Staff Editor: Marlo Welshons

Cover Design: Barbara Yale-Read

Interior Book Design: Doug Burnett

NCTE Stock Number 52961-3050

Library of Congress Cataloging-in-Publication Data

Teaching Shakespeare today : practical approaches and productive
    strategies / edited by James E. Davis, Ronald E. Salomone.
        p.   cm.
    Includes bibliographical references.
    ISBN 0-8141-5296-1
    1. Shakespeare, William, 1564–1616—Study and teaching.   2. Drama—
Study and teaching—United States.   3. Drama in education.
I. Davis, James E., 1934–.   II. Salomone, Ronald E., 1945–.
PR2987.T37   1993   92-41813
822.3'3—dc20   CIP

This book is dedicated to
  our great teachers:

Donald W. Baker, Owen Duston,
  Merritt E. Lawlis, Donald J. Gray
                                    RES

John Long, W. P. Covington III,
  James McConkey, Dwight Burton
                                    JED

Contents

Preface

At many levels in our public schools, the popularity of teaching Shakespeare has increased during the last decade or two. From the tentative and puzzling introduction of a Shakespeare play at the middle school through the challenge of generating a receptive attitude during Shakespeare's slot on the undergraduate English survey syllabus, instructors and students in thousands of classrooms across the country confront the playwright yearly. At the secondary level, school boards, perhaps without even knowing exactly why, encourage a complete unit on Shakespeare at the same time that they compress, say, modern British and American fiction and poetry into a single unit. Likewise, college curriculum committees design full-term courses on Shakespeare's comedies, tragedies, and histories at the same time that they list a single course in "American Literature since the Civil War." For whatever reasons, Ben Jonson's comment on Shakespearee—that he was "not for an age, but for all time"—continues to prove true.

The average public school curriculum will expose students to an occasional reading of Shakespeare—usually *Romeo and Juliet* or *Macbeth*, followed closely by *Julius Caesar, Hamlet, The Merchant of Venice*, and *A Midsummer Night's Dream*. During the first and second years of college, Shakespeare appears more frequently, often as part of a general survey. Typically, not until the third year (or 300 level) does intensive and thorough study of Shakespeare begin. At this point, most students have settled on a major, they are mature and fairly capable readers, and the instructors tend to be the "Shakespeareans" in the department—a classroom situation that extends through graduate school.

Such a state of affairs both sets the boundaries of this book and underscores its timeliness. The unfortunate reality is that the overwhelming majority of publications devoted to Shakespeare target these uppermost strata of study. Here one finds virtually countless articles on every conceivable facet of Shakespeareana. But at the lower levels, a genuine need exists for practical and accessible pedagogical commentary to meet the needs of students and instructors struggling with the experience of Shakespeare. Thus we offer this text, written by experienced teachers from across the country as a resource for the teacher attempting to make the encounter of Shakespeare in the classroom an enjoyable and productive experience for today's student.

Our main goal in teaching Shakespeare is to teach him in such a way that our students will want to approach him again and again, either through reading or by attending performances. How to accomplish this goal? That is the question. In many ways, teaching Shakespeare is a great mystery. When we asked them to write about how they teach Shakespeare, our writers—with Hamlet in mind—could have said, "What? Would you pluck out the heart of our mystery?" And we would have answered, "Yes, that's exactly what we're trying to do." We would pluck out the heart of the mystery of teaching Shakespeare in schools and colleges so that the Bard may speak to all of our students. The world that we can open up to them is not only one of logic and reason, but also one of grandeur, magic, and passion.

But where to start? We chose to begin with Samuel Crowl's essay on Shakespeare in the American landscape. Crowl points out how Americans have been appropriating Shakespeare since we began as a nation, how his works influenced the country's founders, and how the plays have historically been a part of American education. Shakespeare speaks, however, in a different manner to each culture and era. Crowl thus offers a number of suggestions for teaching Shakespeare that take students into "uncharted waters and unfamiliar landscapes." He advocates teaching "with curiosity, a touch of bravado, and a healthy sense of play." We agree!

Introduction
Where the Wild Things Are: Shakespeare in the American Landscape

Samuel Crowl
Ohio University

In my work discussing Shakespeare with high school teachers across the country, one of the first questions I am asked is "Why Shakespeare?" A good question, and one frequently asked by students as well. Teachers need to address this issue when launching an individual course or unit of study within a more comprehensive curriculum. If we cannot explain or demonstrate to our students the pleasure, utility, and significance of what we teach, why should we expect them to respect what we do?

For at least the last century, Shakespeare has been at the center of the American high school's literature curriculum. Two recent studies point to *Romeo and Juliet, Huckleberry Finn,* and *To Kill a Mockingbird* as the most widely read works in high schools across the country (Ravitch and Finn 1987; Gallup 1989). In fact, the survey conducted by Diane Ravitch and Chester Finn reported that "students achieved a greater success with the seven Shakespeare questions than with any other cluster in the literature assessment" (97). Ninety percent correctly noted that Romeo and Juliet were hindered by feuding families, and eighty-eight percent correctly identified the first five lines of Hamlet's "To be or not to be" soliloquy. Only five other questions in the history and literature assessments received higher scores. Though the purpose of such surveys often seems more to deplore what our students do not know than to applaud what they do, it is clear that Shakespeare is a prominent component of American cultural literacy.

As anyone who has lived through the Bennett, Bloom, and Hirsch years knows, America does not feature a common high school curriculum. For some this is the blessing of a multicultural society; for others it is the curse of pluralism. But from the advent of the McGuffey

Readers in the mid-nineteenth century to the revision of the canon at the end of the twentieth, Shakespeare has been the one constant fixture in the American high school's English curriculum. In this essay, I would like to try to answer the question "Why Shakespeare?" by providing some of the context for his surprising assimilation into our national culture. I also want to suggest how we might keep alive the dynamics which distinguish that historical assimilation in our current teaching of his plays.

I

By most accounts, Shakespeare entered the national secondary school curriculum through piecemeal inclusion in the McGuffey Readers, though he undoubtedly entered the common culture years before. In his remarkably prescient *Democracy in America* (1842), Tocqueville reports that he discovered that "deep into the recesses of the forests of the New World there is hardly a pioneer's hut that does not contain a few odd volumes of Shakespeare," and that he first read *Henry V* in just such a setting (1966, 2:55).

Gary Taylor, in his recent *Reinventing Shakespeare*, reports that by 1886 Shakespeare had come to completely dominate the top-ten list of works most frequently read in American high schools. *The Merchant of Venice* and *Julius Caesar* were ranked one and two, *Macbeth* sixth, *Hamlet* eighth, and *As You Like It* tenth (Taylor 1991, 204). As most high school English teachers will immediately recognize, this list has changed only slightly in the past century. Although *Romeo and Juliet* goes to the head of the current list, *Julius Caesar, Macbeth,* and *Hamlet* are still among the most frequently taught of Shakespeare's plays. My guess is that *The Merchant of Venice* disappeared after World War II as its anti-Semitism became too painful to explain or contain. Other examples of Shakespeare's comedies also dropped out, generally because teachers thought—mistakenly, I believe—that their conventions were too distant to make fresh and immediate for a modern teenage audience.

If Shakespeare has been a central fixture in our formal high school curricula this century, he has had an even longer impact on the development of our culture. He dreamed our discovery and early colonization in *The Tempest,* which contains echoes of material published in the Bermuda pamphlets detailing the troubles of early attempts to found the Virginia colonies. And his final play, *Henry VIII,* contains a moving prophecy by Thomas Cranmer, Archbishop of Canterbury, as he baptizes Henry VIII's infant daughter Elizabeth, future queen.

Cranmer concludes this prophecy by evoking Elizabeth's successor, James I, and the creation of "new nations" (also the beginnings of British imperialism) under his reign:

> Nor shall this peace sleep with her; but, as when
> The bird of wonder dies, the maiden phoenix,
> Her ashes new create another heir
> As great in admiration as herself,
> So shall she leave her blessedness to one
> When heaven shall call her from this cloud of darkness
> Who from the sacred ashes of her honour
> Shall star-like rise, as great in fame as she was,
> And so stand fix'd. Peace, plenty, love, truth, terror,
> That were the servants to this chosen infant,
> Shall then be his, and like a vine grow to him;
> Wherever the bright sun of heaven shall shine,
> His honour and the greatness of his name
> Shall be, and make new nations. He shall flourish
> And like a mountain cedar, reach his branches
> To all the plains about him; our children's children
> Shall see this, and bless heaven.
>
> (V.iv.39–55)

Perhaps it is only fitting that the leaders—particularly Washington, Jefferson, and Adams—of one of those "new nations" turned out to be Shakespeare enthusiasts. Jefferson kept a commonplace book when he was a student at William and Mary, and the first six quotations he recorded in it are from Shakespeare, including, interestingly, quotations from Caesar and Falstaff that directly contradict one another on the nature of cowardice. Jefferson's remarkably complex intelligence was apparently drawn toward absorbing conflicting ideas, a trait much at the heart of Shakespeare's own genius. Perhaps Jefferson's interest in *Julius Caesar* and its linkage to ideas of revolution was spurred when, at the age of twenty-two, he heard Patrick Henry deliver one of his attacks on the Stamp Act. As Henry pounded home his argument —"Caesar had his Brutus, Charles I his Cromwell, and George III . . ."—he was interrupted by the crowd gathered at the doors of the Virginia House of Burgesses with shouts of "Treason! Treason!" at which point he calmly concluded, "may profit by their example" (Malone 1948, 92).

George Washington was drawn to Shakespeare more in the theater than in the study. We know that he attended a performance of John Dryden and William Davenant's adaptation of *The Tempest* in the summer of 1787 while in Philadelphia to participate in the Constitutional Convention. Later, after he was elected president, he sponsored private productions in the original White House, one of the first being *Julius Caesar* (Dunn 1939, 105–6). Perhaps a line can be drawn directly from *Caesar*'s inclusion in Jefferson's commonplace book and its place on Washington's entertainment schedule to its position of prominence in the American high school curriculum over the past two centuries. The resonances Patrick Henry, Jefferson, and Washington all felt in reading Shakespeare's play through their own revolutionary experiences made its themes bend to the American struggle for independence and the founding of the republic.

One of the tenets of contemporary criticism is that all reading, all interpretation, is fluid, everchanging, and subjective. Such criticism argues that not only are all of our attempts to interpret a text doomed to be misreadings, but also that the very texts themselves are in a constant process of fragmentation as they are absorbed by the reader and transformed by each individual act of reading. Texts, for such postmodern critics, are much like Heraclitus's famous river: never to be stepped in twice. I think these are complex, subtle, and potentially perilous critical waters to navigate, even for our most skillful philosophical sailors. But I do believe that our own experiences, as individuals and as participants in a particular culture, draw us toward some works more than others. Few Shakespeareans would place *Julius Caesar* in the front rank of Shakespeare's major plays. Yet for generations of Americans it has served as a mythic paradigm and warning as it depicts the Roman republican ideal being subverted from both the right (Caesar) and the left (Brutus), leading the way not to increased liberty, but to the establishment of Augustus Caesar as the first Roman emperor.

If Shakespeare, particularly in *The Tempest* and *Julius Caesar,* gets assimilated into the American experience by providing dramatic analogues for our own early colonial and revolutionary history, and then accompanies the movement of settlers deep into the recesses of the New World's forest, by the mid-nineteenth century he had become so thoroughly a part of our landscape that he would emerge at the heart of three definitive works of the American imagination: Melville's *Moby Dick* (1851), Emerson's *Representative Men* (1852), and Twain's *Huckleberry Finn* (1885). Melville acknowledged that he sought to build his great American novel on the twin pillars of Shakespeare and the Bible. Ahab and Pip are conceived as a version of King Lear and his Fool, with the great white whale, Moby Dick, conceived as something as huge and terrifying as Lear's tempest. In both instances, the true terror of the external, whether monstrous wind or whale, is the way in which it is internalized by Lear and Ahab. Melville, in reaching to capture what is both dynamic and demonic in the American imagination, responds to the hyperbolic reaches of Shakespeare's vision and learns from him how to transform landscape into psychology—a key component of American myth and culture.

Emerson, in his *Representative Men*, elevates Shakespeare into the exalted company of such figures as Plato, Montaigne, Goethe, and Napoleon and makes him a partner in fashioning his ideas about self-reliance, nature, and the American character. Indeed, by 1885 Shakespeare had become such a fixture in our national culture that he could pop up literally right smack in the middle of the novel regarded as America's signature work: Mark Twain's *Huckleberry Finn*. Melville and Emerson so successfully enshrined Shakespeare as a key element in our high culture that Twain, with his sly folksy American vernacular style, was able to make Shakespeare—and the high culture he represents—yield to the subversive nature of his humor. The King and the Duke are at once both America's greatest con artists *and* Shakespeareans, and Twain places their hilarious pastiche of lines from *Hamlet, Macbeth,* and *Romeo and Juliet* at the precise center of his novel. In a novel that is merciless, and mercilessly funny, in subverting American society's notions of respectability and civilized behavior, the subversion of Shakespeare is awarded the place of prominence.

America has been appropriating Shakespeare and remaking him in our image and to our purposes from our very beginnings as a nation (Bristol 1990). It should come as no surprise then that Shakespeare should be found at the heart of our greatest, and most defining, work of the imagination. Twain's ability to parody Shakespeare, to see his potential for subversive American humor, is in itself an act of revolution and decolonization. Nevertheless, Shakespeare proved resilient enough to survive Twain's lampooning. So he has proved equally resilient to the transforming powers of the twentieth-century art form most closely allied with America: film.

II

Shakespeare's American legacy has always been twofold: as an author to be absorbed in the study (or classroom) for the moral or didactic revelations of his art and as a playwright to be enjoyed in the theater (or movie house) for the spectacle and passion his plays release in performance. Moreover, the popular outline of Shakespeare's biography has had a deep resonance with the American imagination. In essence, Shakespeare's life is a version of the Horatio Alger myth, in which a young man of modest education and means ventures from country market town to major metropolis to seek his fame and fortune. When both are secured through the labors of his unique talent, he returns home to buy and refurbish the biggest house in town and live out the remainder of his life supported by the investments of his theatrical profits.

American tourists (joined by hundreds of thousands from around the world, particularly from Japan and Germany) flock to Stratford each year as if it were Mecca or Lourdes. Many have never seen Shakespeare performed, and most do not even linger to take in a production by the Royal Shakespeare Company, but they are nevertheless moved to experience something of what they imagine to have been his landscape. This tradition long predates our consumer society; clever Stratford merchants have been cashing in on their most famous son for centuries.

A wonderful example of American tourist curiosity, coupled with Stratfordian market ingenuity, can be found in John Adams's diary account of a trip he and Thomas Jefferson made to Shakespeare's birthplace in April of 1786:

> Stratford Upon Avon is interesting, as it is the scene of the birth, death, and sepulchre of Shakespeare. Three doors from the inn is the house where he was born, as small and mean as you can conceive. They showed us an old wooden chair in the chimney corner where he sat. We cut off a chip according to custom. A Mulberry tree that he planted has been cut down and is carefully preserved for sale. The house where he died has been taken down, and the spot is now only a yard or garden. The curse upon him who should remove his bones which is written on his gravestone (Good Friend for Jesus sake forbear / To digg the dust enclosed here / Blessed be he that spares these stones / And curst be he that moves my bones) alludes to a pile of some thousands of human bones which lie exposed in that church. There is nothing preserved of this great genius which is worth knowing; nothing which might inform us what education, what company, what accident, turned his mind to letters and the drama. His name is not even on his gravestone. An ill sculptured head is set up by his wife, by the side of the grave in the church. But paintings and sculpture would be thrown away on his fame. His wit, his fancy, his taste and judgment, his knowledge of nature, of life and character, are immortal. (Adams 1971, 3:394)

What a splendid sight! How many chairs had already been whittled away, how many genuine Shakespearean mulberry trees had already been peddled by those clever Stratford merchants capitalizing on their most famous citizen. One can almost see Adams mulling over how to get that "carefully preserved" tree back at least to London, if not across the Atlantic.

Yet the Shakespeare flow across the Atlantic has typically operated in both directions. Indeed, the American assimilation of Shakespeare has always been distinguished by our willingness to experiment and take chances with him, particularly in performance. The American assimilation of Shakespeare onto film would prove no different.

The rise of film as the popular art form of the twentieth-century bears a strong resemblance to the power and popularity of the rediscovery and reinvention of the theater in Renaissance London. While scholars continue to debate precisely how extended the social strata of Shakespeare's audience were, no one doubts that the theaters constructed on the South Bank of the Thames drew an eager audience hungry for such entertainment. We know theaters like the Globe were large, holding between twenty-five hundred and three thousand spectators, and that admission could be gained for as little as a penny. Recent excavations of the foundations of the Rose and the Globe on London's South Bank have confirmed many of the modern speculations about the size and structure of such theaters. The floor of the Rose, where the penny-ticket purchasers stood to watch the performance, was even found to be littered with hazelnut shells evidently cracked and discarded by the spectators.

The immediate popularity of both Renaissance theater and twentieth-century cinema meant that raw material needed to be raided in order to be transformed according to the demands of the new medium. Shakespeare and his contemporaries plundered every available source for plots and materials to be reshaped for the stage. In Shakespeare's case, such sources included, most prominently, both Hall's and Holinshed's chronicles of English history, North's translation of Plutarch's *Lives* (which gave him access to Roman history), Ovid's *Metamorphoses*, Italian tales and English pastoral romances, as well as earlier plays. Film faced a similar need for stories to be translated onto the screen. Not surprisingly, Shakespeare was one of the first places it turned to for material. Robert Hamilton Ball (1968) has catalogued over four hundred instances of Shakespeare as a source for silent films alone, and Kenneth Rothwell and Annabelle Melzer (1990) have just released their monumental listing and description of film and video adaptations of Shakespeare, with 747 entries all told.

The first American sound film of Shakespeare, *The Taming of the Shrew* (1929) with Douglas Fairbanks and Mary Pickford, is acknowledged less for its achievements than for the wonderful chutzpah of a credit line that reads, "By William Shakespeare with additional dialogue by Sam Taylor." Fairbanks and Pickford were the reigning Hollywood stars of their day; it was only appropriate that they would seize upon Shakespeare's *Shrew* as an ideal vehicle, much as Elizabeth Taylor and Richard Burton did forty years later when they made their film version of the play.

Hollywood's second attempt to absorb Shakespeare was far more successful, when in 1935 Warner Brothers produced a version of *A Midsummer Night's Dream,* directed by Max Reinhardt and William Dieterle with a cast loaded with familiar stars from the Warner Studios, including Jimmy Cagney, Dick Powell, Mickey Rooney, Olivia de Havilland, Joe E. Brown, Victor Jory, and Anita Louise. While some elements of Shakespeare's tale—particularly the night's confusion for Bottom and the four young lovers—fail to come alive, Reinhardt and Deiterle are masterful in their creation of the forest world, the broad comedy of the rude mechanicals, and the special effects which accompany Oberon and Titania's appearances, effects that anticipate work later associated with the genius of Walt Disney. As a result, the Warner Brothers *Dream* is the only Shakespeare film of the 1930s that reaches toward finding a visual style that resonates with the rich and suggestive imagery of Shakespeare's poetry.[1]

Shakespeare's full assimilation into film was the result of both English and American productions; it was particularly the result of the films that both Laurence Olivier and Orson Welles made between 1944 and 1965. Olivier's great achievement was to demonstrate that, properly spoken and understood, Shakespeare's language was not fatally incompatible with film. Appropriately, it was the American, Orson Welles, whose visual and technical imagination allowed the camera to become the key ingredient in translating Shakespeare's verbal images and psychological dynamics into moving fragments and images. Welles's work is bolder and more daring than Olivier's, though not always as successful. Again, as an American, Welles was able to take chances with Shakespeare available only to someone outside of Shakespeare's own culture and its theatrical legacy, as transmitted from Burbage to Garrick to Kean to Irving to Olivier.

Welles's great contribution to the Americanization of Shakespeare came primarily through his film productions of *Macbeth* (1948), *Othello* (1952), and *Chimes at Midnight* (1965).[2] But his stage productions in New York City during the mid-1930s—first for the Federal Theater

Project and then for his own Mercury Theater Company—were equally startling in their departure from performance tradition. Arguably the most famous American Shakespeare production of our century was Welles's *Macbeth* (1935), set in Haiti with an all-black cast. The production galvanized so much interest and acclaim—the streets surrounding the Lafayette Theater in Harlem were packed with ten thousand people on opening night—that it not only played to full houses during its New York run, but toured the country as well. Welles was a risk-taker, and when his risks worked, as with this *Macbeth,* the results tapped new energies and possibilities both within Shakespeare and American culture.

Several years later, Welles staged a production of *Julius Caesar* (1937), setting the play in contemporary fascist Italy and thus releasing its ability to speak across the centuries to a modern political context. For some, Welles's work, on stage and in film, placed him closer to the tradition of Twain's King and Duke than to the more conventional work of his English counterparts, Olivier and Gielgud. But he was working in a tradition where Shakespeare is not always treated with reverence. As a culture, we have been freer to play with Shakespeare, to experiment with him, to try to adapt him to new landscapes, than our English counterparts, who must always cast one eye on tradition even as they experiment with innovative approaches.

III

If the American cultural assimilation of Shakespeare has been characterized by invention and innovation, can a similar pattern be seen in our treatment of Shakespeare in the classroom? I believe, at least based on recent history, that the answer is *Yes.* American academics have taken the lead in the past twenty years in championing a performance approach to teaching Shakespeare. The work of critics like Miriam Gilbert (1984), H. R. Coursen (1988), and Jay Halio (1977) has had a great impact not only on the teaching of Shakespeare in our colleges and universities, but in our high schools as well. All three have published widely on performance issues in criticism and teaching, and all have led successful summer seminars for college and high school teachers in teaching Shakespeare through performance. Coursen's seminars use film and video productions as a focus; Gilbert and Halio lead their seminars in Stratford-upon-Avon using the resources of the Royal Shakespeare Company and the Shakespeare Centre. Performance approaches have gained recognition elsewhere too. A special issue of the *Shakespeare Quarterly* (1984, issue five) devoted to essays on teaching Shakespeare was dominated by articles describing the many virtues (and some of the vices) of teaching Shakespeare through performance. That collection highlighted a movement that has been under way since the late 1960s, when younger scholars and teachers began to move beyond the tenets of the New Criticism in their approach to Shakespeare's plays.

Performance approaches liberated Shakespeare from the page and reunited his language with action and gesture. Shakespeare's richly imagistic language remains the chief hurdle for students raised in an anti-rhetorical culture, a culture in which we are accustomed to a dense succession of rapidly changing visual images (witness MTV or any television ad), but not verbal ones. Students need to realize firsthand that Shakespeare wrote for the ear and that the dynamics of his iambic pentameter line are meant to fit the natural rhythms of spoken English. They need to understand that Shakespeare is meant to be played with, by the voice as well as the body. Cicely Berry, the noted voice teacher for the Royal Shakespeare Company, has a number of warm-up exercises that she uses with actors but which can be adapted for use by novice students as well. For example, getting students to chant or shout or whisper a speech in unison can begin to acquaint them with the sound and rhythm of Shakespeare's language. It can also help to break down their natural self-consciousness when speaking the text. A second step might be to ask students to say the same speech, with each student simply uttering one word and then passing that word, like a baton in a relay race, on to the next student, who speaks the next word, and so on around the room. From individual words one can move to alternating entire lines. The issue here is getting students comfortable with the language, getting them to hear and seize upon its possibilities for inventive play long before they begin the search for meaning.

This process will not be an immediate success, as students are rarely asked to respond to the expressive qualities of the literature they study. But I believe that over several class periods it will begin to allay their fears about having fun with a cultural icon. Students should understand that such approaches have long characterized the Americanization of Shakespeare, as the early sections of this essay have tried to demonstrate. If the students have read *Huckleberry Finn*, this might be a time to reintroduce Twain's pastiche-parody of Hamlet's "To be or not to be" solioquy and give it the same verbal treatment they have been using on Shakespeare. And if a particular class seems to respond eagerly to this exercise, I recommend that you cut them loose in developing a rapid-fire condensed version of the play you are studying. The English playwright Tom Stoppard, best known for his *Rosencrantz and Guildenstern Are Dead*, has also written a wonderfully funny fifteen-minute version of *Hamlet* that you might wish to use as a model. All the lines are lifted from Shakespeare, but they are piled on top of one another in such a dizzying fashion that the action resembles a film played at fast-forward speed.

I think an important step between group work with Shakespeare's language and getting students on their feet and at work on a specific scene from a play is to ask each student to memorize a speech of at least ten lines. Once again, catching the language up from the page and turning it around on the tongue can, for some students, be the key to unlocking the barriers to that language as it lies dense and inert in the text. Many high schools, having made great strides in their efforts in teaching writing over the past decade, are now recognizing the importance of creating more opportunities for their students to build confidence and ability in public speaking as well. Asking each member of the class to recite ten lines from memory and to briefly describe why they chose those lines or what difficulties or discoveries they encountered in the experience will again draw their attention to the special qualities in a language written to be spoken. As Miriam Gilbert (1984) has pointed out, "the anxiety (even panic) created by actually having to speak the line works for both professional actor and student performer; there is a real *need* to know what those words mean, and so students take the trouble to find out" (603).

Another step along the way to using a full-fledged performance approach, one which asks students to exercise their visual as well as verbal imaginations, is to challenge them to use or describe the use of a particular prop in a specific scene. In each case, the students should be asked to explain how the prop could be used to reveal some element of the scene latent in its language. In some instances, the prop might be one called for by Shakespeare: Macbeth's bloody daggers, Yorick's skull, the masks worn by Romeo, Mercutio, and Benvolio at Capulet's ball. In others, the prop might be one supplied by the teacher. What if Rosencrantz or Guildenstern should be carrying a basketball when they try to pluck out the heart of Hamlet's mystery in II.ii? How might it be used as the three pass around limp undergraduate witticisms about the nature of fortune? And how might Hamlet seize and redefine such a prop as he launches into his "What a piece of work is a man" speech? How might the dynamics of the Nurse's exchange with Mercutio, Benvolio, and Romeo in II.iv be heightened if she were carrying an umbrella and were quite prepared to use it to parry their aggression? How might the Porter in *Macbeth*, when he enters at the sound of Macduff's knocking, make effective use of a large flashlight to illuminate his metaphoric suggestion that he is opening Hell's gates and introducing us to Macbeth's dark and murky world?

In classrooms where a hands-on performance approach does not seem congenial, many teachers have taken great strides in the past decade to incorporate film and video productions into their teaching of Shakespeare. I do not believe such productions are wisely used simply as an opportunity for students to passively view one version of a Shakespeare play. I find many of the BBC video productions deadly, and if used only as an alternative to several hours of class interaction about the play, they will more likely bury Shakespeare than praise him. Nevertheless, as I argued in an earlier article on this topic, one can turn the experience of viewing a film version such as Zeffirelli's *Romeo and Juliet* or Polanski's *Macbeth* into an active classroom exchange by having students pool their communal observations and descriptions of what they have seen (Crowl 1976). Here their experience as members of a culture dominated by film and television works to an advantage, as they often prove more willing and more perceptive readers of visual images than of verbal ones. I find that if you divide the class into several groups, each responsible for providing details on an aspect of the production—camera work, decor and landscape, costumes, music, major textual excisions or reorderings, and acting—that you will discover a wealth of details in their responses. Those production details can then become the basis for a concrete discussion of the play's images, characters, and themes.

It can be even more enlightening to expose students to a pair of productions of the same play. I recommend contrasting the Warner Brothers 1935 *A Midsummer Night's Dream* with Peter Hall's 1968 version of same play. Laurence Olivier's *Henry V* takes a very different interpretive angle on the play than does Kenneth Branagh's 1989 film. And Tony Richardson's 1969 version of *Hamlet* with Nicol Williamson stands in constructive contrast with either Olivier's 1948 *Hamlet* or Franco Zeffirelli's 1990 film starring Mel Gibson and Glenn Close. In each instance, students will quickly grasp that productions are as much versions, or interpretations, of the play as are the critical analyses that fill the Shakespeare shelves in our libraries. Each production responds to and highlights different themes and values and issues embodied in the text.

Shakespeare, like any protean artist, speaks in a different manner to each culture and era. Those of us fortunate enough to have spent a lifetime reading and writing and talking about his plays with others find that our responses to individual works shift and change with the times and our own growth and development. Studying film and video productions of Shakespeare can allow students to see that when Shakespeare's text is dramatized, caught up from the page and translated into action and gesture and sound by the actor's art and director's design, it becomes open and fluid and plastic. The text comes to life in the interaction of actor and audience. Actors are acutely aware when a given audience is transfixed by a performance, when its energy creates a dynamic tension with that of the actors, just as they are equally aware of audiences whose members sit like lumps passively letting the performance wash over them.

Similar experiences exist for each individual act of reading a text. Readers know the difference between those moments when one's mind and imagination are actively engaged by a text and those other, often wearying, experiences when one's mind fails to make active connections with the page and what one reads is reduced to "words, words, words." Employing a variety of performance approaches to Shakespeare, approaches which depend upon making students participate in the process, may thus make them more active and engaged readers.

I think it is important for our students not only to be aware of how and why Shakespeare has become such a significant part of the American landscape, but to imagine him within our current culture as well. Many popular American films have appropriated Shakespeare for his plots, if not his language, much in the same manner Shakespeare raided his own sources. *Forbidden Planet* (1956) is a science fiction version of *The Tempest*. *Joe Macbeth* (1955) moves *Macbeth* into Chicago's gangster world. Paul Mazursky's *Harry and Tonto* (1974), starring Art Carney, is a gentle reimagining of elements of *King Lear.* And Mazursky's *The Tempest* (1982) creates a modern version of Prospero, this time a burned-out modern architect who goes into self-exile on a Greek island accompanied by his daughter, Miranda, played by Molly Ringwald in her first film role. Howard Hawk's *Bringing Up Baby* (1938) and Woody Allen's *A Midsummer Night's Sex Comedy* (1982) are both brilliant rhapsodies on a series of Shakespeare's comic themes. And the very recent *Men of Respect* (1991) revisits *Macbeth* from the perspective of *The Godfather.*

I would encourage high school students to imagine and defend their choices for American settings for the Shakespeare plays they read. Determining a particular historical moment and geographical landscape in which to set a play provides students with a familiar context for making suggestions about assimilating props, costumes, and action into a specific locale. Asking them to cast the plays with television, film, and stage actors with whom they are familiar also begins to stimulate their visual imaginations; suddenly Shakespeare's words are conceived as flowing from a specific voice and body.

These suggestions—from working with Shakespeare's *spoken* language, to imagining how props and settings can help to localize and define a possible context for the play's action, to viewing and discussing film and video productions of the plays—all aim at making students become more actively engaged with Shakespeare's various worlds. The American approach to Shakespare has never been to regard him as, in Hamlet's words, "weary, stale, flat, and unprofitable," but to greet him with Miranda's innocent enthusiasm: "O Brave new world / That has such people in it!" In our teaching, we need to keep alive that long-standing American tradition of treating Shakespeare less as a classical relic than as a fellow pioneer in exploring the mysteries of individual psychologies and social dynamics.

One of the enduring works of contemporary American culture is Maurice Sendak's *Where the Wild Things Are*. Like all great works of the imagination, it invites us to journey into alien territory where we encounter the fears and fantasies of our dreams and nightmares. Shakespeare's plays—particularly frequently taught works such as *A Midsummer Night's Dream, Romeo and Juliet,* and *Macbeth*—invite us to take a similar journey into uncharted waters and unfamiliar landscapes. We must engage those worlds and the wild things they contain in much the same manner as Sendak's young hero Max does: with curiosity, a touch of bravado, and a healthy sense of play.

Notes

1. The Hollywood of the 1930s produced a string of sophisticated comedies, like *The Philadelphia Story, The Lady Eve,* and *Bringing Up Baby,* that contain themes and patterns very reminiscent of Shakespeare's festive comedies. Stanley Cavell, the Harvard philosopher, has written a wonderful book on these films, *Pursuits of Happiness: The Hollywood Comedy of Remarriage* (Cambridge: Harvard University Press, 1981), that details their Shakespearean resonances while managing to be a witty and elegant exploration of marriage as well.

2. Welles was also an early leader in bringing American films out from the Hollywood studios, which dominated the medium from the 1920s to the 1950s, and into the international arena. His films of *Othello* and *Chimes at Midnight* were both shot on location in Europe and Northern Africa and featured actors from America, Ireland, Canada, England, Italy, and Spain. One of the unintentional but delightful rewards of such international casting occurs in *Chimes at Midnight,* where the great French actress Jeanne Moreau, playing Doll Tearsheet, finds herself perched on Welles's (playing Falstaff) gigantic lap while purring into his ear, "Thou whoreson round man . . .": her "whoreson" emerges with a distinct Gallic flavor as "Orson."

References

Adams, John. 1971. *The Works of John Adams.* Vol. 3. New York: AMS Press.

Ball, Robert Hamilton. 1968. *Shakespeare on Silent Film: A Strange Eventful History.* London: George Allen and Unwin.

Bristol, Michael D. 1990. *Shakespeare's America, America's Shakespeare.* London: Routledge.

Bulman, J. C., and H. R. Coursen. 1988. *Shakespeare on Television: An Anthology of Essays and Reviews.* Hanover, NH: University Press of New England.

Crowl, Samuel. 1976. "The Arm'd Rhinoceros and Other Creatures: Shakespeare's Language and the Reluctant Reader." *Focus* 2: 19–25.

Dunn, Esther Cloudman. 1939. *Shakespeare in America.* New York: Macmillan.

Gallup Organization. 1989. *A Survey of College Seniors.* A poll conducted for the National Endowment for the Humanities.

Gilbert, Miriam. 1984. "Teaching Shakespeare Through Performance." *Shakespeare Quarterly* 35: 601–8.

Halio, Jay. 1977. "This Wide and Universal Stage: Shakespeare's Plays as Plays." In *Teaching Shakespeare,* edited by Walter Edens. Princeton, NJ: Princeton University Press.

Malone, Dumas. 1948. *Jefferson the Virginian.* Boston: Little, Brown, and Company.

Ravitch, Diane, and Chester E. Finn, Jr. 1987. *What Do Our 17-Year-Olds Know?* New York: Harper and Row.

Rothwell, Kenneth S., and Annabelle Melzer. 1990. *Shakespeare on Screen: An International Filmography and Videography.* New York: Neal-Shuman Publishers.

Shakespeare, William. 1974. *The Riverside Shakespeare.* Edited by G. Blakemore Evans. Boston: Houghton Mifflin.

Taylor, Gary. 1991. *Reinventing Shakespeare: A Cultural History, from the Restoration to the Present.* Oxford: Oxford University Press. Weidenfeld and Nicolson edition published 1989.

Tocqueville, Alexis de. 1966. *Democracy in America.* 2 vols. New York: Alfred A. Knopf.

I Approaches (Critical and Otherwise) to Teaching Shakespeare

1 Some "Basics" in Shakespearean Study

Gladys V. Veidemanis
Oshkosh Area Public Schools, Oshkosh, Wisconsin

Come Shakespeare time in the curriculum, Ms. Frantica, the department enthusiast, charges into the arena determined that no challenge be evaded. Her notion of what is basic is everything: Shakespeare's life, the history of the times, literary criticism, Renaissance thought, sources of plot, versification, production history, numberless writing tasks, and independent projects as well. Unfortunately, the Franticas of the profession never know where to stop, and as they slowly expire under the burden of all that must be accomplished, students sink deeper into stupor and other manifestations of "overkill."

Mr. Relevance's primary goal is instant rapport. Consequently, any tactic guaranteed to bridge the four-century culture gap and dissolve resistance to a difficult and alien text passes "go." "Relate, kids, groove!" is the charge. "This chick's boyfriend ain't acceptable to her old man. Should she stick by him or give him the shove? Read *Romeo and Juliet* to see what happens." Or, "This dude's woman thinks he oughta knock off the Boss, and she's willin' to help. But he's startin' to chicken out. Read *Macbeth* for the inside scoop." Mr. Relevance always gets off to a jazzy start, but the letdown is usually jolting once students discover themselves back in the dialect and society of Elizabethan and Jacobean England.

Ye Olde Gradgrind is as misguided at the other extreme, engrossed in pedantry and nitpicking: "Identify three oxymorons. Parse the second soliloquy. Paraphrase lines 100 to 310." Gradgrind busyworks students to death and unwittingly buries Shakespeare in the process.

The Media Slob, wanting to avoid teaching, wheels in the AV cart, covers the windows, and justifies continuous viewing in the name of visual literacy. In the study of *Romeo and Juliet*, for example, the Media Slob may use a filmstrip on Shakespearean theater, the complete recording of the play, the Zeffirelli film, and the BBC videotape all in the same unit. As might be expected, students sit stupefied after four weeks in a dark room, only to be told they will now view *West Side Story*.

The Frustrated Barrymore is generally a sincere and enthusiastic sort, persuaded that a play comes to life only when performed. But he cannot resist arrogating all the action to himself. Actor, director, and producer in one, our reincarnated Thespis struts the classroom boards in solo glory, gesture and delivery a wonder to behold. But even the most energetic performance inevitably palls when students are made to be constantly passive and adoring.

Of course, extreme types like these are laughable. Yet the effective teacher of Shakespeare is most likely a combination of all the persons here mockingly profiled: possessed of the zeal of a Frantica, the scholarship of a Gradgrind, the dramatic flair of a Frustrated Barrymore, the sense of immediacy of a Mr. Relevance, and an enthusiasm for media tastefully employed. Needed in addition, however, given the overcrowded curriculum and frequently disrupted routine, is a clear sense of teaching priorities and pacing to give direction to classroom study and discussion.

Absolutely "basic" is the language of the play: the vocabulary in context, metaphors, recurrent images and motifs, and a sense of spoken emphasis, tone, and pace. Comprehension of the language, in turn, enables analysis of four essential elements of the work: plot (including handling of time), character, structure, and theme. This analysis can be enhanced by the use of records, scenes on video or film, oral reading or enactment of selected scenes, and, when possible, field trips to live productions. Meanwhile, as appropriate—and often "incidentally on purpose"—a great deal of "decent erudition" can be passed on about plot sources, Shakespeare's theater and life, the Renaissance world view, and critical perspectives on the play. Research papers, independent study, and time-consuming projects such as theater construction, dramatic production, and costume design belong in the realm of "above and beyond": all worthwhile activities, but to be done only as time and student ability permit.

Reading Shakespeare is not easy for students of the nineties; nor was it easy for those of previous decades. Many teachers are thus justifiably concerned about getting a class "ready" to read a play. Some have even resorted to workbook-type exercises aimed at developing the kinds of reading skills a Shakespearean work demands. But vocabulary and comprehension exercises done in isolation quickly become deadly. A person learns to read Shakespeare only by coming to grips with the text at hand.

This is not to say that a few reading pointers are not of value. For one thing, students are helped by having wide exposure to poetry *before* they deal with a Shakespearean play. They need to be reminded of such fundamental matters as reading to the period instead of pausing at the end of every line and paying attention to repeated lines and images. Students need the most help with determining metaphoric equivalents. Just what does Shakespeare mean by referring to a person as a "waterfly"? Or by talking about the need for a balance of "blood" and "judgment"? Typing up short passages rich in metaphor and asking students to do oral or written paraphrases before tackling an act as a whole is one way of anticipating and preventing reading problems.

For that matter, selective paraphrasing, though not a technique to be overused, must be regarded as "basic" in Shakespearean study to clear up thorny comprehension problems. Wallace Bacon of Northwestern University tells the story of a student who paraphrased Iago's statement "your daughter and the Moor are now making the beast with two backs" as "Othello and Desdemona are now riding out of the city on a camel." He concludes, "Not only did this young man's picture of Venice seem odd for *any* century, but he seemed to me to need some instruction in human relations" (Bacon 1973). Similarly, asked to paraphrase the lines

> Then senseless Ilium,
> Seeming to feel this blow, with flaming top
> Stoops to his base, and with a hideous crash
> Takes prisoner Pyrrhus' ear

from the Player's recitation in Act II of *Hamlet*, literal-minded students invariably miss the metaphor and erroneously conclude that Pyrrhus's ear has been cut off during the heat of battle. No doubt every English teacher could supply comparable examples of gross distortion of the text as further evidence that the teacher's starting place has to be close and careful study of the words on the page, with reading problems handled at the time of encounter.

But what text should students read? Every year new advocates of a "simplified Shakespeare" surface, along with "Shakespeare Made Easy" texts. Led by scholars of the eminence of J. R. Rouse, such advocates argue the desirability of a "minimal" translation to simplify complex exposition, dense stylization, and obscure wording. Granted, the notes and critical apparatus of a scholarly edition of the plays can seem overwhelming and distasteful to the beginning reader, and a simplified text could possibly facilitate more immediate accessibility.

But as a close analysis of any "simplified" text reveals, even a "minimal" translation is likely to result in

- Distortion of meaning
- Destruction of the original meter and metaphor
- Elimination of significant imagery
- Removal of important connotative meanings
- Needless rewriting of lines most readers should be able to understand
- A warped sense of the distinctive speaking styles of the various characters

In short, what is destroyed is the *poetry*, and thereby the essence of Shakespeare. No competent teacher expects students to understand every word and allusion in a play, but the text to use is a reputable edition of the one Shakespeare gave us.

In our devotion to the written word, however, we must not ignore the spoken dimension, a fault to which many English teachers, short on theatrical background or, like Lamb and Hazlitt, disdainful of Shakespeare in production, would have to plead *mea culpa*. Wallace Bacon, in his essay "Problems in the Interpretation of Shakespeare," reminds us that "in Shakespeare, the actor, among other things and with particular significance, *speaks*." Consequently, "it is not simply a question of how Hamlet or Lear feels, but how those feelings sound; it is the felt language, the felt sensing, which matters above all" (Bacon 1973). Indeed, the reading of a play calls not only for the decoding of written symbols, but also for the enacting of that work in the theater of one's imagination, and to that end, oral reading and scene dramatizations are a must.

As Peggy O'Brien of the Shakespeare Folger Library repeatedly preaches and demonstrates in her theater workshops, Shakespeare is most successfully taught "vertically," with students on their feet enacting scenes and lending their voices to the action. To introduce *Julius Caesar* to a classroom of sophomores, for example, O'Brien suggests class dramatization of III.iii, the short scene in which the bloodthirsty mob, enflamed by Antony's funeral oration, encounters Cinna the poet and rips him limb from limb. The teacher can start with individual volunteers, then involve increasingly more students until the entire class is vocally and physically engaged. Moving from this mob scene to the opening scene of the commoners on holiday is an exciting and natural progression. With classes having few competent readers, the teacher can use choral reading for group scenes—whatever it takes to get students on their feet, speaking lines, and making decisions about movement and tone.

Yet another technique for highlighting the spoken dimension of the plays is to pick out short scenes that are subject to diverse interpretations and ask three or four student teams to present their readings. For this assignment, speeches rich in innuendo or irony work especially well. For example:

Macbeth:	My dearest love, Duncan comes here tonight.
Lady Macbeth:	And when goes hence?
Macbeth:	Tomorrow, as he purposes.
Lady Macbeth:	O, never Shall sun that morrow see!

In their first attempt, students are likely to be very matter-of-fact, not perceiving that husband and wife are here intuiting their "most black and deep desires." A fruitful analysis of needed vocal emphasis and tone can thus ensue.

Another good selection for team readings is the "What a piece of work is a man" speech from *Hamlet*. After students have performed, recordings of Olivier, Gielgud, Burton, and Jacobi giving their dramatic interpretations can prove enlightening. Students may be astonished to hear the same speech read to convey profound melancholy and awe as well as mordant cynicism and self-loathing. A delightful follow-up is the recorded version of this passage from the musical *Hair*. Of course, the purpose of all such comparisons is, besides "tuning" the ear, to lead students back to the text for a closer look at character, imagery, and dramatic situation.

For most teachers, plot has always seemed the most accessible element of a Shakespearean play. Even the dullest student seems able to respond to an exciting story and, later, retell what happens. But too often the tendency is to expend all energy on a passage-by-passage elucidation of the text, leaving no time for putting all the parts together. A "basic" task, then, has to be examination of a play's overall structure and design once scene-by-scene study has been completed.

The most popular tool for plot analysis is the famous Freytag Formula, which calls for identification of the introduction, an exciting force, rising action, a climax, falling action, and a catastrophe or denouement. Applied to a story or play, it compels students to examine the work as a whole and come up with a compact summary of events, as demonstrated by the following application of the formula to *Hamlet:*

Introduction:	The recent death of Hamlet, Sr., the threat of invasion from Norway, and the appearance of a ghost on the parapets establish a mood of mystery and uneasiness. Holding their first court, Claudius and Gertrude appear controlled and commanding, in contrast to the sable-clad, dejected prince.
Exciting force:	The ghost of Hamlet, Sr. confirms young Hamlet's suspicions about Claudius's role in his father's death and incites him toward a course of vengeance.
Rising action:	Hamlet languishes while affecting an "antic disposition." Polonius, Rosencrantz and Guildenstern, and Gertrude and Claudius spy on Hamlet, hoping "by indirections to find directions out." The arrival of the players motivates Hamlet to action: the play within a play. During "The Murder of Gonzago," Hamlet "probes" Ophelia, Gertrude, and Claudius, provoking the king into emotional flight.
Climax:	Hamlet fails to kill Claudius when he comes upon him at prayer.

OR

	Hamlet slays Polonius in his mother's bedroom and is dispatched to England.
Falling action:	Ophelia goes mad and subsequently drowns herself. Claudius and Laertes conspire to plot Hamlet's death. Returned from his aborted trip to England, Hamlet struggles with Laertes by Ophelia's grave.
Catastrophe/ Denouement:	Hamlet, Laertes, Claudius, and Gertrude perish in the duel scene, leaving Horatio to tell the true story. Young Fortinbras, returned from Poland, orders a soldier's funeral for the slain prince.

Besides calling for an ordering of events, such an exercise in mapping design invariably stimulates lively debate over what constitutes the point of climax. For instance, in *Hamlet,* is it Polonius's death or, instead, Hamlet's failure to slay Claudius when he comes upon him alone at prayer?

As far as possible, however, students should be urged to go beyond a single formula to an exploration of other designs in the text that give the overall work unity and power. For example, students could profitably explore the following artistic patterns operative in *Hamlet*:

- The alternation of public and private scenes
- Scenes of masking/unmasking, "seeming"/"being"
- The dominant metaphor of health/sickness, order/chaos: "the poisoned kingdom"
- The archetypal pattern of "Loss of Innocence"/"Journey to Manhood"
- Hamlet as "mirror" of the Danish Court and its chief characters
- The arrangement of scenes as a sequence of "triptychs," reflective of the emblematic art of the period (See Mark Rose's *Shakespearean Design*, Harvard University Press, 1972, for a fascinating analysis of Shakespearean structure based upon spatial form.)

Of course, the purpose of any such discussion of structure and design is to enable students to perceive the play as a unified whole instead of as a collection of isolated speeches and happenings.

"Basic" in the study of character in Shakespeare, as with any literary work, is helping students draw appropriate inferences, trace character development, and make meaningful comparisons. Equally important is sensitizing young readers to the way Shakespeare's characters reveal themselves through their speech. In Shakespeare, language always reflects a character's true nature. For example, in *Othello*, Iago's words are so poisonous and perverting that Othello's language and actions eventually become as warped and demonic as those of the fiend obsessing him. In *Julius Caesar*, the plain-speaking, high-minded Brutus is no match for Antony, the master rhetorician and devious manipulator of mobs and emotions.

Analysis of speaking styles is especially important for an understanding of *Hamlet*. In Act II the young prince carefully instructs the visiting players to "suit the action to the word, the word to the action" because he knows himself to be surrounded by people who use words as a mask to distort or misrepresent both themselves and the truth. Polonius, the nation's chief counselor, is a man habituated to double-talk and double-dealing, one who uses words for their sound rather than for their meaning, and who thereby gets lost in the labyrinth of his own convoluted rhetoric. A "chip off the old block," Laertes is addicted to hyperbole and public grandstanding, whether at court or at his sister's gravesite, where he is rightfully shown up by Hamlet for his emotional superficiality and insincerity. Claudius's speech is artfully controlled, the rhetoric of a shrewd and calculating individual who prides himself on his use of "reason." But in a guilty aside he confesses to having to conceal his ugly deeds behind the "painted word," like a harlot "beautied with plast'ring art." In Act V the pretentious and affected Osric "apes" court talk in an attempt to impress Prince Hamlet, but succeeds only in eliciting a contemptuous parody of his grandiloquent style that he is too dim-witted to comprehend. Over and over again throughout the course of the play, Hamlet mimics the speech and actions of his adversaries to expose duplicity and affectation and to show up what "seems" for what "is."

Shakespeare's themes, at first, seem clear-cut: power corrupts, appearances are deceiving, evil begets evil, "heavy lies the crown," and so forth. And there is something deeply satisfying in being able to conclude a unit with a tidy list of "universal ideas to be pondered." But, on deeper thought, we find ourselves as puzzled as Macbeth after the visit of the witches, aware that "nothing is / But what is not." Steeped in ambiguity, the plays always raise more questions than they answer. How, really, do we explain the perversion of Brutus's lofty idealism, the depth of Iago's malignity, the cruel tyrannizing of Juliet by parents who so obviously dote on her? Why does Bertram spurn the beautiful and virtuous Helena, "noble" Macbeth murder a man he admires, Lear turn on the dearest love of his life? Yes, there are explanations, but students need to be told that every reading of a Shakespearean play is likely to raise new questions and modify initial assumptions.

For example, writing about *Hamlet* in his essay "The World of *Hamlet*," Maynard Mack (1964) points out that "the first attribute that impresses us . . . is mysteriousness." Scene after scene is charged with questions, riddles, and controversies that will be disputed as long as the play is read. Why does Hamlet delay? Is the ghost to be trusted? "To be or not to be"? What constitutes right action in a world of deceiving appearances, moral corruption, and ephemerality, a world in which " 'would' changes, / And hath abatements and delays as many / As there are tongues, are hands, are accidents"? David Bevington (1988) calls *Julius Caesar* "an ambivalent study of civil conflict" that "reflects a dual tradition: the medieval view of Dante and Geoffrey Chaucer condemning Brutus and Cassius as conspirators, and the Renaissance view of Sir Philip Sidney and Ben Jonson condemning Caesar as a tyrant." As for *Romeo and Juliet*, are we meant to regard the doomed lovers as playthings of Fate or, instead, as victims of their intense infatuation and reckless impetuosity? In *Macbeth*, is Duncan truly as virtuous as Macbeth describes him or, as some readings suggest, power-hungry, personally weak, and possibly senile? How do we account for Banquo's continued loyalty to Macbeth after Duncan's murder? "Nothing is but what is not."

In the crowded high school curriculum, how much time should be spent on a Shakespearean play? The title of a lively article on the teaching of Shakespeare offers a guideline worth heeding: "When Thou Teachest Shakespeare, Do It Fast." The underlying assumption is sound: lively pacing is crucial. Still, anything less than three weeks on a play is likely to be ineffectual. Given their length and complexity, both *Romeo and Juliet* and *Hamlet* require a minimum of four weeks, possibly with extra days to accommodate writing activities and viewing of films or videotapes. Shorter works like *Macbeth* and *Julius Caesar* can be studied in three weeks if energetically paced. But teachers who wish "The Shakespeare Experience" to be something more than a blurred and superficial exposure must be flexible in providing the necessary time for discussion, reflection, and synthesis.

Memorization appears to have gone out of style, relegated, along with formal grammar, to the educational dustheap; but a reevaluation seems in order. Memorizing is not just a "rote" activity, but a way of acquiring what E. D. Hirsch (1983) has termed "cultural literacy," the shared knowledge that unites members of a literate society. Memorizing further enables students to experience for themselves the shape and sound of the Shakespearean line and the effect of spoken emphasis on the meaning of a given passage. Most important, memorizing helps students contemplate and store away profound ideas beautifully expressed. As Francis Bacon long ago advised, readers must occasionally go beyond the level of "tasting" and "swallowing" to the "digesting" of ideas, a process memorization can facilitate.

Making memorization an optional assignment is very likely the wisest strategy. Teachers can also sponsor memorization contests, undertake five minutes of choral reading/memorization with a class each day, or plaster the room with quotations and passages artfully inscribed. Recognition of passages games, perhaps within a *Jeopardy!* format, can also make memorizing a passport to lasting satisfaction and a sense of personal accomplishment.

Every Shakespearean play offers rich material from which varied writing assignments can be generated: character studies, comparison/ contrasts, critical analyses of scenes and speeches, paraphrases and interpretations, and so forth. What should not be overlooked is opportunities for imaginative writing that call for students to apply the ideas of the play to contemporary times and their own lives. During the study of *Hamlet*, for example, students might be asked to undertake brief writing tasks such as the following:

1. Try your hand at writing a humorous soliloquy in the pattern of the "To be or not to be" speech. Start by choosing an infinitive for an action requiring wholehearted commitment, such as "to marry," "to diet," "to study," "to save," or "to clean." Then work out the pros and cons of such an action, following the sequence of thought Hamlet goes through in his debate on suicide.

2. Assume that you are Horatio at the end of the play, carrying out Hamlet's dying request to tell his story. Write a detailed report to Fortinbras in which you do so, concluding with a recommendation of actions that require the new king's urgent attention.

3. Using blank verse, write a soliloquy appropriate for Ophelia immediately after she has learned of her father's death and begun the descent into madness.

4. In a paragraph, discuss criteria for evaluating and performing a play (as set forth in Acts II and III) that modern-day thespians would be wise to adopt.

5. Look up the words for the song "The Impossible Dream" in Dale Wasserman's *Man of La Mancha* and compare Don Quixote's goals with those prescribed by Polonius to Laertes. Explain which you would prefer to follow in your own life and why.

6. Throughout your study of the play, maintain a journal written from Hamlet's point of view. Record his changing feelings, problems, and struggle to make decisions. Include his views on people and life as well as his increasing "readiness" to meet what Fate decrees. In the margins of your journal, record *your* reactions to Hamlet's thinking and decisions.

Interspersed throughout the study of a Shakespearean play, assignments like these promote not only writing fluency, but also thoughtful reflection of the ideas and style of the play. Longer analytical assignments are best reserved as a culminating activity for the unit.

By defining and adhering to "basic" priorities, teachers of Shakespeare can achieve important goals: knowledge, imaginative response, pleasure, humanistic insights. But we must not expect too much from a single unit. W. H. Auden once noted that every one of Shakespeare's works is unique, requiring the reader to experience them all to get a proper idea of the Shakespearean world. He also commented that "no one is less a writer for the young, for persons, that is, under the age of thirty" (Auden 1961). Yet much will have been accomplished in any classroom if students capture, if only incompletely, a sense of the complexity, variety, richness, and universality of this drama which transcended its age and indeed all time.

References

Auden, W. H. 1961. "Three Memoranda on the New Arden Shakespeare." *The Mid-Century* 21 (January): 3.

Bacon, Wallace A. 1973. "Problems in the Interpretation of Shakespeare." *The Speech Teacher* 22 (November).

Bevington, David, ed. 1988. Introduction. *Julius Caesar.* By William Shakespeare. Toronto: Bantam Books.

Hirsch, E. D., Jr. 1983. "Cultural Literacy." *The American Scholar* 52 (Spring): 159–69.

Mack, Maynard. 1964. "The World of *Hamlet.*" In *Shakespeare: The Tragedies: A Collection of Critical Essays,* edited by Alfred Harbage, 44–60. Englewood Cliffs, NJ: Prentice-Hall.

2 Teaching Shakespeare's Dramatic Dialogue

Sharon A. Beehler
Montana State University

Because of Shakespeare's status as a cultural icon, and because of the firm position his works hold in school curricula, it is worth considering the impact Shakespeare makes upon those facing adulthood in the United States. Today Shakespeare serves as either the means by which a person enters the dominant society through familiarity with the culture or the model against which one must exercise resistance in order to demonstrate fair-mindedness toward disenfranchised members of society. Both situations have their validity, but too often students cannot relate to these comprehensive issues with any personal judgment or experience. By examining Shakespeare's dramatic dialogues as instances of communication, and thus providing a "hook" for student readers, either of these emphases can be addressed without losing sight of Shakespeare the playwright.

Because students are familiar with the communication problems and components individuals face in their daily lives, these problems provide a nonthreatening context for an area of study that otherwise seems remote and foreign. Moreover, such a context enables students and teachers to address questions of plot, characterization, and performance (in all its communication modes) with greater viability. By regarding the social relations depicted in Shakespeare's plays as instances of communication, we can offer students an avenue of investigation that has immediate familiarity and allows for discussion of historical, cultural, and political issues as well.

Communication, as I use the term with my students, refers to the practice of using various sign systems to exchange ideas among individuals. Dramatic dialogue captures such practice with all its inevitable difficulties. Shakespeare appears to have been especially alert to the range of styles and assumptions informing individual communication. He was particularly sensitive to the consequences of these assumptions and used them to create comic and tragic situations. Perhaps his function as playwright and actor facilitated his understanding of these conditions. As a member of an acting company, he had a definite economic interest in relating to an audience; he had to know the idiosyncrasies of creating receptive listeners. If students become aware of this aspect of Shakespeare—his role as communicator—they can begin to regard his work as similar to their own efforts as writers and speakers. Moreover, thanks to the insights of reader-response critics, students can examine the plays as multidimensional dialogues between dramatic characters, between readers and text, between actors, and between production and audience.

Such an approach encourages critical thinking by raising questions about what works and what doesn't in the various conversations. These questions help students develop a better sense of what communication means to them, how individuals can manipulate communication for self-gain, and how self-expression in both speech and writing can be made most effective. Matters of careful listening, discourse assumptions, subtext, feelings, and trust necessarily come to light through such thinking.

To make these points more concrete, let me turn to *A Midsummer Night's Dream*. Although this play has been popular with college instructors for some time now, it has only recently begun to achieve acceptance among secondary school curriculum planners. Its witty repartee and outrageous confusions make it especially suitable for a communication approach, and students at both levels can find it enjoyable.

To introduce the communication focus, I give each student a slip of paper with these instructions:

1. Arrange the following words into a logical sentence.
   movie   you   to   to   with
            I   the   go   want
2. Determine where you would place the stress in the sentence.

Students (native speakers) who complete the exercise usually agree on the arrangement of the words, forming the sentence "I want to go to the movie with you." But they disagree about where to place the stress. Their agreement on the sentence structure indicates the degree of influence exercised by conventions of grammar and usage. Nevertheless, the disagreement over emphasis indicates a more complex influence, that of imagined circumstance, something that will differ among individuals depending on their past experiences and knowledge. In particular, students faced with this exercise must draw upon their background, their own emotions and motivations, an imagined listener (including that person's relationship to the speaker and his or her point of view and background), an imagined situation, and the conventions of inflection, gesture, and facial expression.

The grammatical and social structures of spoken discourse receive attention in most English classes. Yet communication also has to do with the assumptions we make about how language actually works to establish ideas in conversation. The work of the Russian theorist Mikhail Bakhtin (1984) is useful here. Bakhtin was fascinated by questions about how communication occurs. His thinking led him to conclude that language never conveys meaning in some pure state from one person to another. Because language already belongs to a public realm, it cannot be wholly appropriated by a speaker to serve a private need. Language carries with it a host of prior contexts for both speaker and listener, and these "traces" of former usage interfere with any direct conveyance of thought. Meanings are produced between conversers as each participant contributes his or her understanding, his or her background. What is heard will never be exactly what was "intended." Thus, according to Bakhtin, discourse is always *dialogic*, that is, subject to the interplay of voices and prior meanings. A speaker who respects this feature of discourse is said to speak *dialogically* and understands that he or she cannot impose or close meaning. A person who assumes that language *can* convey an intended meaning and that a listener is essentially an empty vessel to be filled with the speaker's thoughts is said to be a *monologic* speaker. These types of conversers are familiar to all of us; many students see adults as inflexible monologic speakers. Because students do recognize these types, they can read a Shakespeare play with critical focus on the characters who exemplify the types. What becomes exciting for students is the growing awareness that they too practice monologic assumptions in their conversations and that such assumptions (as illustrated by the plays) often lead to trouble.

Another idea that contributes to the understanding of communication is that of the *interpretive community*, an idea developed by literary critic Stanley Fish (1980) and others. An interpretive community is a group of people who share common experiences, beliefs, and understandings. This allows them to communicate with each other more readily than they would with outsiders. Their interpretations, in other words, are conditioned by mutual experiences. This manner of communicating calls attention to the dialogic condition of language by emphasizing its collaborative features.

The sentence produced by the above introductory exercise would no doubt occur in a more complex situation than its isolated state here suggests. The choice of where to place stress hints at the motivations, or subtext, that inform the statement. For instance, the sentence might be a test (how will you react?), a lie (I don't really want to go with you), a misunderstanding (I thought *you* wanted to go), or an excuse (. . . but I have work to do). These subtexts are often buried or repressed, deliberately or involuntarily, and yet they still interfere.

Actors and directors deal with subtexts all the time in order to determine motive for characters, and they are aware that these subtexts shape the communication which seems to occur between the dramatis personae. By helping students to identify possible subtexts and consider the dialogic/monologic assumptions characters seem to practice, we can make them more alert to the importance of the same phenomena in their own lives. They can see that hidden subtexts and monologic assumptions can have evil consequences, as between Iago and Othello; tragic ones, as in the Lear-Cordelia relationship; or comic ones, as between Maria and Malvolio. Monologic speakers discount the importance of the interpretive community and believe that their subtextual motives are invincible.

Once this groundwork has been laid, students are ready to look at III.ii.122–344 of *A Midsummer Night's Dream*. This scene depicts the frustration and confusion between Hermia and Helena and Lysander and Demetrius as a consequence of Puck's mistake with the love juice. The two men, both of whom had been in love with Hermia, have awakened to the sight of Helena and, under the influence of the potion, have fallen madly in love with her, rejecting Hermia altogether. Helena concludes that the other three have conspired to mock her, and she expresses her resentment of that treatment even as Lysander and Demetrius insist upon their passionate devotion to her. Hermia, finding herself cast aside by the men and scolded by Helena, seeks desperately for an explanation of the bizarre events, only to despair when Helena's attacks become vicious and the men go off to fight a duel.

This scene, while humorous to an audience in the know, has tragic elements; certainly the anger and frustration felt by all four characters is poignant. Students reading the scene quickly recognize the complexity of the characters' anxieties. Asking students to identify the factors that create the confusion can help them sort out some of this complexity. What they will find is that certain features of the discourse have aggravated the situation. Among these features are (1) the failure of the characters to consider alternative explanations to the ones they fasten upon initially, (2) jealousy, (3) male pride, (4) disloyalty, (5) self-centeredness, (6) suspicion, (7) Petrarchan conventions in excess [not always known by students to be "Petrarchan," however], (8) mistaken conventions of the joke or prank, (9) disbelief in vows and promises, (10) anger, (11) name-calling, and (12) a sudden shift in expected behaviors. The factors aggravating the characters' discourse thus range from specific linguistic elements (e.g., name-calling) to emotions (e.g., anger) to inadvertent psychological impulses (e.g., self-centeredness). The violation of the sanctity of the interpretive community also plays a part when Petrarchan conventions become excessive, familiar personal behaviors disintegrate, and the conventions of a joke seem to be operating. Challenging students to articulate these features results in an awareness of how performers must think about their roles in order to create believable and familiar characters and situations. It can also make them more appreciative of Shakespeare's skill as a dramatist and creator of dialogue.

In addition, asking students to consider whether any of the characters speak monologically in the scene focuses their attention on the basic discourse assumptions that each character makes. As the circumstances become more confusing, each character finds himself or herself separated further from the others. This breakdown of the community virtually forces monologic thinking. No longer can the others be depended upon to engage dialogically; each one seems to have lost touch with the others. Were they all to seek preservation of the community and attempt understanding through negotiation, much of the tension would be released. Of course, then we would not have the comedy. In our daily lives, such negotiation would be preferable; but in the work of dramatic art, tension must occur. At any rate, Shakespeare's sense that threats to an individual's place in the community often lead to monologic thinking can be seen in other plays as well, and by helping students examine this condition of the dialogue, we can simultaneously urge them to consider the consequences of their own choices when faced with alienation.

While secondary students prefer to address the issue of communication as a matter of plot and characterization, college students enjoy going a step further and examining the ways in which political and social practices find expression through the dialogue. For instance, power often figures in instances of communication, with one character exercising, or attempting to exercise, power over another. Gender, class, race, and age influence the degree of power allowed in a given case. The shift to a monologic style of speech often signals a seizure of power, as is the case when both Hermia's and Helena's confusions are dismissed by the men as irrelevant to their chief concern: winning Helena's acceptance. This occurs most noticeably when, following Helena's declaration of her love for Demetrius, Lysander pulls away from Hermia and urges Demetrius to the duel:

> Now she holds me not;
> Now follow, if thou dar'st, to try whose right,
> Of thine or mine, is most in Helena.
>
> (III.ii.335–37)

It would seem from this that Helena's preferences have little to do with who has a "right" to her. Lysander's words, in fact, echo the manner of thinking that dominates Athenian law, which, as we learn in Act I, requires a woman to accept her father's will in the choice of a husband. Such a patriarchal system does not foster dialogic assumptions.

To make this scene more vivid for my students, I show them a clip from the 1935 film version of the play. Because we are dealing with a videotape, I can stop, start, and rerun portions of the scene that students wish to examine more closely. Ideally, students should have the opportunity to see the scene performed by more than one group of actors. This can be accomplished by having the students perform the scene in small groups that adopt different interpretations, by having amateur actors visit the class to perform the scene, or by showing clips from other productions. If a live production is available locally, a class trip to the theater might be in order. Witnessing several versions of the same scene calls attention to the variety of interpretations possible to actors, thereby taking the negotiation of meaning outside the playworld and into the domain of reader and text and production and audience.

I have also designed several activities connected with the communication approach to *Dream* to enhance students' critical thinking and writing abilities. For example, I ask students to identify both the questions asked in the scene and the answers given. Here is a sampling of relevant lines:

Sample I

Hermia: But why unkindly didst thou leave me so?

Lysander: Why should he stay whom love doth press to go?

Hermia:	What love could press Lysander from my side?
Lysander:	Lysander's love, that would not let him bide—

> Why seek'st thou me? Could not this make thee know,
> The hate I bear thee made me leave thee so?

Hermia:	You speak not as you think.

(III.ii.183–86, 189–90)

Sample II

Hermia:	[*to Helena*] What have you come by night And stol'n my love's heart from him?
Helena:	Fine, i' faith! Have you no modesty, no maiden shame, No touch of bashfulness? What, will you tear Impatient answers from my gentle tongue?

(III.ii.283–87)

What students immediately recognize after examining such passages is that most of the questions that characters ask are either not really expecting an answer or not wanting one; that is, they are rhetorical questions asked primarily for effect or as expressions of incredulity. This is a sign of the characters' failure to attempt mutual understanding; each character *declares* his or her thoughts and does not really "hear" the others. Having observed this phenomenon, students can then begin to explore the causes of it.

Another strategy that works well is to have the students articulate the assumptions under which each of the characters is operating. Here too such articulation brings to light the reasons for the characters' misunderstandings. When Helena, for instance, says,

> If you were men, as men you are in show,
> You would not use a gentle lady so—
> To vow, and swear, and superpraise my parts.
> When I am sure you hate me with your hearts

(III.ii.151–54)

she makes several assumptions: (1) that Demetrius and Lysander cannot be serious, (2) that gentlemanly behavior includes disguising hatred, (3) that the two men hate her, (4) that she is a "gentle lady," and (5) that vowing, swearing, and flattering are the behaviors expected from men in love. It is the first assumption, however, that underlies the others and makes understanding impossible. The next question, then, must be, why cannot Helena entertain the possibility that Demetrius and Lysander are serious? This question helps students get at the complexity of Helena's situation and her effort to find an explanation, however painful, for a terribly confusing event. It points out how desperate people can be to make sense of their experience.

Having students write alternative scenes can also help them develop new insights about the communication phenomena in the play. Here are four changes that can encourage creative thinking:

1. Write a dialogue that resolves the scene by avoiding the threat of a duel.

2. Continue the scene by showing how the situation would end if Oberon and Puck did not intervene to correct Puck's mistake.

3. Imagine how the scene would develop if the potion had been placed on Hermia's eyes (instead of Demetrius's) and that the first person she saw on awaking was Demetrius.

4. Play the scene as if Helena is right: all three are mocking her.

These changes in the playtext call attention to Shakespeare's dramatic choices, helping students appreciate the complexity of those choices and their theatrical effectiveness. Moreover, the revised scenes reflect students' growing awareness of the subtleties of communication through dialogue. The first option, in particular, requires that students show sensitivity to effective ways of avoiding conflict through discourse.

There are, of course, many other scenes from *Dream* that lend themselves to investigation of communication problems. The opening conversation between Theseus and Hippolyta can be played in numerous ways, depending on the assumptions we make about the relationship. Has Hippolyta fallen in love with Theseus and therefore as eager for the wedding as he is? Is she resentful of her military defeat and therefore bitter about her impending marriage? Is she thoroughly deflated by Theseus's victory and consequently rather listless and indifferent about her future? Or is she, perhaps, conniving so as to make Theseus vulnerable and, ultimately, her pawn? Each of these possibilities requires a different behavior from the actress playing Hippolyta and a different sense of the communication that occurs in the dialogue.

The scene between Oberon and Titania in which they argue over the changeling boy also offers good opportunity for critiquing communication. Oberon tries a variety of methods to appease Titania, but when none of them work, he resorts to threats, which only inspire her scoffing. In the forest, magic alone can resolve the conflicts. No dialogic engagement can occur, except by Bottom, who accepts his transformation and the oddity of his situation as Titania's paramour with little reluctance, demonstrating that alienation from normal circumstance does not have to lead to closed-mindedness. Unlike Helena, he does not frantically seize upon an explanation. Were he in Helena's position, he would probably greet Lysander and Demetrius with open arms. Bottom so strongly believes in himself that such a change of affection would merely be perceived as his due.

The last scene of the play, during which the mechanicals perform their version of "Pyramus and Thisbe," provides yet another opportunity for discussion of communication. Here we have several different components of the communication spectrum: the mechanicals demonstrate their sense of how characters in a play communicate; the newlyweds demonstrate the type of communication that occurs between an audience and a production and among the audience members themselves; and the Pyramus and Thisbe story recalls the earlier confusions of the forest. While the newlyweds make fun of the mechanicals, we remember our own laughter at the plight of the lovers. This awareness raises the question of how comedy and tragedy are constructed. What phenomena of communication allow an audience to see the same events as tragic in one instance and comic in another? For Oberon and Puck, the mortals are fools, and as audience members, we tend to share that view. Yet the Pyramus and Thisbe episode recalls not only our earlier delight in the forest confusions, but also our probable distress over a play written at approximately the same time: *Romeo and Juliet*, in which similar incidents are treated tragically.

Questions about the ways in which productions communicate with an audience inevitably arise from focusing on this concluding scene of *Dream*. As we move out from the mechanicals' theater space, we move beyond the newlywed observers to the fairy world that oversees the human realm, and with each step outward we change our perspective until the fairies too become part of an inner space, that of the theater itself, and we are left outside with our multiple views and our questions about whether we too fit within the frame of some other consciousness.

Communication between individuals is always subject to this unsettling blend of perspectives. By examining a play like Shakespeare's *Dream*, we can increase our sensitivity to the dialogic condition of discourse and, consequently perhaps, improve our abilities to communicate effectively with one another. If, as teachers, we help our students reach these same insights, we will have taken a small step toward enhancing human relations and a large step toward establishing a sound foundation for teaching Shakespeare, the communicator.

References

Bakhtin, Mikhail. 1984. *Problems of Dostoevsky's Poetics*. Edited and translated by Caryl Emerson. Minneapolis: University of Minnesota Press.

Fish, Stanley. 1980. *Is There a Text in This Class?: The Authority of Interpretive Communities*. Cambridge: Harvard University Press.

Shakespeare, William. 1988. *A Midsummer Night's Dream*. Edited by David Bevington. New York: Bantam Books.

3 Shakespearean Role Models

Ruth Ann Gerrard
Austintown Local Schools, Youngstown, Ohio

Certain Shakespearean characters have definite potential as student role models. Although these characters may not all be "good influences," they do provoke young adults into considering a variety of intellectual and emotional options as they make life decisions. Indeed, in the process of growth, students seeking direction for their futures may well evaluate, consciously or unconsciously, the choices of such individual figures as Richard III, Henry IV, Falstaff, Hamlet, and Lear.

Richard III, with his fascinating manipulation of individuals and ruthless destruction of innocents on his path to the crown, is surely not someone for students to emulate. Nevertheless, his motives and intellect demand close examination for the political and personal insights they give into shrewdness and power. Richard, by his own description, is supremely ugly:

> Cheated of feature by dissembling Nature,
> Deformed, unfinished, sent before my time
> Into this breathing world, scarce half made up,
> And that so lamely and unfashionable
> That dogs bark at me as I halt by them

> (I.i.19–23)

Yet this Tudor-created monster is a most successful intellectual schemer. From his Act I wooing of Anne to the premeditated, sequential deaths of his two older brothers to his assumption of the role of Protector of his minority-age nephew to the slaying of anyone in his way, Richard's dramatic acquisition of the throne is an excellent opportunity for watching a master "operator" at work. Indeed, even after Richard instructs his kingmaker, Buckingham, to align the citizenry and nobility for him, he still plays "hard-to-get":

> Alas, why would you heap this care on me?
> I am unfit for state and majesty;
> I do beseech you, take it not amiss,

I cannot nor I will not yield to you

(III.vii.204–7)

In this the mastery of all political manipulation is immediately obvious, fraught with possibilities for both oral and written response from students as well as for personal reflection. Richard's ultimate defeat at Bosworth also provides multiple possibilities for reaction to the rise and fall of shrewd manipulators. In essence, students must ask, Do they and those around them seek a positive or a negative path to power?

Richard III represents choice. The biography of Richard would have been that of a little known prince who lived out his life as a minor royal brother had he not chosen to seek the throne by whatever means. As teenagers are faced with decisions—and as they recognize that the dubious decisions of political adults may one day be their problem—they are intrigued by the moral and social responsibilities inherent in the freedom to choose. Many of the leaders of the twentieth century have found themselves considering such weighty responsibilities, especially as they set paths not just for themselves, but for others as well. Of course, throughout recorded history, there have been leaders of nations who have ignored these responsibilities and who have ended up as destructive as Richard III. Richard's character thus provides material for personal reflection on long-range choices. This reflection can easily lead to essay comparisons of those world leaders whose choices shaped an age, for good or for ill. Had there not been a Richard III to proclaim, "I am determined to prove a villain / And hate the idle pleasures of these days" (I.i.30–31), or had there not been a Buckingham to help Richard to the throne only to regretfully say, "Made I him King for this?" (IV.ii.120), the history of England would have been quite different. Indeed, had there not been positive and negative leaders who made choices in every country of the world's history, leaders such as Caesar, Lincoln, Churchill, and Hitler, the evolution of human society would be greatly altered. Herein lies the value in studying Richard III.

Striding through three plays—*Richard II* and *Henry IV, Parts 1 and 2*—Henry IV offers student readers a fascinating look at the process of climbing the executive ladder and succeeding in office. Beginning in Richard II as Bolingbroke, the banished cousin of the reigning monarch, Henry returns from exile to play upon popular dislike for the incompetent king and to justify his claim to his inheritance. By Act IV of that play, he has accomplished the unthinkable: deposing

God's "anointed king" (III.ii.55) and establishing himself upon the throne. In his new role, he must demonstrate the ability to make wise decisions, cope with adversity, and plan strategically.

Shortly after his ascent to the throne, Henry IV shows both wisdom and humor in his handling of a family problem with his cousin Aumerle, concern over his son's lively social activities, and growing guilt for his deposition of the king. All of these are to be fully developed in the two plays given to him by the Bard as he develops the administrative role.

The first play focuses on the Percy Rebellion, as that family rues the day that it helped Henry to the throne. Nevertheless, King Henry IV is steadfast in his rule over the country, his resolution to defeat the insurgents, and his domination of the military. He tries to be equally strong in his role as father, but he constantly fears the potential disaffection, even disloyalty, of his carousing son, Prince Hal. Hovering over all of this is his own guilt for having usurped the throne from God's rightful ruler, Richard II. In an effort to assuage his guilt, he constantly talks of a trip to the Holy Land. The second play depicts the resolution of much of this, as the rebellion ends, the son becomes honorable, and the father's guilt diminishes. Still, Henry continues to know the sleepless nights that perhaps plague every burdened administrator: "Uneasy lies the head that wears a crown" (III.i.31).

With many young men and women looking ahead to management careers, the burdens of capable administration, family responsibilities, and ethical considerations in the climb to the top are very real concerns. King Henry IV is an ideal look at just such a "manager," delighted with his position yet burdened with its multifaceted responsibilities. For personal journals, for classroom discussions, and for essays, Henry IV is an excellent subject.

Falstaff is an opportunity for hilarity, both in the staged robbery of *Henry IV, Part 1* and as he assumes the role of the king in his role reversal with young Prince Hal. His military manipulations in the same play can nevertheless create disgust. And his speech on honor is an excellent commentary on the true significance of life in cowardly, yet practical, terms. In all, he is one of Shakespeare's most beloved characters, a personage in his own right and a prelude to the playwright's fools. Yet to leave Falstaff at that stage would do a disservice to his potential as a role model, for in his evolution is a fated story that gives students cause for reflection on their own place in friendships and the social order.

Early in the *Henry IV* plays, Falstaff is with the "in crowd."

With the hilarity of his highway robberies, bragging of conquests, and lively patter in the gathering places, he lives a boisterous, partying existence. This existence has the added appeal of royal connections that make privilege a way of life. And his confidence that he will always be a royal confidant only adds to his sense that he has secured the "good life." Indeed, in the reversal scene with the madcap Prince Hal, Falstaff counsels him, "there is virtue in that Falstaff. Him keep with, the rest banish" (II.iv.435–36). Despite a growing sense that he irritates the maturing Prince, Falstaff remains confident of his place and practical in his self-preservation: "What is honor? A word. What is in that word honor? What is that honor? Air—a trim reckoning!" (V.i.136–37). Consequently, after the death of Henry IV in the second play, Falstaff is most confident of his joyous future: "I know the young King is sick for me. Let us take any man's horses; the laws of England are at my commandment" (V.iii.139–41). But a short time later he is utterly rejected by the new king:

> I know thee not, old man. Fall to thy prayers.
> ....
> I banish thee, on pain of death,
> As I have done the rest of my misleaders.
>
> (V.v.52, 68–69)

In this evolution lies the folly of the clown, the meaning of a life spent in dubious pursuits that come to naught. While there is inherent sympathy for the rejected "buddy," there is also the inevitable lesson of poor choices and wasted time.

Thus far, Shakespeare's characters all seem to build up to the complex, intriguing Hamlet. As one young man observed, "I may have college and career choices to make, but nothing as difficult as Hamlet faced." All young people are aware that life sometimes calls for decisions that may well have serious, even grave, consequences. When Hamlet ponders the question "to be or not to be" (III.i.64–96), he is questioning life itself, the worth of human existence. Yet the decisions that Hamlet is called upon to make are as real as those of any man or woman burdened with the responsibilities of life; Hamlet the character and *Hamlet* the play encompass the full range of life's eternal issues.

Hamlet—as a young man coping with his father's murder, charged with proving that his uncle is the villain, despairing over his mother's hasty remarriage, frustrated with women and punishing Ophelia for her own femininity, and blaming himself for his inability to act decisively—faces all the overpowering circumstances that life could present. Still, he is all too aware of his responsibility: "The time is out of joint. O cursed spite / That ever I was born to set it right!" (I.v.215–16). He must, as the son of the father, as the Prince of Denmark, set it right by whatever choices are available. He thus vows to "catch the conscience of a king" (II.ii.614), and his plotting becomes a model for control of circumstances and seizure of opportunities. Even so, his course of action is fraught with debates on the nature of man:

> What a piece of work is a man! how noble in reason! how infinite in faculties! in form and moving how express and admirable! in action how like an angel! in apprehension how like a god! the beauty of the world, the paragon of animals! and yet to me what is this quintessence of dust? (II.ii.319–23)

Hamlet is the philosopher in the midst of horrendous problems. As the play evolves, he continues to debate his existence, especially in his speech on suicide, the "to be or not to be" soliloquy. Nevertheless, he also designs the perfect trap for the guilty king and uncle, proving his point, his manhood, his reason, and his control—and losing his life.

Hamlet represents the ideal Renaissance prince. Yet when he appears (or is) mad, he seems to have lost all the perfection he once had shown, much to the chagrin of Ophelia, who enumerates his former virtues; he was, she says, a courtier, a soldier, and a scholar with the "glass of fashion and the mould of form" (III.i.161–63). Hamlet, like many young people, has lost his image. As part of a contemporary world that depends upon outward appearances and often ignores inner realities, young people can begin to scrutinize the shams with which they must often cope and see not only the harsh reality of losing the superficial, but also the worth of genuine self-examination. Within his visibly shattered self, Hamlet provides a provocative guideline for personal insight through journal-style notation and casual conversation. Indeed, this sort of reflection may well be the impetus for growth toward a stronger self-image and increased self-esteem.

Because Hamlet exists in both the public and private world, because Denmark serves as a microcosm of society at large, and because the individual and the state are inextricably intertwined, the character Hamlet and the play *Hamlet* direct thought to the dual existence that most professional roles in adult life demand. Many students who seriously study Shakespeare's *Hamlet* will one day carry the burden of representation, whether political or professional. With an appreciation of Hamlet's trials as a prince whose every move affects the "distracted multitude" (IV.iii.4), students can analyze the public self, learn coping skills for that role, and make the career determinations that best reflect themselves.

The tragic story of Hamlet is ultimately about decision making, existence, significance, potential, ruin, representation, love, and pain; it is about life in all its joys and agonies. This play is the thread of the Shakespearean canon that puts life into perspective, into a system of values, into eternal meanings.

Hamlet might well stand as the epitome of Shakespearean role models if it were not for the complex, yet universal, structure of *King Lear*. In the sense of unbelievably powerful decisions and themes, *Hamlet* is at the apex of the canon; but in the sense of individual lives, *Lear* supplies the "placement model" that illustrates for the student a family situation fraught with love and conflicts, a situation just as real in the contemporary world. Caught in a web of generations, jealousies, and intrigues, both the family of Lear in the main plot and the family of Gloucester in the subplot give young students models for the roles that they presently embody—sons and daughters, grandsons and granddaughters—as well as for those ahead of them—husbands, wives, parents. Somewhat stereotyped characters interwoven with this tangle of human emotions make the realities and directions of humanity all the more clear.

Viewed with the contemporary concern over care for the elderly in mind, a concern that students may comprehend in watching their parents and grandparents (as well as in shadowy thoughts of their own future roles), Lear's proposal to divide his kingdom in exchange for care is of debatable wisdom. The ensuing chaos that afflicts both Lear and Gloucester, his parallel, is the embodiment of reality in a world where "baby boomers" are advancing in age and care for the elderly is a reality. Questions of preparation, of rights, and of planning are excellent subjects for discussion.

With experience in the daily situations of sibling rivalry, whether clothing and car hassles or custody and will battles, students are well aware of the problems that exist for children and their parents. While Lear may lament, "How sharper than a serpent's tooth, it is / To have a thankless child!" (I.iv.290–91), his daughters still plot against him and among themselves. On the other hand, the beautifully loyal Cordelia in the main plot and a comparable Edgar in the subplot remain faithful, despite the fact that both have been disowned by their misguided fathers. In watching these extraordinary individuals, students have an opportunity to look at the essence of compassion and debate its logic and validity.

Competitions for power, position, love, attention, material goods, and land are so much a part of families and nations that students are automatically led into rich, full discussions by this play. Equally important, they are led to a realization of Shakespeare's skill in portraying humanity. This play, whether in its presentation of individual characters or in its larger picture of humanity in general, offers greater potential for analysis than any in the Shakespearean canon. From Cordelia's perception of a daughter's role,

> You have begot me, bred me, loved me; I
> Return those duties back as are right fit,
> Obey you, love you, and most honor you
>
>   (I.i.102–4)

to Lear's query "Is man no more than this?" (III.iv.107–8) to Kent's "Is this the promised end?" (V.iii.314), *King Lear* epitomizes Shakespeare's presentation of the psychological, sociological, and cosmological link between individual, family, state, and universe.

Shakespeare's plays give us ageless role models. The debatably negative, captivatingly shrewd Richard III, the controlling and managerial Henry IV, the frolicking yet pathetic Falstaff, the burdened, indecisive, and overpowering Hamlet, the simultaneously ordinary and cosmic family of Lear—all stimulate open-ended classroom discussion, debate, and composition. And beyond classroom exercise is the message of life, of a world of individuals who share the joys and concerns of ordinary youth struggling for direction in the midst of complexity, a world unfolded in a grand style that gives each student a sense of the majesties of literary art, of historical progression, and of human evolution.

4 The Use of Quotations in Teaching Shakespeare

Leila Christenbury
Virginia Commonwealth University

Like most teachers, I have changed instructional strategies and emphases over my years in the classroom and, like most, I think about those changes. Some alterations, no doubt, have resulted in improvements in my teaching and understanding; some, possibly, merely reflect my own shifting interests and interpretations. I know, for instance, that I have lost the love of "symbol hunting" I tried to instill in my students and now prefer a less targeted approach to literature discussion (why was it students never found *my* symbol anyway?). I have also decided that, for complex and relatively long works, students do not need to understand or know everything (and just what *did* happen in that scene and what *was* the name of the hero's dog?); this sensible tolerance for the big picture was wholly dictated by students who demanded to be treated as readers, not fact machines. Finally, I have lost what I call my "classic mania"; once a medieval studies major who began teaching high school believing students should replicate my slow advance through the centuries, I now strongly advocate American regional and contemporary literature.

Regardless of this last change, I have not abandoned my love of probably the most traditionally revered writer in the language arts curriculum. I firmly advocate Shakespeare and think that probably every student should, though in varying intensities, be exposed to the magic of his writing. I rate Shakespeare above anything or anyone else in the canon, and I will give up time with some of the best new writers to have students read and respond to his sonnets and plays. While I do not want to symbol hunt or make sure every student knows every aspect of every scene, Shakespeare is eminently worth both my time and that of my students.

For me, the major reason is the language. Even across the centuries, it stands and endures and calls. Shakespeare has crept into our conversation, phrases, quips, and titles—from "all the world's a stage" (*Hamlet*) to "green-ey'd jealousy" (*The Merchant of Venice*) to "hark, hark, the lark" *(Cymbeline)* to "double, double, toil and trouble" *(Macbeth)* to "sharper than a serpent's tooth it is / To have a thankless child" *(King Lear)*. Our students know to "beware the Ides of March" *(Julius Caesar)*, they can complete the line "Romeo, Romeo, wherefore art thou Romeo," *(Romeo and Juliet)*, and "the winter of our discontent" *(Richard III)* may strike a vague chord of recognition. Most of our students, consciously or unconsciously, know some Shakespeare. On a more elevated level, the words of Shakespeare often give shape to the inchoate and have, even in the latter part of the twentieth century, a freshness and sharpness worth our attention and study. In *An Essay on Criticism*, Alexander Pope writes, "True wit is nature to advantage dress'd; / What oft was thought, but ne'er so well express'd" (11. 297–98). Shakespeare is the essence of true wit to advantage dressed.

Consequently, using the language of discrete quotations to structure study and discussion can be a helpful tool in approaching Shakespeare's plays in the English classroom. There are literally thousands of quotations that illuminate not only the plays, but also life itself. Using quotations to teach Shakespeare:

- Makes students focus on the specifics of the language

- Helps students deal with the complexity of the plays by using smaller units as a focus for discussion

- Provides students with a structuring device, the part for the whole

- Encourages students to memorize—or own—the language

While the details of having students focus on the specifics of the language are explored below, it is here useful to note that the broad range of the plays themselves can be highly intimidating to our students. Reducing a scene to the consideration of a single quotation can thus help students "manage" the play. Furthermore, the consideration of the smaller idea within the quotation can provide a handle for larger considerations. While it is, of course, a fallacy to blithely assume that the part can stand always and conveniently for the whole, a more limited observation, a more circumscribed comment, can sometimes illuminate a wider field. Finally, close work with a small number of quotations can encourage students to familiarize themselves with, if not actually memorize, the language. Students can thus "own" the words of Shakespeare, the effect of which can be long-range and electrifying.

Using Quotations to Teach the Plays

When I first started teaching Shakespeare in high school, I used a widespread and pragmatic technique to help my students understand the bare bones of the action. I had students, after reading a number of scenes, summarize events and facts by writing a one-sentence précis for each scene. To add a bit of creativity to the assignment, students had three choices of how they could write their scene summaries: in standard English, Elizabethan English, or school slang or street talk. Each choice yielded somewhat different results.

The summaries in standard English seemed to be straightforward attempts to understand the facts of the scene. The summaries in Elizabethan English gave this same advantage, but could also be hilarious, wildly inventive, and occasionally almost frighteningly close to the original language. Finally, summaries in the latest version of school slang or street talk could result not only in factual appreciation of the action, but also in unusual language that occasionally provided subtle and witty comment upon the play itself. Obviously, however, such an emphasis on scene summaries—on what happened—tended to make students concentrate on plot, requiring them to sketch the broad outline of action more than to digest and understand the subtlety of subtext.

Accordingly, my teaching of Shakespeare changed. I moved away from summary to quotations, having students pick out from each scene the lines that they felt encapsulated the most significant thing expressed in that scene. Students would then write a brief paragraph justification, including who said what to whom in what context and why this quotation, over others, was their choice.

With this exercise, as opposed to the summaries, students can discuss what they picked and why. Putting two or three choices on the board or overhead projector and opening the floor for comments or having students who chose the same quotations work in groups (or, for that matter, students who chose different quotations) yields lively discussion.

Choosing a Quotation from *Othello*

After students have read or acted out scenes in class, it is also possible to have the class as a whole agree on a central quotation and discuss why it would be the majority choice. Why, for example, did my students want to argue that, in V.ii of *Othello*, "I that am cruel am yet merciful; / I would not have thee linger in thy pain" (ll. 86–87) was a more significant line than the famous "Put out the light, and then put out the light" (l. 7) or even the more well-known "one that lov'd not wisely but too well" (l. 344)? Just what was cruel, what merciful, and what Othello perceived as lingering in pain was part of the discussion. The light imagery, with all its resonance, was not, for this class at least, of interest. And perhaps the very famous loving not wisely but too well comment seemed hackneyed and, furthermore, so patently false that it was not worth consideration: how could this murderer be accused of loving, at least on a surface interpretation, "too well"?

In addition, students also passed up Emilia's poetic and powerful incremental repetition of "My husband!" as she listens incredulously to Othello's accounting of just how he knows of Desdemona's betrayal. Students similarly gave barely a glance to the "as ignorant as dirt" (V.ii.164) quotation (an insult still used widely in my region). Nor did they care to linger upon the powerful justification Iago makes for his own perfidy: "I told him [Othello] what I thought, and told no more / Than what he found himself was apt and true" (V.ii.176–77). For these students, the "cruel yet merciful" quotation was of central importance. We thus discussed Othello's assessment of his own character and actions and his stubborn refusal, at this point in the scene at least, to see the truth of Desdemona's fidelity.

Discussing a Quotation from *Julius Caesar*

To look at another quotation, let us turn to II.ii of *Julius Caesar.* There are, arguably, a number of quotations students could focus on, among them these six:

> "Nor heaven nor earth have been at peace tonight" (l. 1)
>
> "I never stood on ceremonies, / Yet now they fright me"
> (ll. 13–14)
>
> "When beggars die there are no comets seen. / The heavens themselves blaze forth the death of princes" (ll. 30–31) "Cowards die many times before their deaths; / The valiant never taste of death but once" (ll. 32–33)
>
> "Alas, my lord, / Your wisdom is consum'd in confidence"
> (ll. 48–49)
>
> "And so near will I be, / That your best friends shall wish I had been further" (ll. 124–25).

Let us take a look at the "cowards die" quotation and consider, if a class chose it, what we might discuss.

Caesar says to Calpurnia, attempting to calm her fears regarding his planned trip to the Senate, "Cowards die many times before their deaths; / The valiant never taste of death but once." Certainly Caesar means this of himself; in a subsequent line, he notes that death is inevitable and thus thinks it "strange" that people fear it. Brave words, indeed, but does Caesar really live them? Is this the comment of a great ruler, a man impervious to fear? Is Caesar, then, the valiant man rather than the coward? Does he indeed postpone going to the Senate not because of any doubts he might have, but because he is acceding to his wife: "And, for thy humour, I will stay at home" (II.ii.56)? It is possible.

But what if Caesar is not sincere? Why then, immediately following this declamation to Calpurnia, does a new, less gruesome interpretation of Calpurnia's dream by Decius sway Caesar—not to mention the not insignificant news that the Senate will be awarding Caesar a crown that very day? Has Caesar intimate knowledge of the coward dying a multitude of deaths? Is his comment wishful thinking on the part of a politician whose very life is often at stake when he goes in public?

If this interpretation is true, what are we to make of a man who pronounces certain people cowards and others (clearly himself) valiant when it seems likely that he is tailoring his words to fit his own self-serving actions? Regardless, how does this single quotation illuminate the character of Caesar? Is he a truly brave man? Or is Caesar, on the other hand, a boastful dolt? And, if he is the latter, does that fact in any way justify his subsequent murder and thus exonerate his murderers? Is self-deception or lack of self-knowledge—or even pompousness—so serious a character flaw that assassination is justifiable? Or can we absolve Caesar, recognizing that while he is not valiant, he at least wishes he were?

The context of Caesar's remark is also of interest. We know that immediately after this ringing declaration, Caesar receives new information that sways him. What does that mean? Also, would the meaning of the quotation be different if it were said to a wider audience and not, as it apparently is, to a spouse in a relatively private observation?

Looking at the language, the first line of the quotation is a straightforward subject/verb construction. The second line uses the unusual verb "taste" and then the rather less emphatic "but once" for the modern equivalent "only once." By using the plural noun "cowards," Shakespeare must use the plural "deaths" as the object of the preposition; "the valiant," however, does not require such a plural, and Shakespeare can use the more elevated and almost metaphorical "death." Thus cowards "die many times"; the valiant encounter the cosmic one death.

Turning to the verbs, why do cowards just "die" but the valiant "taste of death"? How does the verb (like the noun death/deaths) exalt death for the valiant? Finally, is there a conceptual difference in *dying* and *tasting of death*? Is Shakespeare implying that the death faced by the valiant is less permanent than that faced by cowards? What subtle distinction may there be?

This consideration, albeit brief, of a single quotation from one scene in *Julius Caesar* demonstrates how rich the consideration of just a few lines can be. Caesar's statement to Calpurnia, an offhand comment of sorts, not only illuminates his attitude toward himself and his life, but also, in its language, heavily accents the gulf between coward and valiant. Of course, the real value in interpreting this quotation comes from the fact that its consideration opens up the play. Just what does Caesar's comment tell us about his character?

Acting Out Quotations

Certainly the use of dramatics, or performance-based teaching, is an important part of considering the plays. In performance, students can experiment with the inflection and intonation of the quotations they choose, a process that necessarily brings to light alternative interpretations. Miriam Gilbert (1984), in her essay "Teaching Shakespeare Through Performance," recommends "deprivation" exercises, in which students not only mime lines, but also "telegram" them, "reducing [the lines] to the smallest number of words that will convey the message" and then performing them. She reminds us that "performance-based teaching needs to work toward discussion," which will reveal the number of interpretations any group of students will find in Shakespeare's lines.

Using Quotations in Testing the Plays

As quotations can be used to discuss the plays and their implications, so they can also be used with essay tests. It is possible to present students with a number of quotations on a requisite list and have them pick out a fair number (for example, five out of twenty or seven out of fifteen) on which to write. Student responses should include who said the lines, to whom they were said, and at approximately what juncture in the play the lines occur. Students should also discuss the significance of the quotation and its wider meaning. Context—who, to whom, and when—can be most interesting, and even if students are mistaken in their memory or judgment, they can still consider just what that quotation might mean and why. The wider significance is helpful in that it asks students to consider the contextual ramifications of the lines both before and after the actual incident.

In selecting such a list of quotations, students should have some familiarity with the range of lines before the test; to present students with a list of relatively unknown quotations—regardless of the possibility of choice—is, I think, self-defeating and anxiety-producing. The point is to look at the line or lines and see context and wider dimension. Indeed, a similar test might simply ask students to choose a limited set of quotations (possibly one for each act or a central single line) and write on why their chosen quotations are important.

Choosing Quotations

Shakespeare provides us with a universe of great lines, and every teacher has a number of favorites from the plays. For works that are, for whatever reason, less familiar, a number of handy quotation compendia, organized by author and subject, are on the market and in the library reference shelves. Yet rather than shoulder the burden of choosing quotations or selecting them from something such as *The Oxford Dictionary of Quotations* (whose third edition devotes seventy-six pages to Shakespeare), we as teachers can start with our students and ask them to select, from a limited range of lines, what quotations are most significant to them. Allowing students to select what is most important not only gives them control over the discussion, but also encourages them to consider just what is important and what is not.

Conclusion

In "The Aims of Education," Alfred North Whitehead (1929) railed against the widespread examination of students on the works of Shakespeare; it caused, he felt, in the England of the 1920s, the "certain destruction of [students'] enjoyment" and resulted in no less than "soul murder." Letting students choose quotations and then discussing them in context can, I think, keep the study of the plays away from the particular type of testing and parsing many of us found ourselves confronted with; the language thus becomes more than the "words, words, words" Hamlet sighed over (II.ii.194). The language of Shakespeare is, like the beauty of Cleopatra, what "age cannot wither . . . nor custom stale" (II.ii.239), and by exploring and celebrating that language in the study of quotations, we enjoy the infinite variety of one of the world's great language masters.

Acknowledgments

Thanks to Dr. C. W. Griffin, Department of English, Virginia Commonwealth University, for sharing ideas.

References

Gilbert, Miriam. 1984. "Teaching Shakespeare Through Performance." *Shakespeare Quarterly* 35:601–8.

Shakespeare, William. 1942. *The Complete Plays and Poems of William Shakespeare.* Edited by William Allan Neilson and Charles Jarvin Hill. Cambridge, MA: Riverside Press.

Whitehead, Alfred North. 1929. *The Aims of Education and Other Essays.* New York: Macmillan.

5 Getting to Know a Play Five Ways

Martha Tuck Rozett
The State University of New York at Albany

We have all tried to come up with topics that do not lend themselves to plagiarism but that do inspire thoughtful and analytical commentary—commentary free of clichés and oft-repeated characterizations of the Hamlet's-fatal-flaw-was-indecisiveness variety. After about fifteen years of teaching Shakespeare almost every semester, I developed a new assignment for an upper-level Shakespeare course; I call it "Getting to Know a Play Five Ways."

In devising this assignment, I tried to accomplish three major objectives:

1. To challenge students to read every line, every speech, and every stage direction in the play very carefully, and so compel them to come to terms with the whole work, not just the plot and major speeches and themes.

2. To give them an opportunity to do something imaginative, even fun, that requires analytical and communicative skills but that avoids the anxieties attendant on arguing an interpretive thesis using standard essay-writing techniques and academic diction.

3. To get them to think about a Shakespeare play as it might have been performed in 1600 by a company of actors constrained by theatrical conventions, economic considerations, and the technology of the times. These actors were speaking their lines, to be sure, but they were also entering and exiting, performing various kinds of stage business, wearing costumes, and carrying props.

To these I might add a fourth objective: I wanted to make the paper-grading process less repetitive, less predictable, and less riddled with the nagging sense that I had not gotten my students to do their best work.

The full text of the assignment, in its most recent form, reads as follows:

Getting to Know a Play Five Ways

Choose a play from among the plays on the syllabus, or choose another play by Shakespeare that you have read or would like to read. Then explore the play using two (or more, if you wish) of the five ways listed below. This assignment will be discussed in some detail in class using one of the plays on the syllabus as an example. I would be glad to consult with you during the planning stages to help you choose plays that lend themselves to the various approaches.

1. You are in charge of props for a production of a Shakespeare play. Go through the play carefully and compile a list of all the props that will be needed for the production, with indications of when and how they are to be used. Accompany your list with an essay on the thematic or symbolic significance of key props, or groups of props, including, if appropriate, some discussion of what they might look like. Avoid inventing props, aspects of scenery, or costumes that are not called for in the text.

2. You are the leader of an acting company in 1600 and are staging one of Shakespeare's plays. You have a company of seven trained professional actors, or shareholders, but will need to hire boys for the women's and children's parts and men for the nonspeaking and smaller roles. How will you arrange the doubling of the parts to make this work most efficiently, that is, with the smallest number of hires? Include an essay on the possible dramatic effect of using the same actor for two or more roles and make some suggestions about how that actor might look or act.

3. You are compiling an annotated concordance for a Shakespeare play and are preparing entries for key words used several times in ways that contribute significantly to the play's meaning. Using the Shakespeare concordances in the library as your starting point, write sample entries for at least three such words, indicating (1) how the words change in meaning depending on context and speaker, (2) how the words possess metaphorical or symbolic meanings as well as literal ones, and (3) how Shakespeare uses these words to set up thematic patterns in the play. Make sure you record each occurrence of the words you choose, including variants (e.g., *honor/honorable* or *love/lover*), and choose words that seem to be important to the particular play.

4. You are preparing a Shakespeare play for a university production. You need to divide it into two acts and cut approximately fifteen

percent of the lines in order to keep each act to about one hour and ten minutes. You may decide to cut scenes or sections of the play, but many of your cuts will probably be small groups of words or phrases which either seem too difficult or confusing for your actors and audience or else which could be regarded as redundant or relatively unnecessary to the development of plot and theme. You may also want to add or elaborate on some nonverbal stage business. Using a photocopy of our text, a colored marker, and extra space for your notes, present your cut version of the play, indicating (1) where the intermission occurs and why; (2) where the extra stage business occurs, what it consists of, and what you want it to convey; and (3) your rationale or defense of the cuts, that is, how you feel they help you emphasize what is important in your version of the play.

5. You have been offered the opportunity to do an experimental adaptation of a Shakespeare play for an off-Broadway theater. The purpose of the adaptation is to shed new light on an accepted cultural icon—a well-known, often-taught classic—in a way that makes a social, political, or aesthetic statement. You can be as radical and daring as you like in transforming the play and its characters, but you must be prepared to explain why you have changed them. Submit an outline or synopsis of your adaptation, accompanied by (1) short comments on or descriptions of each character, (2) a sample scene, and (3) an explanation or critical statement of what your play means.

Each of these exercises can be used separately, or all five can be assigned over a period of several weeks or months, combining individual and group projects. I can envision a small group of students working together to map out the doubling exercise, which becomes very complicated for a play like *Richard III*, since Shakespeare brings back most of the "killed-off" characters as ghosts in the final scene and so prevents those actors from being doubled as soldiers. Students could also work as a group on the cutting exercise, talking over the advisability of alternative cuts as they read the lines aloud to one another. Such an approach might be particularly effective with a class reading Shakespeare for the first time, as it would compel the students to figure out the syntax and purpose of a speech so that they could then decide which parts of it, if any, were dispensable. Small groups could also work on the props assignment while preparing staged readings of scenes; similarly, they could develop adaptations or transformations and stage them for a class composed of potential producers or first-night critics.

Of the five parts of the assignment, the props exercise might be most successful with students who are not quite ready for the other four. It requires a certain degree of close reading, both of the text and of the stage directions, but any text will do; students do not need to be using *The Riverside Shakespeare* or a comparable college edition in order to find references to the swords and letters and purses and rings in *Twelfth Night,* for instance. By locating such props and looking at how they are used, students might become aware of, and able to write about, Viola's inability to become convincingly masculine in the duel scene. Or perhaps they will discover the bond of trust and affection signified by Antonio's loan of his purse to Sebastian and his subsequent feelings of betrayal when Viola does not recognize him. Whichever props they do locate, the props that students overlook often reveal much about the differences between reading and seeing a play. Neither of the papers I received recently on *Richard III* included Hastings's head among the props in otherwise admirably complete lists, although both students did include the strawberries Richard asks Ely to send for, an "offstage prop" that is probably never seen. If these students had seen a performance of the play, they would surely have responded differently. Several papers on *The Two Gentlemen of Verona* left out Launce's staff, the source of some very bawdy joking in II.iii ("It stands well with him, it stands well with her," and so forth). Another student, however, who submitted a splendidly annotated cutting exercise, paid close attention to this scene and marked the text to indicate a series of comic stage directions.

It is frequently difficult to detect and assess the genuine effort that goes into term papers and critical essays. Every teacher, I am sure, has given an A to an articulate student who dashed off an interesting essay and a B or a C to a less talented student who labored long and hard over a rather dull one. The "Getting to Know a Play Five Ways" assignment enables me to recognize and give credit to the careful, conscientious student who takes the assignment seriously. Someone who does the cutting exercise, for example, does not have to write a sustained argument, but can explain in marginal notations his or her problem-solving strategies and their effect on the play as a whole. I recently read a project that cut *Richard III* by deleting all references to Jane Shore and the events in the *Henry VI* plays. The student felt that these would require explanatory footnotes not available in performance and that their omission did not detract significantly from the play's effect. She went through the play line by line, paring away additional lines, suggesting stage directions to indicate the characters' tone of voice or facial expressions, and substituting more familiar words for obsolete ones, yet paying close attention to the rhythm of the lines as she did so. Another student, whose test grades were roughly the same, clearly devoted far less effort to the assignment. Her cuts left unfinished sentences, retained responses to deleted questions, and were accompanied by little marginal commentary beyond "unnecessary" or "redundant." I had no qualms about giving her a much lower grade.

More difficult to evaluate are the decisions students make to cut the text on critical or ideological grounds. A student who started early, asked for help repeatedly, and did an excellent job on the project as a whole decided to cut out all of IV.ii in *Twelfth Night,* the scene in which Feste, as Sir Topas, visits the "lunatic" Malvolio. She found this to be "overdone" and commented, "Malvolio becomes pitiful; I do not think there is any reason to carry the prank this far." To be consistent, she carefully deleted the references to the letter and Sir Topas in the last scene (although she overlooked one, when Feste quotes Malvolio's words "By the Lord, fool, I am not mad"). I respect this young woman's decision to soften what many of my students over the years have viewed as an excessively cruel practical joke, though I did point out in my comments that an audience familiar with the play would notice the omission. I was much less tolerant, however, of a student who quickly amassed her allotted number of cuts by deleting virtually all of the Clown's lines in *All's Well That Ends Well,* apparently without thinking about the effect this would have on the Countess's role or the rhythm of the play as a whole. Nevertheless, students who choose the cutting assignment generally try hard to make the cuts work. It is quite fascinating, actually, to sit down with four or five versions of the same play and compare the students' decisions.

The doubling exercise will seem deceptively easy for plays with small casts and daunting for plays with large and complex ones. It can be fun to see students discover for themselves famous instances of doubling—Cordelia/Fool or Theseus/Oberon and Hippolyta/Titania, for example. To do this project successfully, the reader has to track a character's exits and entrances and figure out how much time an actor needs to change from male to female attire, as compared with, say, the time needed to change from the livery of one noble household to the livery of another. A theater major wrote a very interesting essay for this assignment in which she pointed out that "comic characters have a tendency to dominate on stage and audiences remember them. Because of this, I did not double the roles of Speed and Launce . . . the audience will always see the comic character acting the doubled part." Students less inclined to visualize the play sometimes come up with inappropriate doublings; for example, someone once suggested that the actor playing Charles the wrestler in *As You Like It* double as Adam, who has to be carried onstage by Orlando. Because I discuss such issues during the two class sessions I devote to explaining the assignment, I feel justified in assigning lower grades when students succumb to these and other pitfalls. Often the nameless servants and messengers (as in *Antony and Cleopatra*, for example) pose more of a problem than the main characters. This exercise thus serves to work against our tendency to concentrate on a few important characters in class discussion.

The concordance exercise is chosen by fewer students than the props, doubling, or cutting exercises, perhaps because it requires going to the library, or possibly because it more closely resembles a conventional critical essay than the other three. English majors well trained in reading for poetic imagery have written wonderful papers on sometimes surprising word combinations, but even fairly unsophisticated students can succeed at this assignment if they let the concordance (and their notes from class) guide them to the play's major images. I recently received a paper on the words *moon, dream,* and *night* in *A Midsummer Night's Dream,* a rather obvious but nevertheless effective choice; another explored the word *light* in *Romeo and Juliet,* in contrast to both *heavy* and *dark.* One of the best papers I ever received examined Shakespeare's use of the words *fool, love,* and *nothing* in *King Lear.* Since the Spevack concordances do the work of going through the play and finding all the occurrences of a word and its variants, the student writer can concentrate on developing an analysis of patterns of meaning. This can lead the most industrious among them to the *OED* and other research tools and will alert them to the ways in which words carry multiple associations or change over time. When I discuss this part of the project in class, I try to draw my students' attention to unusual words that recur only in a particular play, like *fashion* in *Much Ado about Nothing,* or words with highly charged Elizabethan connotations, like *honest* in *Hamlet.*

The last option in "Getting to Know a Play Five Ways" produces, as one might expect, the greatest variety of results. Not many students choose this exercise, and some who do simply "translate" the play into the present. Yet I have received some memorable responses over the years: some attempting blank verse, some posing probing questions about Shakespeare and the values or expectations of his culture, and some serving as an outlet for the students' own impatience with the difficult language and obvious artifice of the plays in their original form.

A few effective transformations have come to the defense of Shakespeare's female characters as a way of questioning the patriarchal assumptions under which the plays were originally written and performed. For instance, one carefully adapted and reconstructed version of *Antony and Cleopatra*, written by a senior English major, was designed to "make a statement about women in power." In Act I Antony responds to the news of Fulvia's military activities by angrily asking Enobarbus, "What right has a woman to do battle in her husband's place?" The scene with the soothsayer has been altered so that Iras and Charmian react indignantly to the suggestion that they might want to know about their husbands and children; these women are interested only in Cleopatra's political fortunes. In an added scene between Octavia and Caesar, Octavia proposes the marriage to Antony, for her own political as well as personal gain. Caesar dismisses the idea scornfully, then publicly presents it as his own. The other scenes in which Octavia appears are altered so that she appears "more assertive"; for instance, in III.iv, she leaves for Rome "a woman who knows what she wants and won't put up with Antony's behavior." Enobarbus's famous description of Cleopatra on her barge has been changed only slightly, with "an anecdote describing a strategic maneuver she once used" added to emphasize her "intellect." Moreover, Cleopatra is distraught but not childish in the scenes with the messenger and gives good reasons for her flight from the sea battle in III.xi. When Enobarbus decides to leave Antony, it is because he is frustrated that his master does not see when Cleopatra is right; this blindness, Enobarbus realizes, will bring about his downfall. In Act IV Charmian "will really have to push" Cleopatra to send Antony news of her death, and in their final scene together at the monument, Antony acknowledges his stubbornness as the cause of the tragedy. Caesar treats Cleopatra contemptuously, "as a prize and a toy," but she dies "with dignity and grace."

In her commentary, the author of this transformation explains that she did not want her Antony to come across as a "male chauvinist pig":

I want him to know what is right. I want the audience to see him strive for that, but he is human and falls short. In this day and age, I don't think there are too many "pigs" out there. I feel most men are like Antony; they are struggling with what they know is right. However, they are fighting against their upbringing.

Enobarbus and Dollabella, she adds, are the kind of men who "can look at Cleopatra as their peer without feeling insecure around a powerful woman." This young woman is using her transformation to steer a middle course through the intensely debated sexual politics of her generation. She deliberately avoids a reductive portrayal of men as "the enemy" and dwells instead on the strong women in her play. Octavia is important to her transformation, she remarks, because unlike Fulvia and Cleopatra, she does not die: "I didn't want to leave the impression that death was the successful woman's fate." The commentary ends with a justification for adding a new character, Caesarion:

> There is a myth that the "working" woman cannot be a good mother. I wanted to contradict that. I looked at a biography of Cleopatra, which said she was indeed a good mother. She loved Caesarion very much and she tried to secure his rightful place as Caesar's heir.

The most radical transformation I have received was by an English honors student who said in her final exam that she had become interested in the multiple roles characters assume (Hamlet, for example) and in the way those characters are endowed with the ability to reinvent themselves. Her transformation was entitled

The Reawakening of Juliet
1989
Hey! Romeo Is a Jerk

The first scene takes place in a college classroom, where about twenty students are reading aloud in unison from their Riverside Shakespeares. "Suddenly in one of the back desks appears a ghost-like apparition in the form of Shakespeare's Juliet." As the students read Romeo's lines about Rosaline in I.i, Juliet "jumps out of the play and into the front of the classroom," demanding to know "who this other woman is." The astonished students and professor attempt "to shut her up," so that they can proceed in an orderly way to prepare for the final exam. Juliet will not be silenced, however, and continues to comment acidly on Paris's intentions ("all he thinks about is mothering") and Romeo's pathetically self-indulgent behavior. Finally she announces that "I'm not doing the tomb scene today. It is just too much to handle after all of this misery and faithlessness." Yet once the students stop worrying about what they need to learn for the exam and support her position, she returns to the play and the reading continues. When Paris appears at the tomb in V.iii, there is Juliet, alive and waiting for everyone to arrive so that she can deliver the final speech. In her commentary, the author explains that she intended "to hand the authority of her fate and Romeo's over to Juliet." Juliet is "awakened to Romeo's childish characteristics and saves both of them from impending doom," thus creating an "updated comedy that retains the tragic framework of the original." In her final speech, Juliet announces that "I am going to eat, drink, and be merry because the next time that a student picks up this play I will let myself die. It is much easier that way and whenever I feel the need I will change the play again because now that I have the knowledge, the authority is mine."

What makes this transformation especially interesting is the way it formulates the idea that a text does not need to be the "same" each time it is read or performed and that its variants can reflect the need—here projected onto the character—to assert oneself in the face of authorial authority. The cutting exercise has a similar effect; for some students, it produces a great sense of empowerment, though others have difficulty allowing themselves to tamper with what they perceive as Shakespeare's inviolate text. I have come to believe that giving students these opportunities for self-assertion and intervention, although certainly not the only way to teach Shakespeare, serves as a constructive balance against other kinds of examinations and assignments. Not only do the students get to know the play they choose, but they also start thinking about how *Hamlet* or *Romeo and Juliet* or *Twelfth Night* is constructed by an ever-expanding community of readers, adapters, actors, directors, stage designers, filmmakers, editors, critics, teachers, and students—a community to which they belong.

6 Toward a Teachable Shakespeare Syllabus

Robert F. Willson, Jr.
University of Missouri–Kansas City

I have been teaching Shakespearean drama in college classrooms for twenty-six years. Armed with the tools of both New and Genetic Criticism, I began my career with a split personality. Students left my classes with a thorough understanding of both the clothing imagery in *Macbeth* and the growing commercial role of England in the Renaissance. Still, if there is a connection between these two bodies of information, I am not sure that early victims of my method ever grasped it.

I was the product of undergraduate and graduate professors who rode their hobbyhorses while I watched and took notes. Only in the last ten years or so have I discovered that it is impossible to teach Shakespeare's plays according to principles mandated solely by my graduate training. For example, I now regularly spend a good deal of class time identifying and illustrating those qualities that define the genres of comedy, history, tragedy, and tragicomedy. Not only do I want students to acquire a better understanding of these dramatic forms, I also want them to appreciate how Shakespeare the playwright improved his handling of them. A strictly thematic approach to the canon tends to marginalize the topic of Shakespeare's evolution as a professional writer. It also prevents students from appreciating how certain types of scenes (e.g., trials, eulogies, spying) and characters (e.g., cholerics, melancholics, fools) recur, often in only slightly modified contexts. Discussions of imagery, tragic or comic heroes, and such concepts as time, nature, justice, and mercy are of course necessary and inevitable. Yet they prove of little value unless we glimpse how Shakespeare's skill in dramatizing these topics—not just poeticizing them— improved over years of good service to his company. It goes without saying, then, that a roughly chronological organization of my ideal syllabus is essential.

Students should be encouraged to develop a firm purchase on the historical facts of Elizabethan-Jacobean life and culture. Here I am reasserting the value of the method learned in my graduate training, though I give greater emphasis to the place of public theater in English court and city life than did my former professors. My goal is to highlight Shakespeare's image as a man of the theater. Such material is often referred to by lecturers as "part of the general introduction," which students are generally urged to read on their own. My practice is to explore thoroughly the makeup of the Lord Chamberlain's (subsequently the King's) Men and to outline in detail the chief features of the Globe. Students should appreciate Shakespeare's habit of writing for particular actors with whom he worked to achieve the success of the corporation. Once my charges begin to perceive a family resemblance among such fat fellows as Bottom, Touchstone, Sir Toby Belch, and Sir John Falstaff, they can easily understand that there must have been a corpulent clown for whom box-office-conscious Will wrote those parts.

To make such connections, students need an overview of the makeup and tastes of Shakespeare's audience. That the Globe pit was peopled by a fair number of law students helps to explain why so many of the plays feature legal language and themes. Publishing practice is another topic of some significance; since no autograph manuscripts have survived, we know the plays only in published form. Indeed, the striking differences between the first and second quartos of *Hamlet* provide useful insights into the practice of pirating. Most important, teachers should emphasize dramatic and poetic conventions so that their students are easily able to identify soliloquies, scene-ending couplets, apostrophes, metaphors, and similes. The rhythmic patterns of blank verse can be explored in samples from selected plays to illustrate Shakespeare's skill in fitting sound to sense. Without this careful preparation, students will have difficulty grasping the growing sophistication with which this consummate playwright used his tools.

Shakespeare employed these tools in what might be called signature ways. For example, no other Elizabethan or Jacobean playwright relied so consistently on the theatrical metaphor. Metadramatic effects abound in the plays, and much of my classroom time is spent in pointing these out. Allusions to "cues" and "poor players," plays-within-plays, tyrants depicted as "ranting Herods," and the favorite Globe/globe pun--all these devices suggest that even as he created his plays Shakespeare was reflecting on the riddle of life as art, art as life. No discussion of *Hamlet* can ignore the hero's fascination with the theater, with actors, with the yawning gulf between "acting" in a play and "acting" as a revenger. When Macbeth calls life a "poor player," he seems to realize that he has usurped the "part" of a king and performed it badly. And Prince Hal acts the part of both prince and king in the Eastcheap tavern, rehearsing for his all-important reunion with his father. These are but a few examples of reflexiveness in the plays, but they should suffice to prove that Shakespeare regularly challenged his audiences to contemplate the theater's power to invoke distinctions between illusion and reality, role and true identity.

The identity of a true king is another favorite Shakespearean topic. In fact, the question of what a ruler is to be recurs across the corpus of plays. The differences in personality between Hal or Duncan and Richard III, Claudius, or Macbeth are legion; these characters stand as figureheads at opposite ends of the spectrum of rule. Still, it should probably not surprise us that the question of government was so fascinating to a writer in an age that so feared the spectre of anarchy. Indeed, Shakespeare similarly examines the bond between parent and child, reminding us that fathers should be wise if they expect to be obeyed and that children must pay allegiance to that invisible bond of loyalty if they expect to be appreciated. Within the individual, this same concern for government motivates explorations of reason's relationship to the will and the passions. Perhaps no other writer in Western culture so powerfully dramatized the terrible consequences to the individual (madness, suicide), family (estrangement, disowning), and state (rebellion, civil war) when government is lost.

Shakespeare also seems to instruct us that self-government must be present in the hearts of lovers. Yet this is only one aspect of that complex emotion that fascinates the playwright. That young love is blind, fickle, and spiteful seems to be a given in romantic comedies like *A Midsummer Night's Dream* and *Love's Labor's Lost*. Nevertheless, these comedies also give us characters like Theseus and Hippolyta, who appear to represent the ideal balance between reason and imagination that underpins true love relationships. In Lady Macbeth and Macbeth or Antony and Cleopatra, we witness the destructive power of love; these are associations between mature persons who prove unable to control the external and internal forces that threaten their relationships. And how distinct and different are the ties between Beatrice and Benedick or Angelo and Isabella, characters whose love is built upon contention, yet who are nonetheless forced through confrontation to realize certain truths about their own natures. Shakespeare combines the talents of both poet and psychologist in depicting characters caught in love's vexing grip.

These are obviously only a few of the elements of Shakespearean drama that should be pointed out to beginning students. The best way of combining a discussion of these topics with an analysis of Shakespeare's growth as a dramatist is the elusive goal of my ideal syllabus. To begin, I realize that I must choose about a third of the corpus—twelve or thirteen plays—in order to meet my admittedly ambitious goal. I find, however, that no more than ten or eleven texts can be profitably read and discussed in a fifteen-week semester. Recognizing this fact, I usually give students the opportunity to read and report on one or two plays outside of class.

After about a week of introductory lecturing, I begin with *Richard III*. It serves many of my purposes and generally seems to arouse student interest (most have not read it in high school), mainly because of the hunchback's impressive gift for doing evil unrestrained by a nagging conscience. Granted, most students are unfamiliar with the details of the War of the Roses, but the play stands alone as a powerful dramatic set piece and comprehensive study of a villain-hero whose persona anticipates those of Iago, Macbeth, and Edmund. Richard's opening soliloquy (I.i.1–41) yields rich profits for those interested in the rhythms and poetic richness of Shakespeare's early blank verse. The soliloquy's bombastic, melodramatic tone, its character-revealing details, its establishment of an intimate (even sympathetic?) relationship between Richard and the audience—all are reasons enough for beginning with this play. In addition, we encounter the Senecan revenge theme, prophecies of doom, and menacing ghosts. The figure of Margaret stalking the palace and serving brilliantly as the rhetorical nemesis of Richard establishes a mood of tense confrontation found in slightly different form in plays like *Hamlet, Macbeth,* and *King Lear.* The scene (V.iii) in which the ghosts of Richard's victims condemn their murderer and praise his vanquisher, Richmond, contributes a morality-play strand that Shakespeare skillfully stitches into the tragedy's Senecan fabric. Given that the central role was probably Richard Burbage's first stage success, helping to make it Shakespeare's first box-office hit, we have in *Richard III* a good beginning to the discussion of themes and structure in Shakespearean tragedy.

Of special interest in this play is the scene in which Richard woos and wins the Lady Anne (I.ii). This classic test of wills, an early "battling lovers" episode, attests to the playwright's skill in creating dialogue sparkling with wit and insult. We are also led to contemplate how Richard's other victims will be able to resist him if he can so easily win over a woman whose husband and father-in-law he openly admits to killing.

Such audacity is also found in the character of Petruchio in *The Taming of the Shrew,* the comedy to which I turn as my second play on the syllabus. Here is an early comedy following Plautine form in which clever servants assume disguises to aid their masters and dupe their betters. Here too we find the aged pantaloon, the merchant turned wooer, the Beatrice-like goddess, and the animalistic shrew. When Petruchio vows to outwit Kate in II.i, we are treated to a comic rendering of the battling lovers scene in *Richard III.* Kate's shrewishness, however, turns out to be a humor-caused disease; Petruchio's "suppose," or disguise, serves the end of a doctor out to cure this troubled but beautiful woman. Her transformation into a dutiful wife, which is documented in her controversial capitulation speech (V.ii.138–81), likewise illustrates the metamorphic quality found in most comedies. Finally, *Shrew* reveals Shakespeare's talent for managing a dual plot that is resolved in an ingenious and surprising manner.

Though a wedding feast ends *Shrew,* it is not a truly festive comedy marked by the Petrarchan excesses that characterize the form. *Love's Labor's Lost* and *A Midsummer Night's Dream* are better choices of this uniquely Shakespearean style of farce. In my ideal syllabus, I chose *MND* over *LLL* for a number of reasons, not least because it can be paired so readily with *Romeo and Juliet.* This pairing principle is a critical component of my play list; it helps students see how Shakespeare employed similar devices in both comic and tragic contexts. In *MND,* both the main plot and the "Pyramus and Thisbe" play-within explore the comic potentialities of the Romeo and Juliet story. Instead of dying through tragic accident, Hermia and Lysander are victims of the mistaken application of a love potion. The only feud that parts them is the quarrel that stems from their own jealousy. "Bad acting" could be said to dismantle the relationships of these lovers, and of Pyramus and Thisbe as well, a truth that we in the audience are allowed to glimpse while the married lovers poke fun at the mechanicals' theatrical ineptitude. *MND* gives us a multiple plot, disguise, mistaken identity, and love as a humor-caused disease; it ends happily because a benevolent god finally takes pity on the sufferers.

Romeo and Juliet, on the other hand, are victims of a feud whose death-dealing tentacles, unrestrained by the hand of providential power, destroy even the innocent. In fact, the force of destiny actually appears to drive the terrible events of this play, causing accidents and quarrels in a patterned, not capricious, way. The tragedy emphasizes as well the dangers of a sick state, one in which rule has been given over to fighting in the streets. Old Capulet's sudden change of heart is another instance of a father whose blind imposition of his will threatens the very child he hopes to protect. At base, though, both *Romeo and Juliet* and *MND* depict, often in sonorous, stylized poetry, the potential for fulfillment or destruction inherent in the passion of love.

The Merchant of Venice deals with love as well; nevertheless, Shakespeare also uses this alternately gritty and romantic tale to explore the more profound question of mercy's role in defining justice. The same theme interests him in *Measure for Measure*, another problem comedy that I recommend for study (although this play is best examined after reading the major tragedies, as students are better prepared to grasp a complex type like Angelo after encountering personae such as Claudius and Iago). *Merchant* also satisfies another important goal: the need to analyze Shakespeare's representation of outsiders and minorities. The Jew and Moor were obviously figures of great fascination to the playwright and his audience. Shakespeare's presentation of Shylock in particular, while emersed in traditional, anti-Semitic prejudices, is rich and problematic ("Hath not a Jew eyes . . ."). Shylock and Jessica also emerge as yet another of the many father-daughter pairs that are found throughout the corpus. That Shylock is the blocking parent as well as a despised, anti-Christian usurer is worth emphasizing to students who may not immediately glimpse the plot's romantic roots. Finally, the skill with which Shakespeare manages *Merchant's* dual plot, shaping symbolic words in Venice (Hell?) and Belmont (Heaven?), demonstrates his maturing talent for creating complex and allusive dramatic structures.

Such a complex structure is also evident in *Henry IV, Part 1*, the history play of choice from Shakespeare's second tetralogy. I teach this play rather than *Henry V* because I want to illustrate how the use of a comic subplot aids the purpose of conveying historical fact and legend. This tract on the education of a prince whose character achieves the Aristotelian mean between Hotspur's intrepid but blindly ambitious valor and Falstaff's phlegmatic counterfeiting is the most accessible of the histories. Here are ample pointers about the ideal king, one whose essential goodness is wedded to healthy circumspection and the ability to disguise one's true intentions. The imagined worlds of the court, tavern, and rebel camp facilitate Shakespeare's goal of demonstrating how the true prince functions in and ultimately rules all three. And to prepare us for Hal's coming-out, of course, we are treated to that delightful rehearsal—and reversal—in II.iv, an episode that the future king punctuates with the chillingly prophetic "I do, I will."

The question of rule and the psyches of rulers is a preoccupation of the major tragedies: *Hamlet, Othello, King Lear, Macbeth,* and *Antony and Cleopatra.* Some might argue that attempting to teach all these classics inclines the scale of the course too heavily in favor of tragedy. Yet these are the plays most students expect to read in such a course, and they are likewise the works most frequently alluded to by other authors—and teachers. Most compelling, these works represent the crowning achievement of Shakespeare's art. With the possible exception of *Antony and Cleopatra,* they are rich veins of poetic and dramatic ore that can be mined with great reward.

Turning to *Hamlet* after *Henry IV, Part 1* reveals how different in temperament two princes can be. A good knowledge of the doctrine of the four humors helps to clarify these differences, since Hal exhibits all the traits of the sanguine individual (optimistic, active, sociable) whereas Hamlet presents the profile of the classic melancholic (pessimistic, passive, alone). Moreover, in *Hamlet* we are invited to explore questions of evil and ambition, flattery and disloyalty, by a persona whose eloquence, sophomoric and hyperbolic as it often is, is unmatched by that of other tragic heroes. The playwright's inspired use of "The Murder of Gonzago" play-within (III.ii) serves as a revealing example of his achievement in plotting and scenic design. Although the interlude is intended to catch Claudius's conscience by replaying the murder of Hamlet's father, the poisoner in "Gonzago" is "one Lucianus, nephew to the king." Hamlet thereby hopes to spring his trap on his uncle by revealing that he knows Claudius is a regicide *and* will stalk and kill him in the same manner and place. As happens so often elsewhere in this ironic piece, however, the trap springs back on the inventor when Hamlet fails to act immediately on his proof. Shakespeare's adroit employment of this play-within reveals that he has found a key to unlock the mysteries of plotting, dramatic irony, and powerful catharsis.

Hamlet is not a good ruler, as his melancholia demonstrates. Neither, one might add, is Othello, but for different reasons. He too becomes a seeker after proof, in this case of his wife's infidelity. By relying so blindly on Iago, the Moor shows how he can be victimized by disguise or image, which he takes for truth. Though an outsider, like Shylock, Othello is nonetheless a sympathetic character; in recognizing his personality flaw, we are compelled to see how it is shared by all the other major characters. This tragedy of blind passion yields much, therefore, as a study of Satanic evil and spontaneous scheming. A particularly useful exercise is to compare Iago's soliloquizing with that of Hamlet. Through such a comparison, students begin to recognize how readily they too are seduced by "honest" Iago. This domestic tragedy also provides further illustration of the tempestuous and tragic love affair that we glimpse full-blown in *Antony and Cleopatra*. And here is another blocking father in Brabantio, warning Othello about his wayward daughter's ability to deceive.

Lear too is a father deceived by his daughters. This familial association forges a serviceable link with *Othello, Romeo and Juliet,* and even *The Merchant of Venice*. Yet the chief strength of this tragedy is its arresting depiction of madness in the king, played out against the backdrop of chaos in the state and nature. The success of the dual plot, which traces the journey of two pitiable, blind old men through suffering toward self-knowledge, marks *Lear* as Shakespeare's most comprehensive tragedy. And here is yet another variation on the play-within motif. Lear's mock trial of the absent daughters (III.vi) is followed by a horrific "bear-baiting" trial (III.vii) in which Gloucester suffers the fury of unrestrained bestiality. In *Lear,* students encounter the anarchic state of "nothingness" so feared by Jacobean audiences. They also experience the overwhelming poignancy of Cordelia's death, a sacrifice of innocence almost beyond bearing.

Sacrificing innocents becomes the habit of ambition-driven Macbeth as well. Though many students are required to read this tragedy in high school, few have had the opportunity to compare it with *Richard III,* which likewise features a murderer of innocents. These villain-heroes are intriguing types worth comparing. Macbeth's conscience, however, makes him a more believable and sympathetic character than Richard, though he lacks the lugubrious wit and inventiveness of his predecessor. And Macbeth's complex bond with Lady Macbeth, marked by impassioned debates over manliness, offers an enticing opportunity for comparison with the Richard-Margaret pairing. Moreover, the banquet scene (III.iv) can be regarded as a frustrated play-within, as the poor players of the monarchic roles watch their well-rehearsed state dinner break up into a mad dash for the exits. Finally, key to comprehending the husband-wife dynamic here is the observation of Macbeth's decline from morally sensitive thinker to robotic, Herod-like killer and Lady Macbeth's transformation from ruthless schemer to sleepwalking, conscience-stricken victim. It is as if they have changed roles.

A similar transference can be traced in the characters of Antony and Cleopatra. He begins the play with speeches about the heroic quality of love and ends trapped in Egyptian fetters proclaiming his

Roman nobility in death. The witty, puckish queen, stinging her Antony with taunts that turn into jealous threats, becomes a monarch delivering Roman eulogies after the death of her lover. In this relationship, too, we witness a lively debate on manhood, though, unlike Lady Macbeth, Cleopatra harps on the sexual rather than the political. Though difficult to teach, this play deserves a place on any syllabus, if only because it requires students to accept as hero and heroine characters who more closely resemble the bickering, unromantic types in comedies like *The Taming of the Shrew* and *Much Ado about Nothing*. Much fruitful discussion time can also be spent comparing Antony and Cleopatra with Romeo and Juliet, a comparison that reveals how different the tragic worlds of the two plays are. As for the play's dramatic structure, I have found that the rapid-paced, fragmented third and fourth acts can be analyzed successfully using the language of cinema. The short scenes are like jump cuts that create a mood commensurate with the sudden, time-eating collapse of the lovers' empire.

Given the emotional scope of *Antony and Cleopatra*, I find the return to a more cerebral, debate-style play like *Measure for Measure* something of a restorative. Looking back to *The Merchant of Venice*, students can appreciate Shakespeare's continuing interest in the quasi-legal question of mercy's relationship to justice. Moreover, in II.ii and II.iv we have confrontation scenes of extraordinary tension, recalling the mood of scenes between Othello and Desdemona (V.ii) and Lear and Cordelia (I.i). That Angelo can be forgiven his loutish attempt to seduce the novice Isabella, as well as win the hand of the fair Mariana, yields rich material for a lively discussion of the Shakespearean problem play. Furthermore, with its disguised duke, lecherous Lucio, and underworld apostates like Mistress Overdone, *Measure for Measure* is a good example of the decadent style of entertainment that was beginning to fascinate jaded Jacobean audiences.

Tragicomedy is of course further evidence of a significant shift in audience taste that Shakespeare was eager to satisfy. For this reason, *The Winter's Tale* or *Cymbeline* would appear to be good examples of the new form. But these plays are difficult to teach; their romance conventions require fuller explanation than I can provide late in the semester. *The Tempest*, on the other hand, meets many requirements of a satisfactory "closer." The Prospero-Miranda tie recalls earlier father-daughter pairs, but it hints at a happy resolution impossible to achieve in the world of the tragedies. Indeed, the emphasis in *The Tempest* is on reconciliation, not alienation; Ferdinand is after all the choice of both father and daughter. Prospero's marriage masque (IV.i) is another variation on the play-within formula, here prompting the father/magician/artist's memorable speech on the end of revels and faded, insubstantial pageants. This tone poem on forgiveness and the healing power of art also addresses the compelling question of rule. By abjuring his magic and his lust for revenge, Prospero affirms that "the rarer action" for both father and ruler "is in virtue than in vengeance." Realizing this truth, Prospero will return to his dukedom with a more optimistic view of human nature and a strengthened faculty of reason so vital to any monarch. That *The Tempest* can be read as both a farewell to the stage and a reaffirmation of human goodness seems to me—and to perceptive students—an inescapable truth.

Whether this proffered syllabus is teachable is a matter for the reader to decide. It works for me, and I boldly assume that, in fact, these are the plays (with a few substitutions) that most teachers of Shakespeare cover in their introductory classes. If students who read these plays in this order and from these perspectives come away with a greater appreciation of Shakespeare's gifts as a professional playwright, I will congratulate myself on having truly fulfilled my assignment for this volume.

II Performance?

7 Shakespeare off the Page

J. L. Styan
Northwestern University

My Classroom for a Stage!

"Shakespeare off the page"—because that is the object, to deal in people, not print, to bring the dead alive, legs, arms, ears, eyes, and all. "Off the page," but not, alas, all the way on to the stage—because that is so often how it is, off the page but still in the classroom. Nevertheless, Coleridge condemned Shakespeare's stage as a "naked room" with "a blanket for a curtain," and that description perhaps fits very many of the classrooms we have all known. If it was right for Shakespeare, it could be right for us.

The true discipline of drama study is to find out how drama works, how it performs under the conditions for which it was written, how it communicates and affects an audience. For any point or meaning a play may carry lies in that electric circuit constantly flowing back and forth between stage and audience, where it is a felt experience. The object, then, is to provide an avenue for performance, and the best part of this essay will be to make suggestions for this. First, however, some principles may be welcome.

Death by Ketchup: Some Principles

The best way to learn to swim is to get into the water; and so one gets involved with performance in order to know something about a play. Yet the object is not necessarily to learn how to act or direct or design, but to confront the elements of the art form as they apply to the particular piece under scrutiny, to discover their importance. This ought to be the target at every level of education, even in graduate school. All other knowledge of a play risks being peripheral, even misleading. Make no mistake: learning by doing is hard work and (to deliberately steal the old terminology of the New Criticism) a matter of "close analysis," a kind of "practical criticism" with a perceptual bite. Only then will it stand the test of transmission, reception, and response. Of course, this process consumes time, but it is time well spent, time that keeps the all-essential experience of the play alive and well. And one little scene alive is worth more than a whole play dead.

The principles behind this direct method of teaching follow naturally. If a literary analysis holds to the primacy of the words and asks questions about those a play uses—what kind of words? how do they behave and why?—in drama these questions return us immediately to performance. These same questions—what? how? and why?—justify the regular topics dealt with in literature courses: matters of form and content, the medium and its effect, the audience and its representation, the historical and philosophical background of the work, and so on. In drama, however, these questions do not permit a merely academic approach to interpretation, for if we try to talk about the "idea" or "meaning" behind a play as if it were a logical formulation, it evaporates as soon as the curtain rises. Plays do not have meanings, any more than babies have meanings. But plays, like babies, have a potential function, and can grow to do good.

There is no final way to make a satisfying investigation of a playtext other than to try it out. Reading it, listening to it on a tape, seeing it on film or in the theater—everything helps. But in the end, a play has to be known by testing it in performance, seizing it red-handed in the commission of the act in order to show what it could be and do. Of course, each teacher and each class will know their own best way, and each scene will seem to propose its own treatment. My favorite way is to force it against its nature, with more than one group of actors putting it to the test. "To be or not to be" spoken conversationally, lying down, and puffing on a cigarette is one kind of visual/aural test; intoned and spoken to the sky according to the teapot school of acting is another; either may test the medium. And every time, the response of approval or disapproval, bewilderment or insight, becomes a comment on the words.

By the pedagogical device of performance another desirable end is achieved: nothing comes between the play and the students, no secondhand experience from some stale introduction or instructor advising them what they should think and feel. There will be less pontification and little generalization until after the event. At the same time, students will have had a direct, firsthand experience, and when they see their peers at work, they will be pleasantly alert and critical because they will be involved in the same effort with the same material. The aim of the method is none other than "show and tell."

Are performance devices and subsequent discussion enough to teach Shakespeare? Yes. If knowledge of the period is needed and valid, the encounter with the text will prompt its discovery. When an Elizabethan word or a poetic practice cries out to be deciphered, the demand will be there. If the background of manners and customs or of political and religious attitudes is urgent, it will be researched willingly. If a dramatic convention or technique has surfaced, it will be tested in the best way possible: on a sympathetic audience that can react with perception.

In some small way, the play will have been sampled and felt as a living, growing, changing creature. In particular, performance brings into appropriate prominence those elusive but powerful and essential dramatic elements that no amount of talk can identify, elements like rhythm and style, space and silence. Such things are lost on the page, and without them a play is so far less meaningful that it is close to self-mockery; their absence can make a tragedy into a farce, and any play into a travesty. With performance, students can make genuine value judgments on what they have seen and heard. Those in the audience will be critically engaged, and those on their stage feet will see the "whites of their eyes," an essential initiation. The extraordinary subtlety and interest of a play's power to manipulate an audience and achieve a response, almost impossible to achieve by any other method, emerges when drama is studied as drama. In addition, praise be, the concept of drama as possessing its own discipline of study, multifaceted and drawing on all the other arts, will be reasserted, thereby reversing the schizophrenic division that it has suffered for so long between departments of literature, theater, music, physical education, and what have you.

The intention behind the performance method is not to become a good actor, though perhaps it is to become a good audience. In the making of drama, Meyerhold believed that there was, in addition to the author, the director, and the actor, a fourth creator, namely, the spectator. The super-principle here is that a play is completed by perceiving it. A play is not the book, the text, which is merely a code of signals to be deciphered in its medium. It is for the actors to relay the signals. A play comes alive only when its signals are perceived, the synthesis of all its parts completed, and the circuit of the live experience closed.

From this all things follow: that the code must be known and that it must be capable of being deciphered, particularized, received, and judged. If poetry is making something and drama is doing something, then theater is perceiving something. In this century, psychology believes that perception is not a passive but an active faculty; in theater, then, an audience is essentially required to be creative. We as instructors are educating our students' gift for dramatic imagination and perception—one of the things for which we are in this business of teaching.

If the student of drama has only the text of a play, he or she must perforce be actor and spectator both; the true art of reading a play requires it. Nothing in the world will make readers believe us when we say that *Hamlet* is a good play until they have had some direct experience of it. In 1926, the British Board of Education proposed to offer the public a series of lectures on drama and announced that the first would be on the subject of "comedy." William Poel said immediately what we all know to be true: that no lecture can teach an audience to laugh (unless it is an audience of professors, he added). We should not substitute preaching for teaching.

We cannot forget that there is a glorious mystery in drama, as in all art forms. It is impossible to talk pertinently about a play, about a dramatic form, without its human feeling. Here drama is vivid in its mystery. People do not generally kill their fathers and marry their mothers, nor consult witches when deciding a course of action, nor slip into soliloquy whenever they are alone. Yet we tolerate all this in the name of art. For when it is used on the stage, the cheapest of paste jewelry acquires magic properties and a wound oozing ketchup can cause death. The imagination does not call for scientific proof. So it is that to confine a play to a book is not only to strip it of its immediate sensory qualities, but also of its unpredictable mystery.

A Marginal Comment

Every teacher is different, as every class is different, and one should be wary of laying down any law. But I wish briefly to meet some points that have been raised against this "direct method" of teaching Shakespeare.

It has been suggested that in its rough-and-ready fashion, poor performance will do more harm than good. Nevertheless, this method, I fear, almost depends on poor performance. Some excellent teachers, I realize, have practiced a Stanislavskian approach, working with the "given circumstances" and "magic ifs" of the Method to guarantee a certain quality of performance. Yet while it is a delight to see a good student performance, my emphasis is far less on the actor and what he or she can achieve than on the hypercritical spectator.

To play the devil's advocate for a moment, I would challenge the ghost of Konstantin Stanislavsky in the classroom on two counts: (1) because students are usually nonprofessional, and should remain so, and (2) because Stanislavsky's ways are often uncritical of the play in hand. His great achievement was to reveal the psychological attributes required of an actor in bringing a character to life. Yet in my view, it is this same achievement that makes Stanislavsky an inappropriate guide for the critical activity desirable in a drama class. This is especially true of plays of determinedly unreal situations and characters, like those of Shakespeare.

It is now a matter of history that those who practiced the Method were in danger of asserting their own personality at the expense of the character portrayed. We remember Brando and Gielgud in Manckiewitz's *Julius Caesar,* with Antony searching for his "inner logic" and Cassius resolutely sticking to the rhythm of his lines; it was like watching two different plays that had somehow gotten on to the same stage by mistake. The Method teaches that you can be a better actor by "Being Yourself"—a cliche, Tyrone Guthrie thought, that was inadequate to express any wide range of characters or styles. Robert Brustein once warned that looking for the "subtext" can be a stratagem by which an actor may ignore the playwright's meaning in order to substitute a feeling he or she finds more compelling. And we know that Brecht preferred to expose the spectator to shock tactics, making performance a discussion with an audience.

In my classroom, the students never receive a complete and authentic theater experience, which is bound to be imperfect in any case. The aim is to develop the perception of the student spectator of Shakespeare *at the expense of* performance. To stop and start a performance repeatedly, which can happen if audience perception is the object, is no doubt to batter the sensibilities of the actors, but it can ensure that we see how a play works. The test of style lies in the relationship between stage and audience. When the lovers in the last act of *As You Like It* move into a dance, as their lines suggest, and we are curiously invited to see human love in a special way—partly lyrical, partly reductive—a finished performance works against the critical faculties; only a discussion-rehearsal—painfully slow, never line-perfect, rarely hypnotic—can arrive at this perception.

I confess that my Shakespeare games are therefore nothing like good theater and may seem terribly mechanical. The performers are in competition and contrast with each other, so that the class can see the spectrum of possibilities in a scene or a character or a line. The aim is to create the impression that there is nothing definite about a play. My tricks are thus deliberately provocative, designed to sharpen attention, return us to the text, and prove that a good play is a crucible of unpredictable thoughts and feelings.

Shakespeare on Legs: Some Practice

Ideally, a class should choose its own representative scene and look for a moment in the action that it feels the playwright would not have the audience miss on any account, perhaps a touch of characterization or a quality in the mood or style of a scene. Then, in independently working groups, the class tries to prove the worth of the moment it has selected, one group to another. Such competing units make for lively classroom experiences, and splitting a class into smaller units ensures that everyone is involved in some capacity—"no passengers." In particular, it ensures that theater students do not steal the limelight.

Nevertheless, for students simply to read lines aloud, however badly, and to get to their feet, however awkwardly, sets the eyes and ears to work; responses flow; theater has been initiated. But for this you do not need a lot of theatrical hoopla. Here I have listed a few interesting incidents from recent years and sorted them into categories of a kind—six sorts of activity in the Shakespeare class that often came as a surprise to everyone, including myself.

Show and Tell; or, The Duel Nobody Loses

The injunction is "Do it, try it, show us," with rival teams "doing it" in different ways. Are the opening moments of *King Lear* dull? Gloucester and Kent are having a joke about Edmund's bastardy:

> *Kent:*   I cannot conceive you.
> *Gloucester:* Sir, this young fellow's mother could.

(I.i.12–13)

Edmund is present and hears all this, or he seems to. But if the three walk on together, the lines lose their point. Yet set Edmund apart for us to watch him as we listen to the old men's joke and his silence grows eloquent, since the focus is now powerfully on his feelings.

It will take more than two groups to search out all the nuances from the scene in which Cordelia wakes her father from his madness. The finely scaled-down detail with which Shakespeare conceived this moment awaits the fresh discovery of every student: their physical closeness, the only kiss we see the king receive, Cordelia's hands first on his hair, then on his face, then cradling his head perhaps; eyes straining to see him move, guess his new condition, perceive the pinprick. And who is kneeling to whom? (I'm sure they are both kneeling to one another, father to daughter, subject to monarch.) And only trial and error can arrive at what must happen on "Be your tears wet?"

The ultimate test of the deposition scene in *Richard II* is to try out the purpose of the props called for: throne, crown, and mirror. When is Bolingbroke, when is Richard, sitting on the throne, holding, wearing the crown? The permutations are endless, enough to defeat the best of graduate students and certainly the instructor.

Ringing the Changes; or, The Proliferation Principle

Going round the class studying *Twelfth Night*, and hearing each Malvolio deliver his exquisite line to Olivia—"Sweet lady, ho, ho!"—while in his yellow stockings will suggest a rainbow of noise and a multicolored parody of a lover enough to scare any lady out of her wits. Never spoken the same way twice, the line is powerful poetry. There appears to be no way to get it wrong.

In *Much Ado about Nothing*, the brilliant suggestions that lie behind Beatrice's climactic demand that Benedick "Kill Claudio!" can best be elicited by milking the proliferation principle with several pairs working separately. She is testing his loyalty by an outrageous demand that goes to the heart of the play. But will the audience laugh or be stunned? How is the response to be controlled?

And in *Othello*'s last act, have a sequence of Moors smother their Desdemonas one after another in order to discover the nature of the murder he commits. How much of what he "thought a sacrifice" is what an audience sees?

Vice Versa; or, Hamlet in Pink

If you want to know why the prince wears his "nighted color," let him wear something completely different.

Or, in I.iii of *Romeo and Juliet*, how does Juliet feel when two older women, her mother and her nurse, try to persuade her to marry the County Paris? During Lady Capulet's lengthy harangue, Juliet is silent for thirty lines. When at last she does speak, her response is distinctly ambiguous:

> *Lady Capulet:* Speak briefly, can you like of Paris' love?
>
> *Juliet:* I'll look to like, if looking liking move.

> (I.iii.96–97)

We must assume a substantial pause before this response, but even then it hardly tells us much. One group tried the scene first with Juliet frowning in doubt, then had her laughing with anticipation. Neither seemed right. The last team turned it around again, and Juliet had no facial expression whatsoever because she had her back to the audience. The scene worked, because we found ourselves in Juliet's shoes, wondering how we would have received the Lady's blandishments and the Nurse's bawdy remarks.

Shakespeare tries something like this trick again in *Much Ado*, when in her eavesdropping scene, Beatrice silently receives the news that Benedick is in love with her. A little before, in Benedick's eavesdropping scene, he exposed his weaknesses by talking. The tone of Beatrice's scene is different; her feelings lie deeper.

In *Twelfth Night*, Viola as Cesario is another who cannot express her feelings. But in this play, her embarrassment is turned to delightful comedy when she is cross-questioned by the one she loves. Orsino's teasing,

> My life upon't, young though thou art, thine eye
> Hath stay'd upon some favour that it loves,
> Hath it not, boy?

> (II.iv.23–25)

calls for Viola to supply an amusing facial reaction that we see but that the Duke does not. Managing this to maximum comic effect upon an audience will call for experiment with a variety of spatial arrangements between the two of them, with the class as judge and jury of what works.

Cloning and Clowning; or, Playing Ball with the Bard

Charles Marowitz's strategy in his version of *Macbeth* was to have three Macbeths (analogous to the three Witches) to show the different sides of his character. In the theater this seems unnecessary; but in the classroom a hydra-headed character can provoke debate. For instance, one class, working with the first four acts of *Lear*, chose four Lears to mark his progress round the wheel of fire. They were Lear the tyrant, in authority,

> Come not between the dragon and his wrath;

> (I.i.122)

Lear the blasphemer, challenging the elements and his maker,

Blow winds, and crack your cheeks!
>   (III.ii.1)

Lear the madman, seeing himself in Poor Tom,

>   Didst thou give all to thy daughters?
>   (III.iv.49)

and Lear the contrite, waking to Cordelia's caresses,

>   Pray do not mock me.
>   I am a very foolish fond old man.
>   (IV.vii.58–59)

The four Lears stood in the corners of the room, and we heard the differences, tracking the psychological and thematic changes through the sensory pattern.

In tragedy, the proliferation principle is a challenge; applying it to the role playing of characters in Shakespeare's comedy becomes downright mind-boggling. A class reading *As You Like It*, for instance, had nine Rosalinds; I leave this thought with you.

A more manageable trick I owe to a former student, Professor Douglas Sprigg of Middlebury College. It involves the use of the personal prop. The few such props in Shakespeare are used vividly: Lear's whip, Hamlet's skull, Hal's crown. Or one may invent one's own (temporary) props by which to explore a character. The different sides of Gloucester's character in the opening soliloquy of *Richard III* were revealed by one group using a knife and an apple, although neither is in the text. Fondling the knife and jabbing it into a table on "I am determined to prove a villain" produced a monster. Spoken again without a knife but with a bite of the apple had an electrifying effect, pointing up the villain's cynicism and also his charm (thus preparing for the seduction of Lady Anne).

All Right on the Night; or, Improvise If You Must

In a sense, all drama is to a degree "improvised," but on occasion Shakespeare had the good sense and audacity to set up a situation pregnant with bizarre possibilities and then duck out. In *Twelfth Night*, the duel between Viola and Andrew is anticipated very carefully by undermining what little valor they have. Shakespeare then offers the stage direction "They draw" and no more. But what happens next? The class will joyfully stretch its imagination. Granville-Barker's classic solution was to have each duelist add feverishly to the ceremonial business of saluting in order to delay coming *en garde*.

In *A Midsummer Night's Dream*, Puck's disposal of the lovers for sleep at the end of III.ii by no means suggests that he knows how to arrange them in the correct pairs, unless one grants him a theatrical magic even he is unaware of. Surely the audience must help with advice. And the "Pyramus and Thisbe" play is laden with built-in cues for improvisation, beginning with the delicious interaction of Pyramus and Wall on the hint "The wall methinks being sensible should curse again."

Malvolio's letter scene in *Twelfth Night* brilliantly lends itself to class improvisation. Following Maria's cue, "Get ye all three into the box tree," a decision must be made about where this box tree is to be placed for maximum effect. Better still, consider whether a tree or a bush is needed at all if the *commedia dell'arte* device of farcical "freezing" is used. What if the three conspirators *are* the box tree?

Space and Serendipity; or, Perform and Perceive

Shakespeare enjoyed the empty space of his stage platform, and time and again a line demands spatial treatment. Blessed is the instructor who can open up the classroom or move into an area, indoors or outdoors, comparable to that of the Elizabethan stage.

In *Macbeth*, how should the actors be arranged if King Duncan is to be seen "meeting a bleeding captain"? Does the king enter at the same time as the captain? If not, which of them enters first? And where and how is their meeting effected?

A simple repetition of a word may signal extraordinary business on the stage. In *Hamlet*, how many ways are there to present the prince's "Mother, mother, mother!" as he approaches Gertrude in her chamber? (Try the first word offstage, the second upstage, and the third downstage to her face.) And in *King Lear*, the play reaches its agonizing denouement when the king enters with a dead Cordelia in his arms (or even hanging backwards over a wheelchair, as in London in 1990). Shakespeare marks the moment with three sounds: "Howl, howl, howl!" This time it is the players on stage who will, like a good onstage audience, hear the first sound offstage and react for us, while the last will surely chime with Lear's arrival downstage as he offers the dead girl to the audience directly. Yet there must be many other meaningful ways to arrange this remarkable line.

For one last challenge, this time to students working on *Romeo and Juliet*, consider the ballroom scene. Romeo's fairly long, rhetorical, and expository speech is followed by Tybalt's threat to kill him. Most notable is the sudden action line "Fetch me my rapier, boy!" The boy serves to catch our eye in the first place, but his silent worth is wasted if he now merely slinks away. Yet if he scuttles through the crowd of formal dancers, he can suggest impressively how an orderly and happy occasion may be brought to the edge of disruption. Space is an invaluable asset, and the number of scenes in Shakespeare which use it cannot be counted.

There are no right answers in all this, try as we may. The golden rule is that there are no golden rules. But it does not matter. If drama is a fallible human process of communication, perception, and response, so teaching is also an uncertain human process, one in which, finally, there are only attempts at communication, perception, and response. The art of drama and the art of teaching have a good deal in common.

8 Goals and Limits in Student Performance of Shakespeare

Charles H. Frey
University of Washington

This is a brief plea for more use of student performance in teaching both Shakespeare and drama in general. I end, however, with a caveat concerning certain perceived limits in student performance.

One reason to use student performance in teaching drama is to help students see differences between dramatic and nondramatic forms. Most drama is designed for performance, and students need to understand what that means. Students who read aloud may be encouraged to make the choices in emphasis, tone, and pace that so crucially inform dramatic interpretation. And students who get on their feet to block or perform a portion of a play may discover just how significant the elements of staging that give particular life to a script really are.

Some teachers of single plays in literature courses feel they have all they can do to help students through basic analysis of language, content, and background. But even those hard-pressed teachers might find time to have students memorize a few lines, argue for a ranking of important words in a passage and for alternative ways of intoning them, or indicate what gestures or postures of stage movement would seem appropriate at key points in the play. Indeed, if a teacher is going to devote three or four weeks or more to a play, he or she should be able to teach basic literary analysis *and* divide the class into groups asked to work up a small part of the script for a memorized and blocked performance.

In response to such suggestions, some teachers may object that drama school is the proper place to teach performance. But students were performing drama in English classes before drama schools were even invented. "The play way" of teaching drama in English has a long and distinguished history, reaching back from such current practitioners as Professor Styan at Northwestern through Professor Baker at Harvard and Yale to Caldwell Cook and others near the turn of the century. It is true that some current advocates of studying drama in performance—John Russell Brown, for example—stop short of endorsing full student performance on the grounds that such performance tends to be too excited and too inept to do the theater justice. Yet I disagree with this negative judgment, and I hope that there may be others who have found or will find student performances to be generally instructive, even at times quite skilled and moving.

Other teachers may question student performance on the grounds that some students will resent the forced exposure of performance or may unexpectedly find it too stressful. Again, in watching dozens of such groups, I have not found this to be the case. On the contrary, there seems to be a little ham in everyone, and students who are asked to be responsible for a speech and its physical embodiment as a rule take the work so seriously that they begin to ask on their own what difficult phrases mean, how a speech or scene has been produced, and what sorts of interpretation make sense.

Some skeptics say that students who are not drama majors know nothing of voice production, blocking, and acting skills. Yet such students can quickly gain surprising competence, particularly when they work with more experienced students. Certainly they can rapidly gain an intimate, intricate, and responsible appreciation of how plays come alive on the stage.

Finally, beyond all of these objections lies the harder one: that literary study and performance do not blend well because traditional literary study and teaching have tended not only to be universalizing, spatial, antitemporal, and antidramatic in character, but also based in part upon a conception of student learning—indeed, upon an entire ideology of knowledge—as privatized and competitive. Traditional literary analysis and teaching tend not to allow sufficient collaborative student exploration of the emotional impact and social functions of art. Teaching students to read closely has too often meant teaching them how to interpret a text as certain teachers and critics interpret it. There is, then, a political dimension to the contrast between the literary study of drama and student performance. In fact, student performance often gets associated with the strident theorizing of those who would make creative dramatics the basis of much education so as to validate claims of emotion against reason or claims of dialogic democracy against the authoritarian single voice.

I find in my own experience with teaching through student performance that, yes, it does seem to promote collaborative learning. And it helps students to reappropriate and refashion a piece of their culture in a responsible way, to choose and to create instead of to consume. But also it teaches students more about the meaning of a play and about the nature and functions—including social functions— of drama than they can learn through any other method I know. I therefore heartily encourage student performance of drama.

In teaching Shakespeare, however, the student performance method may have a few drawbacks, as my own experience suggests. I teach Shakespeare to both undergraduate and graduate students. My undergraduate courses typically are at the 200 and 300 level and contain about even mixtures of first-, second-, third-, and fourth-year students; a majority major in disciplines other than English. I average about forty students per class and usually teach courses that meet five days a week (for fifty-minute periods) and that last for ten weeks (one academic quarter). My students typically have studied one or two Shakespeare plays in high school. We ordinarily study four to six plays in the ten weeks, averaging about two weeks per play. Usually we have full-class lecture and discussion on Monday, Wednesday, and Friday; each Tuesday and Thursday, groups of eight to ten students work on preparing (choosing the scene, assigning and memorizing parts, working up blocking, rehearsing) a scene for performance during the last week of class.

Most of my students have little serious difficulty in grasping the standard dictionary, or denotative, sense of Shakespeare's words and phrases. But some students profess themselves baffled by the "Old English," in particular, by the number of unfamiliar words, the un- expected meanings of seemingly familiar ones, the odd combinations of words in phrases, the difficult images, the unusual grammatical and syntactical groupings, the complexity of sentence and paragraph struc- ture, the nature and variety of meters, and above all the tone and emotion to be heard and spoken through the speeches. Because of such difficulties, I always have students study the material on Shake- speare's language in the critical apparatus of the collected edition we use. I also lecture on the history of the English language and pay particular attention to questions on how Shakespeare's English may have been pronounced, on unfamiliar meanings for familiar words, and on obsolete, antiquated, Latinate, bombastic, or bawdy language. I work the class through a variety of exercises designed to show that Shakespeare's language is indeed written in sentences and that the words can be understood, paraphrased, and spoken in their original form with some confidence as to meaning and tone. Finally, I take up questions on puns, ambiguity, irony, indeterminacy, and the like.

If a class appears hesitant or slow to report its own understanding of the language, I may arrange the chairs in a circle and ask the students to read aloud a passage by having the first student read the first word, the next student the second word, and so on, round and round for a few minutes until certain points are obvious:

1. Shakespeare's language can be broken down into very small units of speech and responsibility.

2. Taking one word at a time is a promising way to begin studying the language.

3. In the class, a student does not have to be "an expert" to speak Shakespeare; tiny units of responsibility can be taken on democratically.

After following each other one word at a time, the students may go on to speak successive phrases (any cluster of words appearing between commas or end-stops) or complete sentences. I sometimes encourage students to paraphrase words, phrases, sentences, and passages, either verbally or in writing. We discuss several kinds and aims of paraphrase (whether to seek the letter or the spirit; imitating the syntax, meter, level of diction, tone, and so forth), and we work toward routes that may allow the students to speak the original words aloud with as much genuine emotion as the language warrants.

Because my students often work up the part of a particular Shakespearean character in a scene, I introduce them to the rudiments of actorial preparation. Still, although I was quite enamored of teaching Shakespeare's language through student performance for about a decade, recently I have come more and more to admit problems with the method. Although every student in my class performs, and although none has reported difficulty with hampering shyness or embarrassing incapacity to speak or move with energy and a fair measure of conviction, most students still seem to express the significance and feeling of particular speeches and actions in Shakespeare according to rather tame, safe, culturally endorsed stereotypes of "acting." This behavior mimics, I believe, the behavior of the vast run of film and theatrical actors and actresses. I think there are two reasons for the residual stubbornness of this problem. First, the models of acting, including Shakespearean acting, available to students are often inadequate for conveying genuine and relevant emotion. And second, the potential charge of emotion and significance in much of Shakespeare's language is either too strong or too alienating for communication in conventional classroom settings.

My observation of filmed and live Shakespearean acting suggests that few, if any, actors attempt significant eye contact, voice contact, acting in the present, self-revelation, mind-body fusion, subconscious spontaneity, sustained affection, or any other action that would permit deep and genuine communication between actor and audience. That total responsibility for this situation does not lie with actors should perhaps go without saying; audiences in this culture are not (and probably never have been) educated to look for, demand, or contribute to any but the safest and most constraining routines of theatrical interaction. There is little evidence, in other words, that Shakespearean theater has opened access to emotional realities experienced routinely in any of the many evolving rituals produced in psychodramatic, process-oriented, or other therapeutic workshops, in theater games, in meditation, in prayer, in personal experience with dance or music, or in relations with family, friends, and lovers. As teachers we tend to tout Shakespeare's language as a vehicle of vast cognitive and emotional experience, yet few of our students have discovered any such vehicle.

It may be that students see much of Shakespeare's language as peculiarly at war with itself; countless situations, actions, and speeches in Shakespeare's plays suggest extreme limits of risk, striving, and passion, yet the accompanying language often appears Latinate, artificial, bookish, or tortured. Even when blatant bombast is not at issue, students may find it hard to believe in or find equivalents for exchanges of "passionate speech." The following passage from *Romeo and Juliet* might exemplify this central problem of the posturing emotant:

Nurse: O holy friar, O, tell me, holy friar,
                  Where's my lady's lord? where's Romeo?

Friar Lawrence: There on the ground, with his own tears made
                  drunk.

Nurse: O, he is even in my mistress' case,
                  Just in her case. O woeful sympathy!
                  Piteous predicament! Even so lies she,
                  Blubb'ring and weeping, weeping and
                  blubb'ring.
                  Stand up, stand up, stand, and you be a man.
                  For Juliet's sake, for her sake, rise and stand;
                  Why should you fall into so deep an O?

Romeo: Nurse! [*He rises.*]

Nurse: Ah sir, ah sir, death's the end of all.

Romeo: Spakest thou of Juliet? How is it with her?
                  Doth not she think me an old murtherer,

> Now I have stain'd the childhood of our joy
> With blood removed but little from her own?
> Where is she? and how doth she? and what
> says
> My conceal'd lady to our cancell'd love?
>
> (III.iii.81–98)

For me, in speaking or teaching this passage (and thousands like it), the primary task is to find, feel, believe in, name, and express the passions of the speakers while admitting a sense of linguistic manipulation, of highly self-conscious controls in punning, wordplay, soundplay, and artifice. In what sense is such language to be "taken seriously," "felt in the pulse," "made one's own"? I generally let the anguish in the language languish. I fear that the process of grinding Shakespeare's cleverness or artistry against the situational pain of the characters will simply make it more and more apparent that Shakespeare's language often has little to do with experiencing or learning about what we in our culture identify as genuine, real, empathic feeling. And so I often end up teaching Shakespeare as a master ironist who teaches us to protect our vulnerabilities; at the same time, I must wistfully concede that Shakespeare's characters, more in spite of than because of his language, seem to reach their lives' limits.

Lest any teachers who may read this find too little (or too much) recognition here that after pain a formal feeling comes, let me hasten to add that student performers sometimes display the capacity to mold Shakespeare's often distancing discourse to their own emotions and concerns. The formality, even intellectuality, of the language gives it a useful starch and resistance to conventional sentimentality, street-muddy casualness, or the lobotomous insecurities of the soaps. If students are going to drive real feeling and understanding in any sort of forceful combination through *this* language, they will have to consider it carefully, know what they are about, shape the goals and desires of the characters, and raise up the energy of their passion to the intricacy of each passage. Some students can do that; others cannot and hence swerve themselves into many of the byways commonly inhabited by professional actors (and other interpreters).

A final possibility for enlivening, for incarnating, student reading and performance of Shakespeare lies in attention to the materializing tendencies of Shakespearean imagery and metaphor. Instead of elevating Shakespeare's imagery upward from the sensory ground to the moral tag (wherein blood becomes passion, the eye ego, the heart the soul, and the whole world an allegorical spirit show), a teacher can encourage the student to investigate the literal, experiential ground of the imagery. "Whether 'tis nobler [1] in the mind to suffer / The slings and arrows of outrageous fortune, / Or [2] to take arms against a sea of troubles / And by opposing end them"? Or "Whether 'tis nobler in the mind [1] to suffer . . . or [2] to take arms . . .'"? If we take arms in the mind, what happens to the "mind"? If we take arms not just in the mind, but also out in the world, actionally, then is the sea of troubles "merely" a figure of speech? If we wade out into the sea brandishing our own slings and arrows, will we end the troubles (possibly the opposing "slings and arrows of outrageous fortune")? Or end our taking arms? Or both? Is "To die" (which follows immediately in the passage) a thought consequent upon the suicidal nature of the literalized image, wading in arms into the sea? Is not the play keenly interested in "If the man go to this water and drown himself" (V.i.16)? As Ophelia did? Did the queen go to the liquid knowing that it was quite possibly poison? Did Hamlet take arms "in the grapple" at sea with the pirate ship? Why not "take arms against a sea of troubles" in the most concretely imagined way? What could be lost? What could be gained?

Drama and literature are, of necessity, branches of the greater medicinal tree wherein formal, ceremonial connections arise between our science, or knowing, and our lived experience. Filled with information and feeling, by turns moody and patient as a wise companion dog or cat, the body waits to be listened to and to tell what it knows. The slowed-down, attentive study of Shakespeare could help to close the gap of that waiting.

9 Using Improvisational Exercises to Teach Shakespeare

Annette Drew-Bear
Washington and Jefferson College

One approach to teaching Shakespeare that works well with both beginning and advanced students involves the use of sound-and-movement exercises and parallel scenes. I experimented extensively with these exercises in a January intersession class on Renaissance drama, and I regularly ask for some parallel scene work in my two-semester Shakespeare course at Washington and Jefferson College. These exercises are my adaptations of Miriam Gilbert's (1984) sound-and-movement exercises and Michael Flachmann's (1984) use of parallel scenes. I shall describe how I presented these approaches in my intersession class, and then I shall show, with excerpts from their own notebook accounts, what the students did and how they reacted to it.

In my January intersession class on Renaissance drama, I asked students to do sound-and-movement exercises and modern parallels as preparation for performing unmemorized scenes from *Richard III* and *Volpone*. I also asked them to prepare sound-and-movement exercises and scene performances for *Dr. Faustus*. The sound-and-movement exercises were helpful for all of these plays, while the parallel scenes proved most useful for the often obscure *Richard III*. The students felt that the scenes in *Volpone* were easier to understand and did not really need modern parallels.

Sound-and-movement exercises require students to use movements, gestures, and sound—but no language—to act out what Miriam Gilbert (1984) terms "the central emotional story of a scene" (604). The object is "to deprive the student of language and then restore it" (604) so that the actual performance of the whole scene follows the sound-and-movement exercise and is enriched by it. This improvisation helps students learn that words require movement, gesture, and blocking. In my intersession class, the exercise always carried over positively into the actual performance of the scene, making it less "wooden" and more emotional.

Parallel scenes encourage students to find a modern parallel that captures the essential aspects of a scene and then to improvise contemporary dialogue that captures the sense of the original words, or what Flachmann (1984) calls "the emotional rhythm of Shakespeare's original" (646). The object is to enrich the actual performance of the scene with the experience gained in the modern parallel. To give my intersession students an example of a parallel scene, I showed them a short segment from a videotape put out by the Folger Shakespeare Library called *Teaching Shakespeare: New Approaches from the Folger Shakespeare Library* (1986); it shows what some high school teachers do when they come to the Folger to learn performance techniques for teaching Shakespeare. The portion I showed provides a modern parallel for I.ii of *Richard III*, the scene in which Richard woos Anne. An instructor sketches the modern parallel for two high school teachers, who then improvise modern dialogue in front of the rest of the class. Seeing this parallel scene gives students an effective example of what the exercise requires.

I experimented with having students improvise a parallel scene "on the spot" in class, but this was not as successful as having them devise and practice the parallel outside of class first, since doing so gave them more time to study and understand the scenes. In one case, I provided a modern parallel for the two students who were to do III.vii of *Richard III*, the scene in which Buckingham and Richard play-act for the crown. The student playing Richard was afraid of speaking in class, and he had not understood the scene at first, so I felt that giving him a good modern parallel to work out would stimulate and help him. This scene, in fact, proved to be the most successful of all the modern parallels, and both the class and the performers felt that this example helped significantly to show them what was really going on in the scene.

After each modern improvisation and subsequent performance of the actual scene, students discussed the scene and its relation to the play and wrote about it in their notebooks (regularly outside of class and sometimes for a short period in class). Such analysis generally enriched the students' understanding of the play.

To see how the students felt about the improvisations, I asked them to write about how useful the exercises were to them. Most of the students found these improvisations to be very helpful. One student commented,

The modern version of the scene was very useful in understanding the scene itself. By thinking of the actual scene in terms of a modern equivalent, it was easier to understand the feelings and emotions of the characters. After understanding the characters' emotions, it then became easier to verbalize the original verse lines.

The sound-and-movement exercise and the modern parallel also made it easier to grasp the sequence of the plot. The sequence of events in longer scenes was much easier to grasp when placed in a modern setting. By analyzing the actual scene for indications of movements and gestures, it became necessary to pay close attention to minute details. Also, in attempting to match the scene up with a modern parallel, it was necessary to view the scene from all angles in order for the modern parallel to work effectively.

My favorite use of the modern parallel performed in class was Act III, scene vii. In this modern parallel, Richard became a fraternity brother plotting to become president. Buckingham was the roommate and close friend of the scheming "brother Rich." The mayor was transformed into the brotherhood chairman who was fooled by brother Rich and who tried to convince the other brothers of Rich's great ability. The ironic comedy of the scene was played to the fullest in this modern-day depiction. Rich was pictured as a no-good, unintelligent fake who pretended to be too busy studying the fraternity bylaws to consider running for president but who finally condescended to take the job. Buck and the brotherhood chairman were merely helpful stepping stones leading Rich to the presidency.

Richard's ability to act was clearly shown in this scene. Comic irony was also prominent in the paradox of Richard's true self and his projected self. Finally, the helpless situation of the townspeople was made clear, as they had no real say in whether Richard should take the crown or not.

Another student also felt strongly about the effectiveness of the parallel for this scene:

The modern parallel for III.vii helped me tremendously with the understanding and especially the tone of the actual scene. The immense hypocrisy of the fraternity brother in his reluctance to accept the presidency and his diligence in learning the bylaws carried over to equate with Richard's false humility and religious hypocrisy, both qualities which I missed until viewing the modern parallel.

The student who played the part of Richard in III.vii commented,

I have learned a tremendous amount from staging this particular scene. The modern situation skit stands out in my mind the most. It really enabled me to understand the scene much more. When I read through it the first time, I really did not understand what was going on. But taking it step by step and translating it into a modern situation helped me out tremendously. I knew exactly what expression and feeling to use when I did the silent motion skit and even the actual scene. Everything fell into place after doing the modernized version. The actual scene presentation took a little more work, but still it helped doing the modern version. I have trouble speaking in front of people and having this big part helped me a lot. I worked very hard in rehearsing it, and I hope to improve with each play that I do.

One student discussed another example of an effective modern parallel (III.iv), for which he wrote out the script as well:

When it was performed, the modern parallel for III.iv helped provide a better sense of what each character was trying to accomplish. In playing Richard, I had a sense that Richard should be an excellent manipulator of people in this scene. He can lead a conversation in the direction that he wants it to go. The result of this exercise, along with the sound-and-movement exercise, is to make the scene easier to perform for the players. These exercises allow the performers to grasp the emotions that their characters should express, and they also enhance the overall performance.

The student's script follows:

Modern Version of *Richard III,* III.iv

Mike: Let's get down to business. We need to elect a new godfather to oversee our families.

Johnny: I think Tony would do the best job.

All: Yeah. You're right. I agree.

(Enter Tony.)

Tony: Good afternoon, boys. Sorry I'm late; something came up. Can I talk to you a minute, Johnny?

Johnny: Sure, Tony.

Tony: It seems that Mike and his boys were the ones who tried to bump me off a few years back, and he's turning state's evidence now. We got to get rid of him. *(to Mike)* Hey Mike, how's about sending him out for some coffee and doughnuts, huh?

Mike: You heard him. Take a walk for awhile. What's up, Tony?

Suppose we catch those jerks who tried to waste me a few years back, what should we do with them?

If we catch them, we should dump 'em in the drink.

Tony: If? If, Mike? It was you! I found out you ordered a hit on me. Next time you should make sure your boys do it right.

            Wait a minute, Tony, I—

Tony: Shut up! You two, take care of this garbage. I want it out before I have dinner. I'm hungry. Anyone else joining him or me?
            (Exit all but two men and Mike.)

Mike: I don't believe this. I told everyone to keep quiet.

Man #1:   Come on. The boss don't like to be kept waiting. Besides, you'll be late for your swimming lesson.

Man #2:   Yeah, we're gonna teach you how to swim with cement shoes, all the way to the bottom of the river.

Mike: Tony's number is going to come up. I knew it was a matter of time before this happened. The police have an envelope to open if I disappear suddenly. I might die now, but he'll fry later!
            (Exit two men and Mike.)

Another student remarked on the usefulness of this modern parallel:

> The acting out of the scenes with a modern parallel greatly enhanced my understanding of some of the scenes. The two modern adaptations which seemed to work the best were the Mafia family scene and the fraternity president scene. Adapting Act III, scene iv to a modern parallel of a Mafia family effectively showed Richard's power. Not only did Richard's evil character show through, but the closeness of Richard and Buckingham could also be seen better.

One student summed up the responses of most of his peers when he commented on how the improvisations helped him understand what was often previously obscure:

> I feel that the sound-and-movement exercise and the modern version of the scene helped immensely in making us understand what was happening in the scene. By just reading the scene I often have difficulty in understanding what is happening, and it is easy to get lost altogether. The modern version made us read the lines more carefully and gave us a better feel for what was taking place. The sound-and-movement exercise helped us not only understand the scene better, but also helped us understand what actions the characters were taking on stage. As I watched the different groups perform their scenes for *Richard III*, I could see the resemblance between the actual scene and the modern parallel. Also, going over the scene in so many

different ways really helps us understand the scene better and fit it into the rest of the play. I feel that these two methods of performing scenes are of the utmost importance in helping students understand what they are doing in the scene as well as what the scene is about and how it relates to the rest of the play.

In my two-semester Shakespeare course, I ask for modern parallels for some difficult scenes from the first play we study each term. As in my intersession course, I show the Folger videotape's modern parallel from *Richard III* as an example. Once some students have performed and watched a few modern parallels, they are ready to perform and discuss Shakespeare's own scenes. Other students, however, need more work with parallel scenes and with the process of structured "translations" of lines before they are comfortable with Shakespeare.

Students often respond enthusiastically to the chance to be "creative" with Shakespeare, and they enjoy the task of relating his lines to their own language. Even professional actors and directors sometimes use these techniques in their effort to understand the plays. So parallel scene work can serve all levels of students as a helpful preparation for performing or discussing Shakespeare's scenes.

References

Flachmann, Michael. 1984. "Teaching Shakespeare Through Parallel Scenes." *Shakespeare Quarterly* 35.5: 644–46.

Gilbert, Miriam. 1984. "Teaching Shakespeare Through Performance." *Shakespeare Quarterly* 35.5: 601–8.

Teaching Shakespeare: New Approaches from the Folger Shakespeare Library. 1986. West Tisbury, MA: Vineyard Video Productions. Videotape based on a Teaching Shakespeare Institute that took place in Washington, D.C., in 1985.

10 Enacting Shakespeare's Language in *Macbeth* and *Romeo and Juliet*

Elizabeth Oakes
Western Kentucky University

Shakespeare's greatness lies in his genius with language, yet it is the language that often makes his plays difficult to understand. Although students may have no trouble with the lyrics of a popular song that baffles adults, they can have trouble deciphering the figures of speech and unscrambling the often inverted word order of the plays. Today's Top Forty music may rhyme and have an occasional metaphor or simile, but it is definitely much easier to comprehend than what is essentially a five-act poem by Shakespeare. One strategy for attacking this problem is, I believe, to help students approach the plays in the mode most natural to them at their age. So, because students tend to be more physical than visual and more visual than verbal, I have devised a set of exercises for *Macbeth* and *Romeo and Juliet* that enables a class to approach Shakespeare's language through gesture and movement.

Enacting Meaning in *Macbeth*

In I.vii.1–28 of *Macbeth,* Macbeth debates whether or not to kill Duncan. These lines ("If it were done when 'tis done, then 'twere well" to "And falls on th' other—") are thus some of the most important in the play. To teach this vital but rather imposing speech, a teacher could lead students through the following steps.

    Step 1. After forming the class into a circle, read through the lines, explaining each unfamiliar word and briefly summarizing the passage.
    Step 2. Ask each student to choose a word and to invent a gesture or movement to go with that word. (I sometimes do one to break the ice.)

Step 3. Have each student say his or her word and show the class the action he or she feels expresses it.

Step 4. Read the speech again, asking each student to perform his or her gesture or movement when you say the corresponding word.

Step 5. At this point, ask the students how they would categorize the movements, eventually getting them to notice that some have enacted what one might call "hard" movements and some "soft" ones. "Hard" ones include "blow" (l. 4), "jump" (l. 7), "shut the door" (l. 15), "bear the knife" (l. 16), "trumpet-tongued" (l. 19), "striding the blast" (l. 22), "spur" (l. 25), and "vaulting" (l. 27). "Soft" ones include "kinsman" (l. 13), "subject" (l. 13), "host" (l. 14), "meek" (l. 17), "plead like angels" (l. 19), "newborn babe" (l. 21), "heaven's cherubin" (l. 22), and "tears" (l. 25). Interestingly, "even-handed" (l. 10) does not fit either category, but the motion that students often make—moving the hands up and down—is the visual equivalent of Macbeth debating his choices, as well as that of Justice weighing guilt and innocence.

Step 6. Ask those in the "hard" group to do their enactions in unison. Then ask those in the "soft."

Step 7. At this time, the class might discuss the speech in terms of these movements, which mimic in physical action the choice Macbeth is making: to be "soft" or "hard," good or evil.

Here I point out that Macbeth is a very physical character, unlike, say, Hamlet, who is prone to thought. For instance, instead of saying that he would risk the life to come, Macbeth says he would "jump the life to come" (l. 7). Also, at the end of these lines, Macbeth uses the image of a rider jumping on his horse and falling to the ground on the other side to imagistically encapsulate his usurpation of the kingship and eventual downfall.

This exercise is particularly effective if students are going to view a live or filmed production, as they have a vested interest in their word and listen for it in the speech. Also, although I point out that an actor would not want to make all of these movements, often "Macbeth" will make one or two (moving his hands up and down at "even-handed" is a common one).

Another passage that works well with this exercise is II.i.34–62 ("Is this a dagger which I see before me" to "That summons thee to heaven or to hell"). Enacting this one after I.vii.1–28 is especially effective, as many of the words in this passage demand "hard" gestures, including "dagger" (ll. 34,39), "wolf" (l. 54), "strides" (l. 56), and "horror" (l. 60).

To finish this sequence of speeches, students can do the same exercise with V.v.17–28 ("She should have died hereafter" to "Signifying nothing"). In these lines, most of the words—"creeps" (l. 20), "death" (l. 23), "brief candle" (l. 23), "shadow" (l. 24), "frets" (l. 25), "nothing" (l. 28)—are ones of futility, sadness, or emptiness.

Enacting Poetic Form in *Romeo and Juliet*

Physical action can also be used to break through another barrier faced by students: the plays as poems. Shakespeare uses four styles: prose, blank verse, couplets, and (very rarely) the sonnet. Conveniently, all four are contained in I.v.1–107 ("Where's Potpan" to "Then move not, while my prayer's effect I take") of *Romeo and Juliet.*

Step 1. As before, read through the passage for meaning, explaining unfamiliar words and summarizing the action.

Step 2. Explain the four forms, reading again the section of the passage that is in each respective style.

Lines 1–16 ("Where's Potpan" to "Be brisk awhile, and the longer liver take all") are in prose. In Shakespeare, prose is usually spoken by comic or minor characters, here the servants in the Capulet household (though this is not always the case; for instance, the Nurse's story about Juliet in I.iii is predominantly in blank verse).

Lines 17–44 ("Welcome, gentlemen! Ladies that have their toes" to "Of yonder knight? I know not, sir") are in blank verse, as are lines 55–89 ("This, by his voice, should be a Montague" to "I'll make you quiet, what!—Cheerly, my hearts!"). (Within these lines there are several couplets, as discussed below.) The predominant form in the plays, blank verse is most often used by higher class characters or in important moments (although here too there are exceptions). Capulet's lines sometimes have eleven syllables, perhaps Shakespeare's way of making him seem long-winded.

Romeo's first speech about Juliet in lines 45–54 ("O, she doth teach the torches to burn bright" to "For I ne'er saw true beauty till this night") is in couplets, which Shakespeare often uses at moments of extreme emotion or to end a scene. The couplets in the ensuing argument between Old Capulet and Tybalt (ll. 59–64, "Now, by the stock and honor of my kin" to "To scorn at our solemnity this night") perhaps underscore their anger. And although the scene does not end at line 93, Tybalt's double couplets (ll. 90–93, "Patience perforce with willful choler meeting" to "Now seeming sweet, convert to bitterest gall") have the same effect as a scene change, shifting the tone as attention turns to Romeo and Juliet.

Lines 94–107 ("If I profane with my unworthiest hand" to "Then move not, while my prayer's effect I take") make up an English or, as it is sometimes appropriately called, a Shakespearean sonnet. An extremely rare form in the plays, the sonnet, with its interlocking lines of rhyme, is here appropriate, as the two young people begin to join their lives. Incidentally, the next four lines (ll. 108–11), which make up a quatrain, begin another sonnet, one interrupted by the Nurse. Also, the play begins with a complete sonnet about the two households, as does Act II ("Now old desire doth in his deathbed lie"). The last six lines of the play are quatrain and a couplet, which are also the last six lines of the sonnet form.

Step 3. Divide the students into four groups, asking each group to devise a configuration or movement that expresses one of the forms. (I usually include Tybalt's and Old Capulet's couplets in the blank verse and ask that group to do something different with these lines, reserving only Romeo's couplets for the couplets group.)

Step 4. As one or more students read the passages, have each group demonstrate its movement or configuration. The following configurations seem to be the most common.

The students in the prose group often mill around aimlessly, bumping into each other, scurrying to and fro, which is, I point out, also what the servants in the play must be doing.

In the blank verse group, students will often line up, walk forward (about ten steps) as their line is read, and then disperse. Those who have the couplet lines often wait at the end of their walk until their rhyming partner joins them.

To demonstrate couplets, the students typically form two lines opposite each other. As a line is read, a student walks halfway to the other group, to be met there by the student who has the rhyming line. Since only ten students are needed here, I limit this group to eleven (one reader).

To enact the sonnet form, fourteen students generally divide into three groups of four and one of two. The quatrain groups might then form the pattern of a square. As the first line is read, a student walks halfway to his or her rhyming partner, and so on until all four meet. Then the two students who have the couplet lines walk toward each other. It is nice if they join hands in these groups (and in the couplets group as well), but not necessary. I usually point out that the very structured movement that results resembles the dance in the Zeffirelli film of *Romeo and Juliet,* as, indeed, the prose group's movement does the style of dance today. In fact, if one has an agreeable group, one could ask the students to devise dances that match the stylistic patterns.

At the end of these exercises, students will have a physical as well as an intellectual idea of Shakespeare's language. In addition, they—and the teacher—may also have had quite a bit of fun!

11 Sparking: A Methodology to Encourage Student Performance

Joan Ozark Holmer
Georgetown University

Readers of Shakespearean drama face a number of challenges, including the most obvious obstacle to immediate apprehension, Shakespeare's language. Students today thus need to be encouraged to recover the labor of love involved in "reading" a Shakespearean play not merely once, but several times. Moreover, students need to understand that a good reader is not someone who is necessarily looking for something in particular, but rather someone who remains open and sensitive to what is in the text. The basic skill of reading closely and thoughtfully is fundamental to all my various teaching strategies, but especially to "sparking."

Sparking is a flexible technique that allows for and encourages student performance in various ways but that does not mandate traditional acting. The last decade of pedagogical experimentation witnessed the growing practice of incorporating some form of performance, whether professional or student, into one's teaching of the plays. I have experimented with the option of full-class performance, believing that students will probably understand what makes a play work theatrically if they personally enact it and learn "hands-on" the meaning of "play" and "playing" so essential to Shakespearean drama. But aside from the logistical problems of student performance—let alone how many plays students can reasonably perform in a semester— I find that mandatory acting in a required course, such as mine is, will frustrate at least some students. I thus designed sparking as a pedagogical strategy to address the individual freedom and personal diversity of students while still bringing performance assignments into the classroom.

I call the strategy "sparking," for want of a better name, because it is intended to ignite the interest of its participants, who then generate the opening of a class discussion via their own orchestrated sparking, which runs roughly fifteen to thirty minutes. For their specific sparking assignment, students sign up at the beginning of the semester in teams of two or more people (in order to enhance creativity and promote collegiality). These student teams must tailor their "performance" to illuminate the play we are currently studying, and they must ground their interpretation on textual evidence in the play. Their performance is never an end in itself, but rather a means to an end: the heightened appreciation of the problems and possibilities in Shakespeare's art. Students develop their plans during the course of the semester, and they are encouraged, but not required, to discuss their ideas with me. They must, however, give me advance notice of their intended performance so that plans for class discussion can be coordinated effectively.

The sparkers are always responsible for conducting the discussion that follows their performance. If students decide that their sparking will be a discussion only, then one meeting ahead of their scheduled date they furnish the class with some handout of information and questions that will help everyone prepare for that discussion. Otherwise, I do not require any formal writing in conjunction with this assignment, though I strongly encourage the students to present written material to the class whenever appropriate, especially if they have done considerable research or if they want us to examine closely passages from different works. Because they all find such material beneficial to have, the students almost universally choose to furnish some sort of informative handout in conjunction with their performance.

I urge students to capitalize on their own personally developed interests and talents in whatever fields—music, dance, art, science, law, medicine, international relations, whatever—and responsibly incorporate these into their study of the play. The result of their endeavors has often proved truly astonishing. Indeed, some performances, such as an actual Elizabethan feast prepared by enterprising chefs according to recipes in Madge Lorwin's *Dining with William Shakespeare* (yes, with real rose petals in the salads), are truly exotic. Other, more predictable performances involve presenting research on a variety of special topics—topics such as ghosts, demonology, witchcraft, and magic for *Macbeth* and *The Tempest*, for instance, but also more general subjects involving historical knowledge of Shakespeare's theater, culture, and society. The students can present this research to the rest of the class through a wide variety of formats, including debates, skits, discussions, and interviews. Students may also elect traditional acting and enact scenes, perform particular dramatic moments according to several different interpretations, or write and enact their own adaptation, perhaps, for example, a contemporary version of the casket test in *The Merchant of Venice.*

But whether exotic or not, predictable or unpredictable, these performances must always dovetail with the plays we are studying. The Elizabethan feast not only literally delighted our palates, but also figuratively explored the importance of Elizabethan views on dining and hospitality in light of our plays' recurrent feasts (celebrated as well as disrupted) and Shakespeare's varied use of food, drink, and appetitive imagery. Those students who wrote and performed a witty, modern adaptation of the casket test revealed the gulf that so often exists between theory and practice, between the ideal of human love as suggested by Shakespeare, Spenser, and Milton and the stark reality that Bottom asserts: "And yet, to say the truth, reason and love keep little company together now-a-days" (III.i.143–44). While the need for human love is as important then as now, how we explain and evaluate it can change.

Sparking offers students a range of possibilities. To inform their performance, students can use specific skills and interests developed prior to the course, traditional acting, professional productions, primary or secondary research materials, or outside dialogue for a team-led discussion in class. Those students who derive their primary inspiration from a previously developed talent or interest frequently capture the entire class's attention. An accomplished musician and vocalist, for example, researched the general topic of music for Shakespeare's plays, with a specific focus on *Othello* and Desdemona's willow song, which we were studying at the time. They furnished their bibliography and distributed pictorial and explanatory handouts on Renaissance music and instruments that pinpointed such important issues as differences between Renaissance and modern instruments (e.g., as between the sackbut and the trombone). They also explored the meaning and importance of music, then and now, helping to enlarge our understanding of the broader topic. They then performed Desdemona's willow song as well as some songs and music from *Twelfth Night* and *The Tempest.* In the discussion that followed, they entertained questions about the significance of harmony's dismissal by Othello or interruption by war in *Henry IV, Part 1.*

In another session, focused on *King Lear* but also looking back to *Othello,* some scientifically oriented students with strong backgrounds in biology and psychology decided to perform some visual experiments on the class to explore our dependence on our fallible senses for "knowledge." We were given several different pictures to examine and then were asked to write down what we thought we saw. What we thought was probably the outline of a man's rugged face really turned out to be an outline of a skirted woman wearing a plumed hat. After this experimental opening, these students shared some general scientific information about visual versus perceptual ways of "seeing" as background to their specific discussion of who the "seers" are in *King Lear.* How does evidence from our senses, especially the sense of sight, inform as well as mislead us in our quest for knowing the truth? We were asked to identify some patterns of sense imagery and to make sense of how Shakespeare works with these patterns.

Another team, spearheaded by a talented young woman with a double major in Russian and English, considered the importance of language for appreciating Shakespeare's plays. Citing a series of inadequate English subtitles for the spoken Russian in Grigori Kozintsev's film productions of *Hamlet* and *King Lear,* the team used this evidence as a springboard to examine the problems and possible comparative advantages in studying productions of Shakespeare in foreign languages, concluding that when Juliet asks "What's in a name" (II.ii.43), we might do well to respond, "Quite a lot."

Sometimes sparking provides quite unexpected advantages. An unlikely team of a young poet and a business major got shackled together by fate on the sign-up sheet, surprisingly much to their mutual benefit. The poet wanted to study some of the ways in which Shakespeare's nondramatic verse differs from his dramatic verse. We all learned much, especially regarding gestural implication and scripted signals, but the sparkers also shared with us how much they learned from each other because of the different kinds of questions and backgrounds they brought to Shakespeare's poetry. One of the most memorable sparkings involved the fencing talents of two students who sought to interpret the fatal bout between Laertes and Hamlet during our study of Act V. In this performance, all possible resources meshed brilliantly. After extensive research in three Elizabethan fencing manuals (those of Di Grassi, Saviolo, and Silver) and the critical viewing of four different film and television productions of *Hamlet,* which they summarized for the class in a detailed handout, these students fenced the final duel as they thought it should be played. They also examined how the various productions handled the deception of the unbaited foil and the exchange of weapons, even questioning the accuracy of the editorial stage direction in our text.

The use of traditional acting, although more "traditional," consistently yields its own surprises and benefits. For instance, several experienced male actors performed in juxtaposition the two temptation scenes from *The Tempest*, scenes in which Antonio and Sebastian (II.i) and Caliban, Stephano, and Trinculo (III.ii) plot murder and rebellion. Not only did they ask us to find connections and differences between characters and plots from these two disparate parts of the script, but they also affected our perceptions, as well as their own, by their intentional doubling: Antonio also played Caliban and Sebastian played Stephano. Their choice of scenic juxtaposition was also enhanced by a chance blessing of timing that sometimes occurs in the sparking format. Their acting followed on the heels of a performance that took a contrasting approach to understanding Caliban and his relationship with Prospero by exploring Renaissance travel literature and the history of colonization. Thus our appreciation of Shakespeare's range was deepened by the very juxtaposition of these two different sparkings.

In another sparking, two women decided to perform two different interpretations of Hamlet's final soliloquy. So they cross-dressed, and each woman delivered this soliloquy with distinctly different performance choices. We were then asked to analyze what we thought they were attempting to do and to explain why we preferred one interpretation over the other, whether or not it agreed with our own views on that moment in the play. They also put Hamlet in some theatrical context by furnishing a three-page paper of condensed quotations from their research on history's famous Hamlets, from Edmund Kean to Derek Jacobi. They even tried to explore the history of actresses who wanted to play Hamlet.

One team of students, none of which had done any acting, decided to take the full plunge and reserved the stage in our Gaston Hall to perform on it, as fully as possible (costumes, props, programs, etc.), the nunnery scene in *Hamlet*. They did the scene in two different ways, changing both stage business (particularly whether or not Hamlet is aware he is being watched) as well as the characterization of Hamlet and Ophelia and the emotional tenor of their relationship. We evaluated the relative merits of each version, and they shared what they learned in the process of deciding to do what they did. Some unforeseen developments in the subsequent discussion concerned how the use of a real stage, instead of just the dais in our classroom, influenced our responses to the performance, especially our awareness of space, distance, and sightlines. Another team performed the scene between Desdemona and Emilia (IV.iii.11–105) twice, using different props and swapping roles. They sought to engage the class not just in an evaluation of their performance choices, but also in a consideration of the relationship between these two women, underscored by their exchange of parts. They also asked how and why Shakespeare uses the three women he does in the play.

The sparkers' use of professional productions, whether theatrical or filmic, tends to be sensitive to differences in performance media and to the advantages of multiple comparisons. I encourage this type of comparative perspective by putting on reserve for my students an eye-opening videotape I have had made of four different film and television productions of the same scene in *Hamlet* (I.ii), edited back-to-back so that in one compact hour students can glimpse myriad possibilities. One team used audiovisual equipment to present the same scene in *Romeo and Juliet* (III.ii) from two productions—the Franco Zeffirelli film and the BBC-TV version—in order to increase our understanding of the artistic problems inherent in the interpretation of dramatic meaning when studying Shakespeare on film. Their useful handout introduced the class to helpful vocabulary for discussing the disciplines of literature, theater, and film.

More frequently, however, sparkers gravitate toward film and television as resources for examining characterization. One group, for example, focused on the relationship between Shylock and Antonio (I.iii) by contrasting the BBC-TV and Olivier productions in terms of blocking, costuming, speech patterns, and body language. But they also placed their video presentation within the larger context of stage history by providing a compendium of pictures and photographs that spanned over a hundred years of actors (and actresses) who had played the role of Shylock, including Charles Macklin, Edmund Kean, William Charles Macready, Catherine Macready, Edwin Booth, and Henry Irving. The students noted that a similarly rich resource could not be found for Antonio, and they also cited the very helpful video of David Suchet's and Patrick Stewart's views on playing Shylock ("Exploring a Character") in John Barton's "Playing Shakespeare" series for the BBC. The context they established for Shylock was exceptionally helpful in developing the class's responses to their specific video presentation.

When using theatrical productions, students are more obviously circumscribed by what is available during a given season. Once we were so fortunate as to have two very different productions of *Hamlet* done at local, commercial theaters during the same semester, and as can be readily imagined, students took full advantage of this unprecedented opportunity, becoming especially sensitive to the methods used to involve the audience more directly in the performance. As with the use of film and television, students tend to remain quite conscious of the differences in media, generally concurring that live theater is the most natural medium for Shakespeare's plays, which, of course, were intended for theatrical production. One team analyzed the staging of the blinding of Gloucester in a production of *King Lear* (1984) at the Folger Theater. This production had Gloucester stand with arms outstretched and tied, thereby suggesting a posture of crucifixion. The students led a discussion of the advantages and disadvantages of such blocking, especially in light of other alternatives that would make greater use of the symbolic nature of Shakespeare's physical theater. They particularly discussed a staging that would suggest the symbolism of hierarchical inversion conveyed through a lowering of Gloucester's head beneath Cornwall's heel—the highest sense of sight beneath the lowest sense of touch, the master of the house under the power of his guest, a better nature subdued by a crueler one.

For students who choose to use outside research as their chief resource for their presentation, I encourage the use of primary materials, such as classical and Renaissance literature, over secondary ones. Students thus gain even more exposure to earlier literatures and, like Hamlet, "by indirections find directions out" (II.i.63). Once they have struggled through their own dark woods to emerge with some degree of personal enlightenment, then they may satiate themselves on the overwhelming bounty of secondary criticism that currently exists. Supplemental reading material is on reserve in the library, and students often seek out Bullough's *Narrative and Dramatic Sources of Shakespeare* for a comparative analysis of how Shakespeare transmutes the base metal of his literary sources into his own dramatic gold. One team in particular selected passages from Giraldi Cinthio's *Gli Hecatommithi* (1565) and typed them in juxtaposition with pertinent passages from Act III of *Othello*. This was many students' first exposure to sixteenth-century Italian *novelle* in translation, but more importantly, the apt selection of passages for examination gave the class a more educated sense of the "before" and "after" state of the narrative, as well as of the merits of Shakespeare's poetry over Cinthio's prose. Another team, using the work of Leo Africanus (supplemented by Eldred Jones's

1971 study *The Elizabethan Image of Africa*) researched the Elizabethan image of the Moor in order to have the class ponder how and why Shakespeare uses a black man as *Othello*'s protagonist. And those interested in classical literature have sparked a variety of fine discussions, ranging from a juxtaposed consideration of Virgil's description of Pyrrhus in the *Aeneid* (Book II) and Shakespeare's dramatic version in *Hamlet* (II.ii.450–518) to research on the genre of the masque and how and why Shakespeare uses the classical mythology he does (and does not in banishing Venus and Cupid) for the betrothal masque in *The Tempest.*

Another team responded to the concurrence of a presidential election (1988) with our study of *Henry IV, Part 1* and the question of leadership in that history play. Using books of such ilk as Theodore H. White's *America in Search of Itself* (1982) and conducting informal polls among groups of government majors at Georgetown, this team tried to determine the leadership qualities America looks for in its presidents. Before sharing their findings with our class, however, they polled our views on the same subject. What followed was an exciting and revealing discussion, especially when we took note of what qualities were overlooked. For example, the poll of government majors produced a full list of credible leadership qualities, including charisma, strength, decisiveness, enthusiasm, and humor. Honesty, however, was not mentioned, and honor has become a rather neglected word in our modern vocabulary. Our class identified an even wider range of qualities; still, magnanimity missed the list, even though we had discussed Hal's magnanimous recognition of his foes' brave deeds (V.iv.25–31). When we discussed the importance of moral rectitude, or at least the image of it, students who had studied abroad opened up another perspective by demonstrating how different cultures variously value the importance of a particular quality. What is good leadership, and how do we define "good"? Not only did our discussion make the play more personally and topically relevant, but the class also began to reconsider parts of the play that had puzzled them.

These few examples give an idea of the range of topics that sparking ignites. Although students frequently derive ideas from the specific and general questions I furnish for class discussions, I cannot possibly do justice here to the wide variety of interests students seek out for themselves, covering such heterogeneous topics as cuckoldry and prostitution, symbolic use of costume, the audience in the public theater, botanical references, folly and madness, rituals and ceremonies, and so forth. Probably no examples are needed to illustrate the results of sparking when the primary resource is the students' own close, careful reading or outside discussions that lead subsequent dialogue in class. Although this choice entails less obvious work, the results can be very stimulating. For example, one team, fascinated by the problem of evil, led a discussion on Iago: Is he inherently evil, psychologically sick, or both? What became particularly fruitful was the students' drawing on their own literary and personal resources to forge connections between Shakespeare and other authors they had studied closely who dealt with the same problem, authors as different as Chaucer, Milton, Dostoevsky, Melville, and Faulkner. Indeed, the chief advantage of sparking as a pedagogical strategy is that because it is rooted in student choice and interest, it often yields industri-ous, positive, varied, and even surprising results. And because the format is so flexible within its given structure, students are free to respond to contemporary as well as ancient concerns.

12 Changing the *W*'s in Shakespeare's Plays

Michael Flachmann
California State University, Bakersfield

High school and college English teachers trying to get students interested in Shakespeare's plays face two tough obstacles: the language, which appears archaic and inaccessible, and the dramatic situations, which often seem alien to our own time and culture. "How can we understand and identify with these characters," our students complain, "when we can't understand what they're saying and we have no idea what they're doing?" Most frustrating of all, the harder we try to explain the verse and dramatic situations to our students, the more distance we seem to create between the plays and their reluctant interpreters. Why can't they learn to love Shakespeare as we do? Does the fault, to paraphrase Cassius, lie in ourselves or in our students?

One important answer to these slippery questions may be found in our response to the genre itself. What are we actually teaching when we approach a "play" in the classroom, and how can a clearer definition of this unique art form help us discover equally unique ways to teach it to our students? Interestingly enough, most English teachers use the same word to designate both the printed text and its performance on stage. We say "Have you read *the play?*" and "Have you seen *the play?*" This semantic confusion is quite telling, since it implies that reading a play is just as fulfilling as seeing it performed; neither event is preferable to the other. In fact, if we can trust the semiotics of names, the two experiences must be identical, as we use the same word to denote each of them.

Equally disturbing is the alternate viewpoint, which postulates that scripts and plays are wildly different, like chalk and cheese or "hot ice and wondrous strange snow." In this world of irreconcilable opposites, the term *dramatic literature* becomes an oxymoron similar to *jumbo shrimp* or *Peacekeeper missile*, where never the twain shall meet. Such a dichotomy also sparks vast and arbitrary territorial battles, in which the English department declares itself solely qualified to teach the plays as literature, while the theater department becomes involved only when the play goes from page to stage.

When we teach "plays," however, what we are actually teaching are "scripts" intended for performance. The relationship between the two is sequential and entirely natural. A script and a production of that script are neither exactly the same nor totally different. Unlike novels and poems, which find their most complete and final expression in the quiet solemnity of our mind, a playscript exists to be performed. Its ultimate value goes far beyond the words lying listless on the printed page. The language begs to be spoken by accomplished actors; the dramatic situations need to be seen and felt and taken into our hearts in order to be fully understood. While Shakespeare's scripts clearly have great literary value, the study of that value in total isolation from its theatrical context drastically underestimates the worth of an art form that is larger and more wonderfully complex than the shallow category we English teachers usually assign it to.

The relationship between a "script" and a "play" (that is, between the printed document and its theatrical realization on stage) is in fact similar to several other pairs of objects. For example, a script wants to be a production in the same way a recipe yearns to be a steaming plate of *coq au vin*. No sane person would ever attempt to rip a page out of a recipe book and eat it, yet our teaching routinely implies that reading a script will be just as tasty and nourishing as actually watching a production of that script, complete with well-trained actors, sets, costumes, music, lights, and all the other magic of theater.

Similarly, only a very talented and learned musician can look at a musical score and hear the subtle melodies on the page. Yet we ask our students to respond in the same sophisticated fashion to a playscript by calling upon them to imagine what that script would look like in a fully staged production—despite the painful fact that over ninety-eight percent of high school students and ninety-two percent of college students have never seen a live professional production of any of Shakespeare's plays. Can we compare reading an architectural blueprint to the physical exhilaration of taking an elevator up to the twenty-fifth floor of a newly built luxury apartment building and admiring the skyline? In each of these cases, our viewpoint is severely limited if we confuse the printed document with its more delicious, satisfying, and exciting result.

So how can we accomplish this interdisciplinary approach to Shakespeare, one which sees his scripts as both literary and theatrical masterpieces? Most of us who teach English are not trained in theater. We cannot spend all our time and institutional money carting our students around to see live productions. And we certainly do not want to devote our classrooms to a never-ending stream of videotaped plays. One useful solution is for teachers to integrate into their curriculum one or more pedagogical techniques taken from the world of theater that encourage students to appreciate the dramatic as well as the literary value of Shakespeare's scripts. What we quickly discover when we employ this multigenre attack is that the two seemingly divergent approaches complement and reinforce each other brilliantly. An interdisciplinary approach can also produce stunning results with many types of students who have traditionally had little success appreciating Shakespeare's plays.

One such theatrical teaching technique that helps bridge the formidable gap between our students' language and cultural milieu and that of Shakespeare's time is to pick a scene and have the students experiment, as actors and directors often do, with the five journalistic "W's" connected with it: *who* the characters are, *what* they are doing, *where* the scene takes place, *when* it takes place, and *why* the characters act in the way they do. One scene that works particularly well in demonstrating this technique is the brief meeting between Capulet, Lady Capulet, and Paris in III.iv of *Romeo and Juliet,* in which Paris waits in vain for Juliet to appear and Capulet makes a "desperate tender" of his child's love. This simple but powerful technique can be used in a variety of ways, though the following is perhaps the most effective.

First I split the students into acting groups of five or six persons each, giving each group a secret card with a completely different set of *W's*. For example, one card might say, "The Capulets are an Italian-American family in 1930s New York. They are eating a huge and delicious spaghetti dinner. Paris is the son of a wealthy Mafia leader." Another card could read, "The Capulets are aristocratic Southern landowners in Athens, Georgia, circa 1850; they speak with heavy Southern accents and sit with Paris on the veranda of their home sipping mint juleps." A third might instruct the students that "the Capulets are naked in a Jacuzzi drinking wine (Los Angeles, 1992). Paris is a bit embarrassed and attempts to carry on the discussion without looking at either of them."

Then I either allow the students twenty to thirty minutes in class to rehearse their scenes or I give them till the next class meeting. Each acting group must get together, assign roles, and practice the scene for eventual performance before the entire class. The students can use costumes, props, additional characters, and whatever else they need to make the scene come alive. I also encourage them to revise Shakespeare's language to bring it into harmony with their assigned *W*'s. For example, the Italian-American scene mentioned earlier might include the following dialogue from Lord Capulet: "Things havea fallen outa, sir, so unluckily thata we havea hada no timea to movea our daughter. Passa the spaghetti saucea, per favore."

By working through the scenes as actors, the students immediately and instinctively begin looking for clues to help with characterization and staging, as if they were detectives solving a theatrical mystery. Why, for example, does Capulet say he has had no time to *move* his daughter? Why the word *move*? Why not *convince* or *urge*? Why the awkward little internal rhyme in line 4: "And so did I. Well, we were born to die"? What about Paris's "woe" and "woo" slant rhyme? Is it intentional? Or is it a slight social gaffe? What about Capulet's reference to a "desperate tender" of Juliet's love? What does he mean by this? And why does he lose track of what day it is? To whom does he ask, "Will you be ready? Do you like this haste?" And what in the world does Lady Capulet mean by saying that Juliet is "mew'd up to her heaviness"?

Through the process of rehearsing their scenes, most students will begin to make some pretty accurate decisions about these characters and their motivations in the play. The word *rehearse* means "to re-hear," to say the lines over and over again, trying different vocal inflections and various acting intentions. It also means to ask questions, to be inquisitive about oddities in the lines, like Capulet's use of the word "move" and his wife's allusion to Juliet as "mew'd up." One truth we English teachers often forget is that Shakespeare was an actor before he was a playwright. Consequently, he knew how to write for actors—even inexperienced ones. All the clues are embedded in the language of the script, as if it were a secret map taking us to buried treasure. All an actor has to do, therefore, is rehearse the words with clear, simple, honest emotion to make the scene come alive with meaning.

Thus, no matter what *W*'s are assigned to each acting group, most students will independently come to a number of similar conclusions about this particular scene. They will invariably determine, for example, that the action takes place late at night. Paris has been waiting in vain for Juliet to make an appearance, and both Capulets are embarrassed at her refusal to entertain this wealthy, important suitor. They do not know, of course, that she has secretly married Romeo. (In fact, Romeo is probably in her room upstairs as this scene is being played out downstairs.) Capulet's first speech is formal and awkward; the multisyllable words and artificial diction slow down the actor's speech patterns noticeably. Paris's first speech is likewise strained, betraying his anger (or sadness) over Juliet's rebuff. As Paris turns to leave, escorted by Capulet's wife, Capulet rushes forward and blurts out his "desperate tender," offering Juliet in marriage in the short space of two—no, make it three—days.

Capulet's speech has changed from formal, measured diction to short, abrupt sentences filled with single-syllable words. Has he planned all this beforehand? Has he discussed the offer with his wife? The scene can be played either way, of course, but I think he gets this wild idea on the spot and suggests it to Paris without consulting either his wife or his daughter. Once Paris agrees ("My lord, I would that Thursday were tomorrow!"), Capulet rushes him out the door immediately, sweeps past his befuddled wife, and trots off happily to bed.

What becomes clear to most students as they rehearse this scene is that Capulet is an aged male chauvinist and a preemptory bully who muscles everyone in his household into submission. He uses all the wit and charm of a used car salesman in talking Paris into marrying Juliet, and he attempts to "move" (force) his daughter to wed a man she does not love. In line 22, at least one, and perhaps both, of his solicitous questions are directed to his potential son-in-law: "Will you be ready? Do you like this haste?" Would Capulet care whether his wife approved of his hasty proposal? Undoubtedly not. Paris's wealth and high social connections make him an excellent "catch" for Juliet, and Lord Capulet is not about to let this eligible young man get out the door before the marriage contract has been agreed upon.

Even more telling is Lady Capulet's earlier reference to Juliet being "mew'd up to her heaviness." As most students will learn from their footnotes (another important set of clues), a "mew" was a cage in which hawks and other birds of prey were kept. If we press the analogy further, Juliet becomes the hawk, while Paris is her prey. Since she is an only child, Juliet represents her parents' sole hope of bringing wealth and social respectability into the family through marriage. Her refusal to come downstairs is therefore intensely frustrating to Capulet, as he sees his hopes and dreams for a marital alliance with a kinsman to the Prince of Verona slowly slipping away. This is what motivates his sudden and "desperate" offer of marriage to Paris, an offer which helps precipitate the tragic ending of the play.

When the students perform their scenes in the classroom, the motivations of these characters will be miraculously similar, no matter whether the action takes place over a steaming plate of spaghetti, on a nineteenth-century Southern veranda, or in a Jacuzzi. With minimal help from their teachers, the students will have "discovered" the meaning of the scene through the rehearsal process (rather than having their teachers explain it to them). The real fun begins after each scene is presented and the other students try to guess the set of *W*'s assigned to each group (which are kept a closely guarded secret till after the scenes are presented). Teachers can even award inexpensive mock prizes for such categories as Best Actor, Best Actress, Best Nonspeaking Role, and Best Costume.

In addition to providing our students with an enjoyable, interesting way of learning about specific scenes, this "Changing the *W*'s" exercise leads to a number of important pedagogical insights into the study of Shakespeare:

1. Plays are meant to be acted, and Shakespeare's scripts are most completely realized when they are performed by actors (no matter how untrained and inept) before a live audience.

2. Each scene can have a wide variety of different interpretations depending upon the *W*'s chosen by the director.

3. Some interpretations will be more in concert with the script than others.

4. When we bring Shakespeare into the present or into chronological periods with which we are more familiar than the Renaissance, we "personalize" the plays and more easily identify with the different thoughts and emotions the characters are exhibiting.

5. The process of acting out divergent characters allows our students to "try on" a variety of stage personalities and thereby further develop their own emerging real-life identities.

6. Different societies and social periods can produce wildly distinct ethical and moral contexts for these scenes.

7. In order to act out their scene, the students must dig deeply into the script to understand every word and find every possible acting clue.

8. These scripts are fun to study and perform (which is one reason we call them "plays"—we get to play with words

and characters and ideas in unexpected, invigorating ways when we study Shakespeare).

Most exciting is the fact that this technique, as well as many other performance-oriented teaching devices, seems to work well with many students who have traditionally not had great success with the study of Shakespeare. Generalizing about such matters is risky but interesting. In my own experience, I have found these techniques especially helpful with some boys (as opposed to girls, who seem to have more affinity for Shakespeare in their high school years), some minority students, some athletes, some second-language students, and others. The insights gained from such an approach defy easy categorization, perhaps because these hybrid techniques yoke together two complementary ways of looking at Shakespeare's scripts. And in the final analysis, should we really care whether our students go through a literary or a theatrical doorway to appreciate the plays? The destination is the same either way.

I learn this lesson over and over again whenever I work with students who have never been encouraged to look at Shakespeare's plays as scripts intended for production. One recent experience was particularly memorable. I gave a workshop on Shakespeare at an inner-city school last year during which the students invented their own W's for the third witches' scene from *Macbeth* (IV.i). One set of actors staged the scene as it might have been done by a modern rap group, chanting "Double, double, we be trouble; / Fire burn, and cauldron bubble." The effect was wonderfully funny and instinctively accurate. These students had made the script theirs in a way that no amount of lecturing on my part could have accomplished. Their unique version of the scene also launched us into a lovely discussion about whether the witches contain evil within themselves or whether they simply have the ability to bring forth evil in others. If the witches "be" trouble, then what happens to Macbeth's own responsibility for killing Duncan, Banquo, and Macduff's wife and children? To what degree is he culpable if his actions are controlled by the witches' evil? To what extent are *all* of us fated to play out preordained parts in the drama we call "life"?

Most important, these students genuinely seemed to be enjoying their experience with Shakespeare, which turned out to be interesting, creative, and thought-provoking. Several came up to me after the workshop and asked where they could see a live production of *Macbeth.* They wanted to know how other people presented the witches' scenes! When I see such enthusiasm generated by a few simple theatrical teaching techniques, I always begin asking myself hard questions about why we teach Shakespeare in the English classroom and what we hope our students will discover in the plays—not only about literature and theater, but also about themselves and their place in the universe around them. I do not have all the answers to these questions yet, but I do know that they depend in large part upon our ability as teachers to respond rightly to this unique and challenging art form. We must somehow be able to make the transition between script and performance, between literary and theatrical approaches, when we investigate this interdisciplinary genre with our students. The ability to do so can help clarify more than the language and dramatic situations of the plays. It can also help clarify our students' lives.

III Extratextual Resources

13 Love, Sighs, and Videotape: An Approach to Teaching Shakespeare's Comedies

Michael J. Collins
Georgetown University

I

I shall begin, as I always do when I talk about Shakespeare's comedies, by confessing to a disquieting discovery I made after many happy years of marriage: my wife and I are fundamentally incompatible. On such less important things as using money or raising children, we ordinarily agree. But on one major issue we remain utterly irreconcilable: she likes the tragedies of Shakespeare, and I like the comedies.

Now that discovery would no doubt have remained innocuous had she not gone on to draw a conclusion from it. "You're weird," she said. "Almost everybody likes the tragedies better than the comedies and knows they're more valuable as well. Think about it," she continued. "Aren't the tragedies easier to teach? And don't they face the essential questions of our lives more honestly, more directly, questions about good and evil, the meaning of choice and action, the inevitability of death, and the struggle for dignity? And in any case, the comedies are silly. At the last minute somebody shows up on the stage, has an unexpected change of heart, seems to come back from the dead, and everything falls neatly and happily into place. Life isn't like that, you know."

As if all this wasn't debilitating enough, she finished with an argument that completely disarmed me. "The comedies teach young women bad lessons," she said. "Do you really want our daughter watching comedies? She'll grow up thinking happiness means being married to someone like . . . well, someone like you." I said nothing. I couldn't admit I wanted more for our daughter than that.

And then, one Friday evening at the end of a long week, my wife said she had a surprise for me. "Look what I found at Video Visions today. It's one of my favorite old movies." "What is it," I asked, thinking it might be *Citizen Kane* or Olivier's *Hamlet*. "*Love in the Afternoon*," she said, "with Audrey Hepburn, Gary Cooper, and Maurice Chevalier." I smiled. I suspected she had exposed at last her point of vulnerability.

And indeed she had. *Love in the Afternoon* tells the story of an American businessman, Frank Flannegan (played by Gary Cooper), who falls in love with a young Parisian musician named Arlane (played by Audrey Hepburn). Whenever Mr. Flannegan (she never calls him by his first name) comes to Paris, Arlane spends the afternoon with him, often at his hotel. Their relationship, of course, is entirely chaste; she is young and innocent, and the picture was made in 1952. Slowly, inevitably, and (as is ordinarily the case in these movies) reluctantly, Mr. Flannegan falls in love with Arlane, and although he feels he is too old and experienced for her (he also makes off-camera visits to some twins in Cannes), he must, as the movie moves toward its close, make his choice: marry Arlane or leave Paris for Cannes and the twins, who, he realizes, can never mend his broken heart. He is helped to a decision by Arlane's father (Maurice Chevalier), a lovable blocking figure who arrives to say, "Give her a chance, Monsieur. She's so helpless. Such a little fish. Throw her back in the water." (What any father would say, even if his daughter were thirty-two.) Mr. Flannegan makes his decision. He will do the right thing (which, from the point of view of the audience, is precisely the wrong thing): he will leave Arlane forever.

The final scene takes place at the railroad station in Paris. Mr. Flannegan pays his porter and walks over to Arlane. She seems about to cry, but her words are brave. The train whistle blows. Mr. Flannegan says farewell and, sadly, reluctantly (he clearly wants to do the wrong thing), boards the train. He stands on the steps of the car as Arlane, tears now in her eyes, looks up and tells him about the other men (all fictional) who will soon be with her in Paris. The train lurches forward—chug, chug, chug, faster and faster—as Arlane runs beside it. Music plays in the background. And then, at the last possible moment, just as the train seems about to clear the station (and Arlane to run out of platform), the music reaches a crescendo, and the movie finally gives the audience what it by now desperately wants: Gary

Cooper reaches down, puts his arm around her waist, and lifts Audrey Hepburn onto the train. They kiss, and with tears in her eyes, she smiles up at him as he enfolds her in his arms. The end we knew and hoped would come has come at last, our dreams for Arlane and Mr. Flannegan are finally true, and everyone, except perhaps the twins in Cannes, feels something that feels like joy. And although we already know it, in the final moments of the movie a smiling Maurice Chevalier appears on the platform to tell us, in a voice over, that Mr. and Mrs. Flannegan are now living happily ever after in New York.

I looked at my wife. She was smiling. Her eyes looked as Audrey Hepburn's had when Gary Cooper lifted her onto the train (and as mine felt when he did it). At such a moment, when, thanks to the shrewdly crafted movie we had just watched, the world seemed good, I knew she would be vulnerable. "What cheek," I said. "That's Shakespeare's story, and they even tell it the same way he does. You know what you want and whom you want it for even before the movie begins, and then, when you're about ready to explode with frustration, they miraculously give it to you. If they haven't read Shakespeare, they've surely read Northrop Frye." "Yes," she said, "it's a very silly movie if you take it literally, but it's one of my favorites. It ends just the way you want it to. It always makes me feel, I don't know, happy . . . lucky, I guess." I said nothing else ("golden time convents" too rarely to be swept aside by logic), but I had an idea for my next class on Shakespeare's comedies.

II

If you ask students about the value of comedy (almost any comedy they would ordinarily be asked about in a classroom), they invariably tend to locate it in satire: comedy points up the foibles and pretensions of the characters it presents to us and, by extension, the characters we meet in the world outside the theater. (They answer as they do, I fear, because we who teach comedy are desperate to find reasons for doing so, to make those silly, frivolous, contrived stories as serious, important, and significant as the serious stories we often call tragedies.) But while that answer is to some degree true for some of Shakespeare's comedies, it does not seem to me to take us very far with him. We value Shakespeare's comedies for a different reason, and *Love in the Afternoon* had helped me not only to see more clearly what we do value in these plays, but also to work out what seems to me an effective way to teach them.

The next time I taught Shakespeare's comedies, I arrived, like a teacher from the fine arts department, with a sack, not of slides, but of videotapes, each one rolled to precisely the right place. First the students and I talked for a while about comedy. We defined the familiar progress of romantic comedy, and I set out my wife's arguments against it. Then I asked the students to take a look at a piece of classic comedy. I put in a tape, I pressed the play button; miraculously, it worked. There on the screen before them were Audrey Hepburn and Gary Cooper on the platform of the station in Paris. While the film, in black and white, to some extent showed its age, it worked. Even though the students had not seen the entire movie, the conventional expectations and desires kicked in and, as Mr. Flannegan once again lifted Arlane onto the train and closed his arms around her, sighs of satisfaction (punctuated with some good-natured laughter) moved through the classroom. The students knew the movie had set them up, and they recognized how it did so (the music, the clear possibility that Mr. Flannegan may indeed leave Paris without Arlane, the long-delayed and last-minute lift and embrace), but they all—tough-minded young men, career-minded young women—enjoyed it nonetheless, felt joy in seeing it. Yes, the young women of the 1990s were pleased by a scene that had pleased their grandmothers and their mothers many years before.

My next tape was *Sabrina*, at the end of which (to make a long but familiar story short) Humphrey Bogart leaps onto a tugboat to catch the ship taking (once again) Audrey Hepburn to Paris. The movie embraces all the familiar elements: an older man falling reluctantly in love with a young, innocent woman and deciding, at the last possible moment (even as we see and hear the ship, through a window behind him, moving out of New York's harbor), to marry her; the clear and increasingly disquieting possibility first that he will actually let her go to Paris alone and then that he has decided too late to overtake the ship; a jaunty version of *La Vie En Rose* that comes to a triumphant close as the lovers at last embrace on the deck and thus release all the tension the delay has created in the audience. The resistance of the students to this version of the story was, by the way, no better than it had been to *Love in the Afternoon*; they were happy, as their parents and grandparents had been happy, when, as the movie came to an end, Humphrey Bogart enfolded Audrey Hepburn in his arms.

Then, lest the students think themselves more liberated, more sophisticated, less vulnerable to the contrivances of comedy than their elders had been, I played my third tape. There on the screen, in color at last, was Edward Lewis (Richard Gere) checking out of the Beverly

Wiltshire Hotel in *Pretty Woman*. The manager of the hotel, initially a blocking figure but now a generous and crafty slave, tells him that Rodney, the chauffeur who will soon drive him to the airport in a white stretch limousine, yesterday drove home Miss Vivian, the prostitute (played by Julia Roberts) Edward has fallen in love with. Will Edward do the right thing (which this time is precisely the right thing from the audience's point of view as well): decide to marry Vivian, who only yesterday refused his offer to make her what we used to call "a kept woman" because, as she puts it, she wants it all? The scene shifts to Vivian, packing, saying goodbye to her roommate, telling her (and more importantly us) that the bus she is taking to San Francisco leaves in an hour. The scene shifts back to Edward, sitting in the back of the limousine on his way to the airport, thinking, deciding, unsure (because he feels he cannot love anyone) whether or not to go after her.

As the movie turns to its close, Vivian, at the door of her apartment, about to leave for the bus, hears first the honking of a horn and then an aria from *La Traviata* (the opera she had seen with Edward). She goes to the window, and there on the street below, with his head (and the music) coming through the sunroof, an umbrella in one hand, a bouquet of flowers in the other, is Edward. He climbs up the fire escape to her window (the contemporary equivalent, as the movie has already made explicit, of rescuing the princess from the tower), and they embrace on the metal steps. And although, once again, the man decides how the story will end, Vivian gets the last word, spoken, one imagines, for the women of the 1990s who are watching. "What happened after he climbed up the tower and rescued her?" Edward asks. "She rescues him right back," says Vivian.

In its very last moments, however, the movie takes something of a Shakespearean turn. The camera draws back from Edward and Vivian on the fire escape and, as he crosses the street below, we see and hear a street person—like Jacques leaving the stage at the end of *As You Like It*—deconstructing the comic ending. "This is Hollywood," he chants. "Some dreams come true. Some don't. But keep on dreamin'. This is Hollywood." But we hardly hear his warning; all our dreams for Edward and Vivian have come true, and so, we feel, will our own.

The moment Richard Gere appeared on the screen, the students smiled, and another sigh of satisfaction moved through the classroom. They seemed pleased by a movie that was both familiar and remembered as enjoyable. They also seemed pleased (smiles, sighs, generous laughter) as Edward and Vivian embraced on the fire escape. And whether or not they recognized it at the time, they had already begun to answer one of the questions I put to them once they had seen the three comic endings: Why do we want to have that same comic story told to us—on the stage, in the movies—over and over again? Why does Shakespeare tell it, why does Hollywood tell it, over and over again? What in the story do we value?

III

What we value in that story, whether Shakespeare's version or Hollywood's, it seems to me, are the feelings it evokes in us, feelings of joy, pleasure, celebration, satisfaction, elation (words critics sometimes use to describe what we feel at the end of a well-orchestrated production of a comedy). While the feelings are evoked, as we have seen, by predictable maneuvers (music, the clear and constant possibility that something will go wrong, the eleventh-hour embrace that finally and joyfully releases the tension our frustration and fears have created), and while we in fact learn (as the sighs that filled the classroom made clear) to respond to those maneuvers in predictably appropriate ways, the feelings result as well from our sense that something miraculous has taken place, something at odds with the reasonable expectations our experience has taught us, and we feel joy at what Madeleine L'Engle (1990) has called, in a religious context, a "glorious impossible." Mr. Flannegan scoops Arlane up onto the train; Humphrey Bogart, a shrewd, hardnosed, wealthy, middle-aged, workaholic businessman follows Audrey Hepburn, his chauffeur's beautiful daughter, to Paris; Edward, another wealthy businessman, marries Vivian, a prostitute, and thereby gives her all, the fairy-tale ending she has waited for; Theseus gratuitously chooses love over law and allows Lysander to marry Hermia and Demetrius Helena; Sebastian returns from the sea, miraculously discovers his sister at the house of Olivia, and, putting all confusions to rest, brings about the marriages of two lovely couples; contrary to all reasonable expectations ("Against all sense do you importune her," says the Duke), Isabella, at Mariana's request, intercedes for Angelo, her brother returns from the grave, and she and the Duke are joined together in marriage.

What we value in comedy is the feeling it evokes in us, and we value that feeling not simply because it is joyous or satisfying, but because it gives us hope for our own future and for the future of our world as well. In comedy, Shakespeare's and Hollywood's, our dreams for others come true, and we are brought, through the fairy-tale end of a familiar story (that no one's daughter, once she has left the theater, should ever take literally) and the conventional contrivances that bring it about, to feel joy when they do. That momentary, ephemeral joy makes possible, if only for a moment, the hope, despite all we know of the world, that our own dreams, individual and communal, for ourselves and for our world, may miraculously come true as well. The "glorious impossibles" of comedy, to use the words of Madeleine L'Engle (1990), "bring joy to our hearts, hope to our lives, songs to our lips."

IV

My second question (as well as its answer) may be obvious: Why bother with Shakespeare if *Pretty Woman* does the same thing, evokes the same feeling as, say, *Twelfth Night* does? The answer emerged gradually as we worked our way through some of the comedies: what we value in Shakespeare's comedies is the complexity or ambiguity of feeling they evoke through their consistent refusal to rest easily in the conventions, particularly the conventional closure, of their own genre. Malvolio's exit at the end of *Twelfth Night*, like the disquieting marriage of Sir Toby and Maria (which may suggest what marriages are too often like in our own world), undercuts the comic ending of the play and can leave an audience feeling uneasy with and unsure of its own feelings of joy. Unless the director decides otherwise, Egeus, Hermia's father, may remain outside the new society that takes shape at the end of *A Midsummer Night's Dream*. The assured understanding of Beatrice and Benedick at the end of *Much Ado about Nothing* inevitably tempers the elation an audience feels at the miraculous reconciliation of Hero and Claudio, for it suggests both the continued vulnerability of a woman like Hero in a patriarchal world and the precarious ground upon which she and Claudio have to build their life together.

Shakespeare's comedies characteristically dilute the joy we feel at their endings and to some degree temper the hope they engender with a recognition that miracles are only momentary, that not everyone may share in them, that the world continues to go its familiar way. The elation we feel at the end of Shakespeare's comedies is consistently chastened by the complex of events that calls it forth. But for all their clear-eyed awareness of the reluctance of the world to take the shape we dream for it, Shakespeare's comedies nonetheless affirm, through the feelings they evoke in us, that joy is possible, that dreams can at least sometimes come true, that a man who likes comedies and a woman who likes tragedies can sometimes, like the ass and the fairy queen in *A Midsummer Night's Dream,* find some happiness together during their brief moments on earth, that they can, in the words of the poet John Ormond, with "brief and charmed arithmetic / Prove, for a time, that one and one is one" ("Three Rs," 1969, 42).

V

On November 1, 1990, I caught the next to last performance of the Royal Shakespeare Company's production of *Pericles* in The Pit at the Barbican Centre in London. It was a matinee (the last performance was that evening), and most in the audience were students, mainly American, some British. The production was excellent; both the reunion of Pericles and his daughter and their subsequent discovery of Thaisa were beautifully done and deeply moving. With (I suspect) most of the audience, I felt I might cry with joy. As I left the theater, I walked up the stairs behind two young American women, one black, the other white, both students. As I listened to their conversation (I wanted to know how they felt about the production), the black woman said to her friend, "That was great. It ended just the way I wanted it to. It made me feel like crying." That satisfaction, the pleasure she had had in witnessing her dreams for Pericles and his family come true, seems to me precisely what we value in Shakespeare's comedies. And while she did not say so, I imagine she left the Barbican that day happier, more hopeful than she might otherwise have been, more able than ordinarily to see what is good about our world. What more could her teacher have wanted for her as she went off to see *Pericles* than for the production to bring her the joy out of which she might dare to dream dreams for her own future and the future of our world?

References

L'Engle, Madeleine. 1990. *The Glorious Impossible.* New York: Simon and Schuster.

Ormond, John. 1969. "Three Rs." *Requiem and Celebration.* Swansea, United Kingdom: Christopher Davies.

14 Shakespearean Festivals: The Popular Roots of Performance

Delmar C. Homan
Bethany College

The theater celebrates life; a course in Shakespeare celebrates life in performance. For life is in the meaning of the plays, meaning that depends at least in part upon their ceremonious performance. To help students understand how performance functions, *live* productions are thus best. Still, filmed performances can help students develop their theatrical imaginations so that they can produce scenes in class or so that they can create their own productions in their mental theaters as they read and write (Hall 1987, 735–36; Homan 1990). To attract students to this "performance approach," teachers can use festival performances past and present as an introduction to the celebration of life in performance.

The sheer number of festivals operating today in the United States amazes students; the 1991 spring/summer issue of the *Shakespeare Newsletter* lists fifty-four active summer Shakespearean festivals or summer theater programs with Shakespearean plays, and that list is not complete. With twenty-four states (and Canada) represented, the festivals occur from Hawaii to Maine and Massachusetts, from Alabama and Georgia to Idaho and Ohio. Indeed, the geographical range is so widespread that teachers anywhere in the country should be able to find a nearby festival and make use of both its resources in personnel and history and its performances (a number of which continue into the school year, especially in the fall). Many even have special activities and performances for students. Moreover, new productions spring up regularly; according to a recent brochure, a special production arranged for an "Exploring Shakespeare" course was presented in the summer of 1991 at Mt. Rushmore in South Dakota by Huron University students and teachers in cooperation with members of the London Young Vic. Current reviews of major festivals are also regularly published by the *Shakespeare Quarterly*, and students both enjoy and are enlightened by finding descriptions of various festival performances of the same play.

Also attractive to students are the powerfully motivated individuals who have started Shakespearean festivals across the United States. Just as in Kansas two college students started the Pizza Hut chain with a borrowed $500, so also in Kansas a Kinsley editor and theater buff, Charles R. Edwards, founded a Shakespearean festival in 1912 that spread to four other Kansas towns before World War I ended his dream (Homan 1988). More recently, Angus Bowmer founded the Ashland, Oregon, Shakespearean Festival, Joseph Papp founded the New York Shakespeare Festival (now in New York City's Central Park, but originally held in an old church basement), and Tyrone Guthrie founded both the Canadian Stratford Festival and the Guthrie Theater in Minneapolis, Minnesota, with its many Shakespearean productions. These three festivals continue in popularity and are included in the most recent *Shakespeare Newsletter* listings.

Since I teach in Kansas, my research and teaching have emphasized Kansas, including even the significance to Dwight Eisenhower of a role in a Shakespeare burlesque produced as his senior class play and as part of an Abilene high school commencement celebration (Homan 1976). Teachers in other parts of the country can surely find local or nearby examples. And even more distant festivals may turn out to have local connections. For example, the director of the Kansas festivals, Edwards's friend Gilmor Brown, was a North Dakota native educated in Colorado and Illinois, as well as in Ben Greet's traveling company; he also performed in other touring companies, directed a Shakespearean production in Florence, Colorado, just before his summer in Kansas in 1912, and directed another in Rochester, Minnesota, early in the summer of 1916, just before his return to Kansas; and he went on to California to found the Pasadena Playhouse and serve as its president until his death (Homan 1984).

Because of the availability of excellent resources, I have also emphasized Joseph Papp's festival in New York City and the Ashland, Oregon, festival as coast-to-coast events. The production *Kiss Me, Petruchio*, filmed from a performance of *The Taming of the Shrew* with Meryl Streep and Raul Julia, gives a fourfold benefit to both teachers and students: a brief introduction by Joseph Papp, an excellent performance of the major action of the plot, some idea of the excitement generated by the festival in the audience, and a discussion of the relevance of the play in light of today's redefined gender roles. At present, the production is available for rent and sale as an educational film or video from Films Inc. in Chicago.

The Ashland festival is well described in *The Dream Begins,* a thirty-minute production now available for loan from the archives of the Ashland festival as well as from some local libraries. The film tells of the founding of the festival and of the challenges faced and met not only by the founder, but by the actors and backstage personnel as well; it also includes interviews with the people involved. The film's information and inspiration make worthwhile any effort needed to secure it for use in the classroom.

Also available on the Ashland festival are two excellent books. Angus Bowmer's *As I Remember, Adam: An Autobiography of a Festival* traces the festival from its beginnings to 1975, and an epilogue in the third printing by the producing director brings the festival through the death of its founder in 1979 and into an expanded repertoire. The book includes thirty-two pages of black-and-white plates, from family pictures to pictures of the stage, actors, and productions. The other book, *Golden Fire,* a 1985 fifty-year-anniversary volume by Edward and Mary Brubaker, provides both black-and-white and color plates of the theater, scenes, costumes, and actors; a history of the festival; a festival chronology; a listing of the 1935 to 1985 repertory, including plays, directors, and attendance; and a listing of the festival players over the last fifty years. This book is lush, stirring the hidden ham in all of us, teachers and students alike.

Another area of exploration can be the celebrations especially programmed for Shakespearean anniversaries. The three-hundredth anniversary of Shakespeare's death, for instance, occurring in 1916, has been described by Charles Shattuck (1987, 291–309), with special attention to the New York City pageant in honor of Shakespeare, *Caliban by the Golden Sands,* by Percy MacKaye. Shattuck's book provides plentiful illustrations and complete references for further study. Nevertheless, for a day-by-day impression of the excitement building up to and during the performances, one must read daily issues of the *New York Times* (Shattuck 1987, 329, n. 45), since Shattuck finally emphasizes the poor quality of MacKaye's poetry rather than the enthusiasm of the performers—including Isadora Duncan en route from Paris to South America (*New York Times,* 23 May 1916, 9; "Opening of 'Caliban' Postponed by Rain," *New York Times,* 24 May 1916, 9)—and of the first-night audience of fifteen thousand, who came from "the lower east side to Riverside Drive" to see, and almost without exception to remain to the end for, "an extraordinary pageant, a spectacle of memorable beauty. . . . staggering undertaking. . . . a success. . . . the biggest dramatic entertainment ever presented within the limits of this city. . . . a notable achievement. . . . a fine thing to have done. . . . an unforgettable thing to see. . . ." (*New York Times*, 25 May 1916, 11). For Kansans, there is a local connection; the Kinsley native, Charles Edwards, may have taken part in this event, since he was a member of the Washington Square Players at the Bandbox Theater during the 1915–16 season (Mantle and Sherwood 1933, 560–61; Edwards's obituary, *Kinsley Graphic*, 3 June 1926) and since these players were responsible for two of the interludes ("Masque Rehearsed," *New York Times*, 20 May 1916, 9). Whether in the pageant or not, Edwards was certainly caught up in the New York City celebration of the tercentenary, for he acted in, and served as assistant director for, a production of *Twelfth Night* in New York City presented as an "English Teachers' Association's contribution to the Tercentenary Celebration" (*Kinsley Graphic*, 27 July 1916, 3). In his enthusiasm for Shakespearean celebration, he also directed the Kinsley production of *Twelfth Night* on August 2–5 ("Kansas's Greatest Tercentenary Celebration," according to the ad in the *Kinsley Graphic*, 27 July 1916, 3), while Brown directed several others (Homan 1984, 95; Homan 1988, 12 and n. 43).

The four-hundredth anniversary of Shakespeare's birth, occurring in 1964, was also widely celebrated, although collected information about the many events seems not to have been published. Both the 1916 and 1964 American celebrations are touched upon by Louis Marder in *His Exits and His Entrances* (1963, 325–27); however, since the book was published in 1963, Marder's ongoing *Shakespeare Newsletter* serves as the major source of contemporaneous information on the 1964 celebration, as well as on other festivals throughout the following years. Local newspapers should be searched for other contemporaneous information.

Advanced students can, of course, pursue historical detail, and those especially interested in acting can perhaps imagine founding their own festival companies. But all students can be challenged to see that popular festivals demonstrate the need felt by many throughout the United States to participate in performances of Shakespeare's plays—whether as part of a company or as part of an audience—in order to enjoy and understand them. Moreover, the many different interpretations and stagings and reasons for celebration demonstrate the need for students to be able to imagine their own performances, both to get the most satisfaction from their reading and to get the most celebration out of life.

Note

Since this essay was written, Joseph Papp has died, having earlier designated a new director (JoAnne Akalitis) to carry on the work of the New York Shakespeare Festival. Also, the *Shakespeare Newsletter* has been transferred to Iona College in New Rochelle, New York (John W. Mahon and Thomas A. Pendleton, editors), so that Louis Marder will have more time to give to the computerized Shakespeare Data Bank (*SNL* 41.3 [Fall 1991]: 21–23, 30).

References

Bowmer, Angus L. 1975. *As I Remember, Adam: An Autobiography of a Festival.* Ashland, Oregon: The Oregon Shakespearean Festival Association. Third printing, with an updated epilogue by Jerry Turner, after 1979.

Brubaker, Edward, and Mary Brubaker. 1985. *Golden Fire: The Anniversary Book of the Oregon Shakespearean Festival.* Preface by Jerry Turner. Ashland, Oregon: The Oregon Shakespearean Festival Association.

The Dream Begins. 1983. Bijou Productions, Inc., Medford, Oregon. 30 min. Available for loan from the Archives of the Oregon Shakespearean Festival, PO Box 158, Ashland, Oregon 97520; 503-482-2111.

Hall, Donald. 1987. *To Read Literature: Fiction, Poetry, Drama.* 2d ed. New York: Holt, Rinehart, and Winston.

Homan, Delmar C. 1976. "Dwight Eisenhower and William Shakespeare." *Heritage of Kansas* 9.1: 13–17.

———. 1984. "Gilmor Brown and the Avant-Garde Kansas Theatre." *Theatre History Studies* 4: 82–100.

———. 1988. "Shakespearean Festivals in Western Kansas." *Heritage of the Great Plains* 21.2 (Spring): 1–20.

———. 1990. "The Journal as Performance Explicator of Shakespeare." *Kansas English* 76.1 (Fall): 20–25.

Kiss Me, Petruchio. 1983 (made in 1979). Directed by Christopher Dixon. With Meryl Streep and Raul Julia. Films Inc., 5547 North Ravenswood Avenue, Chicago, Illinois 60640-1199; 312-878-2600. 60 min.

Mantle, Burns, and Garrison P. Sherwood, eds. 1933. *The Best Plays of 1909–1919 and the Year Book of the Drama in America.* New York: Dodd, Mead.

Marder, Louis. 1963. *His Exits and His Entrances: The Story of Shakespeare's Reputation.* Philadelphia: J. R. Lippincott.

"Shakespeare Festivals, Summer 1991." 1991. *Shakespeare Newletter* 41.1–2 (Spring/Summer): 1–2, 18.

Shattuck, Charles H. 1987. *Shakespeare on the American Stage: From Booth and Barrett to Sothern and Marlowe.* Vol. 2. Washington, D.C.: Folger Shakespeare Library.

15 Introducing Shakespeare with First Folio Advertisements

Daniel J. Pinti
New Mexico State University

Every teacher of literature must answer the question, What do I do on the first day of class? Going over the syllabus and course requirements, a necessary first-day chore, rarely takes a full class period; still, though the students have yet to read any of the texts, class time is too precious to waste. In a Shakespeare course, an opening lecture on "background" information is possible, even worthwhile, but it also sets a tone: the teacher talks, and the students listen. I am convinced that even an introductory Shakespeare class made up of freshmen and sophomores ought to include as much class discussion as possible; I do not want the students silent and passive at any class meeting, let alone the first. Rather, since an introductory level Shakespeare course, like any course in literature, is in fact a course in textual interpretation, it makes sense to encourage students to interpret texts from day one. So, on that first day, I give them some brief Shakespeare-related texts to interpret. I would like to share a few strategies for encouraging first-day student participation and interpretation, strategies that I have found to be quite successful in warming up the students' critical faculties for a class in which they will be expected to engage texts as actively as possible every day.

One difficulty that must be acknowledged at the outset is that along with textual interpretation can come the problem of textual intimidation; that is, when it comes to Shakespeare, students are too often easily intimidated by the figure of the Bard, by the prospect of facing a writer whose work epitomizes "great literature" and is, the logic goes, ostensibly beyond their comprehension. Nevertheless, if, like Robert Scholes (1990), "we would like our students to be able to function textually in a society that constantly bombards them with texts" (99), active interpretation must be encouraged from the start. Thus the most useful thing we can do in an introductory Shakespeare course is to demystify Shakespeare, to help the student deconstruct the myth of the Bard and "examine the cultural conditioning that has placed Shakespeare in the seat of greatness" (Beehler 1990, 199; cf. Norris 1985). Poking a little fun at bardolatry doesn't hurt; more important, though, is showing students that the Shakespeare myth, like any other, is a cultural construct, one that in itself can challenge and be challenged by their own interpretive powers. In order to get the students thinking and talking on the first day of class, then, I directly address and call into question the Shakespeare myth and the place of Shakespeare in our culture, and I do so by way of a few facsimiles from the First Folio.

I concentrate on two texts from the 1623 edition: the Droeshout engraving of Shakespeare himself and the letter "To the great Variety of Readers" from the editors John Heminges and Henry Condell.[1] I introduce these materials and discuss them with the students even before I go over the syllabus. Most students seem pleasantly surprised by not being handed a syllabus and having it read to them as soon as they sit down in a new course. Moreover, an opening discussion allows me to establish my own teaching "personality" more readily than does a survey of the syllabus, and it focuses the students' attention on Shakespeare, reading, and culture, rather than on, say, whether or not the final exam is comprehensive. Time enough for the syllabus later in the period.

In any case, I use the engraving first, and I have found two "visual aids" to help me with it. Both are recent advertisements that use a version of the Droeshout image. The first is a full-page ad from the *New York Times* (national edition, 21 May 1990, C16) for James Atlas's book *The Book Wars*, with a caption under the Shakespeare icon that reads, "Look who's being thrown out of college classrooms." The next few lines of copy below the caption read, "Out, Shakespeare! And take your friends Plato and Dante with you. Heresy? Hardly. At least not to a growing number of leading university professors." (I never fail to be amused by the image of Shakespeare, Plato, and Dante as "friends," perhaps sharing a drink and genially joking about the Englishman's "small Latin and less Greek.") The second advertisement is a magazine ad for the Business Committee for the Arts, Inc., with a caption next to the picture declaring Shakespeare to be "the greatest apartment salesman of our time" (*Publishers Weekly*, 25 March 1988, 61). The "apartment salesman" reference alludes to the fact that "with every signed lease, Ballard Realty offered a free membership to the Alabama Shakespeare Festival. Soon, over 80% of the company's units were leased before construction was even completed." Not knowing much about the 1988 housing market in Montgomery, Alabama, I cannot say if the cause-and-effect logic here has any merit; the advertisers, however, insist we conclude that "the arts can help create a positive public image, increase a company's visibility, and improve sales." Advertising is a mode of discourse that students are exceedingly familiar with, and beginning with advertisements is meant to put them at some ease—even as I am at least implicitly arguing for the need to analyze the textual strategies of sales pitches with as much intensity as we employ in analyzing the textual strategies of Elizabethan plays.

After presenting the ads, I jokingly ask the students if anyone can tell me whom these are pictures of. Naturally, they know the answer; we then go on to discuss the ways we can tell how the advertisers can *expect* us (inasmuch as "us" means readers of the *New York Times* or *Publishers Weekly*) to know the answer, why they expect us to recognize a representation of Shakespeare's face when we see it. It is particularly interesting to note with regard to the first ad that Shakespeare is visually recognizable, but that Plato and Dante (despite numerous drawings of the latter) are not. It is also interesting to point out the quasi-religious use of "heresy" and the insidious implications of the phrase "a growing number."

I also ask the students what they think of when they see this picture. We know it is a picture of Shakespeare, but what does it represent? What does it call to mind? In other words, what reactions are the advertisers trying to trigger in us? Common answers to these related questions include "literature," "great literature," "genius," "England" (which of course can lead to a few thoughts about what the cultural connections between England, language, and literature mean for us), and so forth. We come to recognize that Shakespeare is someone whom we have collective ideas about, who has some generally identifiable place in our culture. I point out that presumably this is based on what he wrote—and that is of course a big part of it—but we also discuss how Shakespeare's cultural place is an indirect, heavily mediated one, particularly when his reputation is known even to those who have not read any of his plays. Our subsequent discussion centers around the question: What do these ads, and our responses to them, suggest about Shakespeare's place in our society? The issues broached are broad, perhaps, but pertinent, and they help students on the way to viewing the impending course not as Life's Truths as handed down by Shakespeare (or by me), but as a course of genuine relevance in cultural and textual analysis.

At this point I hand out copies of the engraving as it appears in the First Folio. (If students have a scholarly edition of the text, particularly *The Complete Pelican Shakespeare* or *The Riverside Shakespeare*, they can examine the facsimiles in the edition itself.) I give them a quick sketch of some background to the First Folio, noting in particular its status as the first edition of Shakespeare's collected works and its publication seven years after the playwright's death, and I ask them what they make of the inclusion of such an engraving in such an edition. I point out as well the relative expense of such a collection (as opposed to a cheap quarto of a single play) and the possibility of failure for such a publishing venture (Hinman 1968, p. x). The facsimiles work because most students seem to understand and appreciate the sense of a book as an artifact, produced for particular purposes by individuals whom we can name and talk about. We usually discuss briefly the business of Shakespeare, then and now, and how this business relates and contributes to the reputation over which we are trying to gain some control. At this point, in the context of considering Shakespeare as a member and product of both his society and ours, we turn to the Heminges and Condell letter.

I have the students look at this document in facsimile and read it in my own typed (and somewhat abbreviated) transcription. American students know what amounts to a sales pitch when they see one, and it does not take long before they are fruitfully discussing the rhetorical strategies involved in the letter. I ask them first to focus on the title of the letter: What are the implications of a "Variety" of readers, "From the most able to him that can but spell"?[2] What problems arise when you publish something that anyone (with a pound to spare) can purchase, regardless of his or her interpretive capabilities? I usually mention at this point the comparatively heterogeneous nature of Shakespeare's playgoing audience, and I ask them how they think that audience might differ from a reading audience (although I save the bulk of this discussion for a separate class period focusing on playgoing in Shakespeare's time). We note the importance of "censure," of readerly judgment, in the letter, and how the authors simultaneously invite and attempt to direct individual interpretation (regardless of our wit, our critical acumen, we are implicitly cautioned about judging too harshly and reminded that "these plays have had their trial already, and stood out all appeals.") I ask the students to consider in what ways such a statement might contribute to forming a Shakespeare legend. We also discuss the writers' claims for the value and the accuracy of *their* edition; the mention of "divers stolen and surreptitious copies, maimed and deformed by the frauds and stealths of injurious impostors that exposed them" gives me a chance to characterize briefly the status of playtexts in Shakespeare's London, and it makes a nice transition to the editors' appeal that their presentation of the texts is "as [Shakespeare] conceived them." How Shakespeare's texts became the text they handed over their own money for, and the various reconstructions that were part of the process, can itself be of interest to students. Of course, I am careful not to lose the students in a maze of foul papers, prompt books, quartos, and folios, but I do acquaint them with the existence of very real confusions and unanswered questions surrounding the problem of recovering what Shakespeare actually wrote. The presentation of some mystery, I think, intrigues them.

All of this leads naturally into a fundamental questioning of Shakespeare as, in the words of Heminges and Condell, "a happy imitator of Nature, . . . [and] a most gentle expresser of it." By now they have enough new-found knowledge to recognize the apparent falsity of the editors' claim that Shakespeare's "mind and hand went together, and what he thought he uttered with that easiness that we have scarce received a blot in his papers." We discuss how this image contributes to the Shakespeare myth, and by seeing in this document how the legend begins, the students are by now appreciating the legend for what it is—and with any luck, they are less fearful of it. We often make the greatest headway, though, when we discuss Heminges and Condell's claim that if "you do not like him, surely you are in some manifest danger not to understand him." In other words, if you don't like Shakespeare's work, you just don't get it; if you don't enjoy and appreciate his plays, there must be some short-coming in *you*. In all likelihood, if the students had encountered Shakespeare in the classroom before, this had been at least the implicit message, and they tend to be surprised at finding the same sort of appeal to Shakespeare's inherent genius, and the same sort of subtle rhetorical coercion, nearly four hundred years ago. We try to understand this attitude for what it is, namely, a way of putting the reader on the defensive, an attempt to compel acceptance and approval. The editors' final, idealistic picture of readers—indeed, of "friends"—guiding one another to greater understanding and appreciation of the plays un-derscores Shakespeare's fellow actors' concern with having people interpret the plays both collectively and favorably; the former ideal I can redefine constructively in terms of the class, and the latter I leave as only one choice among many.

Although I realize that such topics might sound somewhat esoteric in the context of high school or early undergraduate classrooms, I believe that, with a focus on the materials in hand, discussion of these contextual ideas can encourage students to adopt a more confident and critical attitude not only toward the plays themselves, but also toward what people have to say about the plays. I do not mean to oversimplify the complexity of Shakespeare's place in the culture of the seventeenth century, or of the long and winding road that takes Shakespeare to where he is today.[3] The point is only for the students to see that Shakespeare's place of reverence is a cultural construct rather than an intrinsic given; thus, by the end of the course, they can be on their way to reconstructing Shakespeare for themselves. I open up questions rather than offer pat answers. As we know, the very authority of Shakespeare's voice, and of the teacher's, can prevent a student from finding and exercising his or her own critical voice, so I try to call into question both sources of interpretive authority. There is a danger to this approach, I suppose: open questions and loose ends can be (but by no means need be) as intimidating as unquestionable authority and looming reputation. But they can more often stimulate excitement and encourage exploration; if handled well, they are not paralyzing. The last thing we want as teachers is to have students unwilling or unable to articulate their own thinking.

In my introductory Shakespeare course, I want students to learn something about Shakespeare and his work, to come to their own understanding and appreciation of that work, and, ideally, to consciously and critically find a place for it in their world—though not necessarily at the top of it. The alternative is for the students to accept having the place of Shakespeare assigned for them. By encouraging the students to exercise their own critical powers on the first day of class, I feel I can start them in the former direction; by doing this through the use of a few materials from the First Folio, I invite them to encounter and examine, albeit in a general way, Shakespeare as a man within his society and as a revered cultural symbol within ours. I hope to prepare them to engage the plays themselves in a similar fashion: ready to challenge, resist, and, yes, even enjoy Shakespeare's work on their own terms, but also ready to have their own ideas challenged, resisted, and revised. Such is the critical dialogue that is, or ought to be, the Shakespeare class.

Notes

1. For a brief discussion of the engraving, see Hinman (1968); Heminges, Condell, and their letter are discussed by Gary Taylor in Wells and Taylor (1987, 69–73) and mentioned by Sanders (1990).

2. Quotations from the letter are taken from Wells and Taylor (1988, p. xlv).

3. For a thorough and engaging discussion on the use and reputation of Shakespeare through the ages, see Taylor (1989).

References

Beehler, Sharon A. 1990. "That's a Certain Text: Problematizing Shakespeare Instruction in American Schools and Colleges." *Shakespeare Quarterly* 41: 195–205.

Hinman, Charlton. 1968. *The Norton Facsimile: The First Folio of Shakespeare.* New York: W. W. Norton.

Norris, Christopher. 1985. "Post-structuralist Shakespeare: Text and Ideology." In *Alternative Shakespeares*, edited by John Drakakis, 47–66. London and New York: Methuen.

Sanders, Norman. 1990. "Shakespeare's Text." In *William Shakespeare: A Bibliographical Guide*, new edition, edited by Stanley Wells, 17–35. Oxford: Clarendon Press.

Scholes, Robert. 1990. "Toward a Curriculum in Textual Studies." In *Reorientations: Critical Theories and Pedagogies*, edited by Bruce Henrickson and Thaïs E. Morgan, 95–112. Urbana and Chicago: University of Illinois Press.

Taylor, Gary. 1989. *Reinventing Shakespeare: A Cultural History, from the Restoration to the Present.* New York: Weidenfeld and Nicolson.

Wells, Stanley, and Gary Taylor. 1987. *William Shakespeare: A Textual Companion.* Oxford: Clarendon Press.

———, eds. 1988. *William Shakespeare: The Complete Works.* Compact edition. Oxford: Clarendon Press.

16 Versions of *Henry V:* Laurence Olivier versus Kenneth Branagh

Harry Brent
Baruch College–CUNY

Teaching Shakespeare's history plays to first-year college students is beset with *a priori* problems. As we are all aware from a cascade of reports about what our students do not know, most college freshmen find even the history of our present century difficult to chart. What then of the late Middle Ages, the era of the history plays? Even many teachers have some difficulty sorting out the reigns of Edward III and Richard II, not to mention the eight Beauforts that lie between John of Gaunt and Henry VII.

As has been recognized, any understanding of the Henry plays requires some knowledge of medieval history (Cartelli 1986; Taylor 1986). The historical context of *Henry IV, Part 1,* the most popular of the history plays, is daunting even to the best of students, as it includes material about internal strife in England and border wars with Scotland, Wales, and Ireland during the reigns of Richard II and Henry IV. An appreciation of *Henry V* requires both familiarity with the "medieval world picture" (Manheim 1983) and some specialized knowledge of late medieval history. After all, not only does the central "serious" action of the play deal with the Hundred Years' War, but much of the important "comic" action again focuses on the internal strife of the British Isles during the late fourteenth and early fifteenth centuries.

Ironically enough, Shakespeare's purpose in including this "difficult" material was to make the play more accessible to his contemporaries. His political aim of rousing national unity is an element of what we might call a "Shakespearean multicultural perspective," an attempt to show how the disparate and feuding groups of the British Isles could work in common cause to face a common foe. To this end, in *Henry V* Shakespeare focuses on the Welsh, the Scots, and even the Irish—as personified by Captain Macmorris, though in a sometimes ambiguous way (Berger 1985)—to show how cultural differences can be transcended.

The irony of teaching an American multicultural class the multicultural lessons of the medieval British Isles was not lost on me when I decided to teach *Henry V* in my writing course. However, given the difficulties of the historical background, rich as it is with lessons about antagonism and cooperation among social groups, I at first gave up on the likelihood of *Henry V* ever becoming a mainstay in my freshman writing course—until I saw the Branagh film and learned that intelligent use of film can make history accessible to students and lead to better papers.

When I saw Kenneth Branagh's production of *Henry V*, I immediately noticed two aspects of the production that I knew would help my teaching. First, Branagh leaves out most of the scenes requiring detailed historical explanation. The hostility between the French and the English is presented in clearly drawn lines that can be understood and interpreted by directly observing the actions of the characters. Second, Branagh adds to *Henry V* some of the most important Falstaff episodes from the previous two Henry plays, chief among them the scene in which the young Hal silently banishes his old drinking companion (*1 Henry IV*, II.iv.470–80). These omissions and additions give the film a compactness and simplicity that transcend its difficult historical background—and ultimately make teaching *Henry V* much easier.

My enthusiasm for Branagh's production immediately brought to mind the other great film version of *Henry V*: the 1944 production directed by Laurence Olivier, who also played the title role. I was at once taken with several points of comparison between the two versions. The Olivier film, released during the final years of World War II, serves patriotism. Henry is an immaculately clad champion who, with the standard of St. George at his side, achieves an unambiguous victory over the medieval French, who, given the date of the film, stand for the Nazi Germans. Branagh's Henry, on the other hand, fights a muddy battle in which knives and axes vividly take their bloody toll from both sides—more the real Agincourt (Holderness 1984; Keegan 1976). The possibilities for comparing the two films became immediately apparent. It also became evident that not much historical background would really be needed for students to see and initiate these comparisons for themselves. As reviews of the Branagh film (Forbes 1989) and Branagh's own comments (1988) have suggested, each version is a product of its time; the two can thus be compared on that basis.

The Olivier version is largely meant to be a commentary on the steadfastness of the British people in the face of wartime adversity. The Branagh version, in keeping with the more individual concerns of peacetime, focuses on the personal growth of the young king into responsible adulthood. This is the most basic difference between the two films and should be kept in mind by anyone who pursues the teaching strategy I am outlining here. Using this central point as a guide, many comparisons between the two films are obvious and immediate. The Olivier version, for example, deftly omits I.ii, which unmasks the treason of Scroop, Cambridge, and Grey. Evidently, Olivier, or perhaps British wartime censors, saw no need to explore the possibility of treason. Branagh, on the other hand, plays this scene with added emphasis. His point is to highlight the world of moral ambiguity in which the young king must operate, a world in which he must turn away from the paths of his youth, and his friendships, if he is to survive.

In teaching the Branagh film, I found it useful to point out that Henry's world is not limited to the early fifteenth century; indeed, it transcends time by incorporating problems germane to any person's moral development. My students, many of whom come from impoverished and crime-ridden sections of New York City, noted that they themselves had to "give up" friends "like Falstaff" in order to succeed in college; they also found that many of their old friends who did not go to college "turned against them." The Branagh film brought home to them essential problems of moral development, problems that they shared with Shakespeare's early-fifteenth-century king.

Comparing the emphasis on political stability in the Olivier version with the emphasis on Henry's personal and moral development in the Branagh version creates numerous possibilities for writing assignments of interest to students. In constructing these assignments myself, I decided not to follow my usual procedure of giving an introductory background lecture when teaching the history plays. My purpose in plunging straightaway into the films was to keep the historical material from getting in the way. I did not neglect that material entirely, however. At the end of each screening, I left about twenty minutes of class time to comment on historical background. This procedure worked much better than an introductory lecture. After watching the events of the play on film, students were eager to ask questions: "Why were the French and English at war?" "What's the Salic Law?" "Did women have any choice in whom they married back then?" "Are the casualty figures for the battle of Agincourt correct?"

"What's a 'Dolphin'?" "Was Katherine a real person?" "Who are those soldiers with funny accents?" I could have given all this information in a lecture, but by getting students to *ask* me (and each other) for it, our discussion became much more interactive—a true dialogue, both between myself and my students and among students themselves.

Instead of lecturing in a vacuum, with students taking notes that had no meaningful reference points for them, I took questions on points my students really wanted to understand. Thus, in response to student questions, I was able to cite John Keegan's brilliant account of the Battle of Agincourt, to tell students what the casualties were, how they were caused, and in what specific manner the prisoners were killed. I talked about the nature of political marriage in the Middle Ages and about how the Welsh, Irish, and Scots were the minority groups of their day. Although I could have lectured on the same material, the films initiated dialogue.

The class watched the Olivier film first; then they watched the Branagh version. This process took four classes of one hundred minutes each, including the four twenty-minute sessions during which I answered students' questions. During those question periods, I also began to suggest topics for the comparison/contrast essay, and I asked the students to develop these topics in their daily journals. After the screenings, I devoted two class periods to finding topics and initiating trial drafts. Some of the students' essay topics follow:

- Duty and mercy in the character of Henry V
- Henry V as a symbolic versus psychological character
- The depiction of women in the two versions
- The depiction of violence, with respect to the historical contexts of the two films
- The limitations of friendship and fellowship
- Loyalty and treason in the two films
- The nature of advice in the two versions
- The depiction of the enemy in the two versions

In the process of arriving at these topics, my students began with several general points of comparison, ranging from setting to character development.

The settings of the two films are vastly different. The Olivier version begins with a camera shot of a scale-model, cardboard, fairy-tale medieval London that never was, shining on the banks of the Thames—a stark contrast to the real London of the time, which had been mauled by the blitz. It is almost as if Olivier is saying "Look what the Germans have destroyed." Food is plentiful in Olivier's storybook city. Indeed, fruit (in limited supply during World War II) is depicted as in ample supply for the audience at the Globe Theater. The Branagh version, striking a more ambiguous note, begins on the empty stage of a modern theater. With the words "O for a Muse of fire" (*Henry V*, I.1.1), Prologue strikes a match, then turns the stage lights on. The set is stark, nearly empty, strewn with the detritus of discarded props. Whereas the Olivier set makes the statement that the play is about *civitas* and politics, the Branagh set suggests less directed possibilities. It is as if anything might happen. Later, I noted for students that in the Olivier version, the French countryside is similarly idealized, whereas in the Branagh version it is muddy, cold, and wet.

Another initial point of comparison is the lighting, which differs markedly in the two versions. In the Olivier version, it is clear and direct, just as the issues (as wartime would want them) are clearly defined. The Branagh landscape, however, is a world of shadows, where motivations are often ambiguous and where Henry sometimes doubts a victorious outcome, as in the "O God of battles!" soliloquy (IV.i.306–21), which Olivier truncates to less than four lines, but which Branagh, as Henry, recites in its entirety, emphasizing the dubious legitimacy of his crown.

The Olivier version is not only more brightly lit, but also more boldly outlines the play's action. The actors in the Olivier version *assume* their roles. They are shown backstage *as actors*. The point seems to be that everyone must be ready to assume a role in the pageant of the nation's destiny, an appropriate wartime message. The actors in the Branagh version, on the other hand, are much more ambiguous human beings. They do not take up a part, as one might take up a place in military service; they *are* their roles. Henry, in the Olivier version, is a knight-errant. He frequently speaks from his white horse, sword in hand, and he has no doubts about his purpose. In the Branagh version, by contrast, he is more a real individual beset by doubt.

In the Olivier version, the comic scenes serve a political purpose. Gower, Fluellen, Macmorris, and Jamy represent the elements of British union (English, Welsh, Irish, and Scot) who sublimate in jest their rivalries in order to better face a common enemy. Olivier goes so far as to adorn Jamy with a thistle, Macmorris with a shamrock, and so forth. The imagery of leeks (the national symbol of Wales) is especially emphasized in that it underlines Henry's own Welsh ancestry and thereby enhances the theme of British unity. In the Branagh version, by contrast, Henry's Welshness is painted in emotional colors. His ancestral connections with Fluellen are the sinews that tie him to the souls of his troops and make his moral leadership possible.

My students were very quick to take up such points of departure in preparing their drafts. It was, however, and much to my surprise, the Falstaffian elements that required some additional explanation. One can easily forget that students have not necessarily read or seen the two preceding Henry plays and that Branagh's interpolations from those earlier plays can be downright confusing for them.

To deal with this problem, I briefly rehearsed the plots of the *Henry IV* plays, with a focus on Hal's maturation from a careless adolescent into a responsible young man. Once students got this point, they were eager to amplify it and to make some analogies to their own lives. Since many of them come from New York neighborhoods where they have abundant chances to fall in with "bad companions," Hal's maturation became real for them. Several students noted that after coming to college it was impossible for them to continue their routines with their old friends. They had to make choices much like those faced by Hal.

On the class day subsequent to the screenings, I held a workshop session in which the students were divided into small groups to discuss the topics they had chosen and to help each other discover strategies for developing those topics. I found this collaborative learning approach to be especially beneficial in the context of the history plays. Individual students later confided that, despite my question sessions, they still felt themselves on unfamiliar terrain and that the group format allowed them to ask "stupid questions" (e.g., "Is his name Henry, Hal, or Harry?"). Each group reported to the class as a whole, presenting the topics they discussed and exploring ways in which they intended to develop their topics. Since some topics were similar from group to group, the students were able to compare different lines of argument and to see possibilities for development that, as individuals, they had not originally entertained. For the few students who had not yet found a topic, this cross-discussion suggested a multitude of opportunities. Both the group sessions and the cross-discussion also allowed me time to help students refine their topics and to steer them away from overly broad and potentially disastrous lines of investigation, such as "The Hundred Years' War as Compared to World War II and the Post-Vietnam Syndrome." After the group work, students drafted their papers, brought them to class once again for a session on final revision and editing, and then handed them in. The following examples taken from my students' completed essays indicate the directions of thought and expression that developed in the course of the assignment's progress.

Most students developed their essays with reference to the contexts in which the two film versions of *Henry V* were produced. If there was an archetypal statement of a thesis, it was Yan Er Ping's (a pseudonym, as are all students' names in this article):

> Filmed during World War II (1944), *Henry V,* starring Laurence Olivier, was designed to heighten patriotism on the English homefront. The 1989 version, starring Kenneth Branagh, was filmed during a time of relative world peace and was therefore open to a freer and more creative interpretation in which the director focused more on Henry's personality. One version is a bright, wholesome, and somewhat edited translation of Shakespeare's play, while the other version is a powerful, dark, and mysterious war epic.

Students typically went on to compare various characters or scenes from the two film versions of the play.

Several students compared the ways in which Henry V was played by Olivier and Branagh. Jilleen Roberts wrote,

> In our modern age we do not expect our heroes to be perfect. Branagh's Henry is thus appealing to today's audiences, in some respects, because of his imperfections, which make him psychologically complex. In the Olivier film, Henry is portrayed by an actor who looks too old for the part. We don't get that feeling of growth, physically or mentally. He is just going through the motions of being the king. I don't get a sense of change, of learning. In the other film, Kenneth Branagh, a seemingly younger actor, portrays Henry as a character who is constantly moving forward, being shaped, and expanding through the course of the film, much as in Shakespeare's original play.

There were not as many papers on the role of women as I had hoped. Indeed, I had primed the class discussion with references to the role of women and especially to the ambiguity of Katherine's situation (Wilcox 1985). Delores McCrum did notice a marginalization of women, especially in the Olivier film. She observed,

> The women of the Olivier version were quite hidden. The importance of women was not emphasized, if acknowledged.

The conspiratorial Archbishop of Canterbury and Bishop of Ely intrigued many of my students. James Duncan wrote,

The bishops' strategy is to divert Henry's attention away from taxing the Church and into war with the French. Olivier uses this scene for laughs. Branagh presents this scene with a sinister flair to it. This scene sets the tone for both of the movies. Olivier's version is light, energetic, and almost uplifting. Branagh's version is more serious, dark, and introspective.

As for the treason scene, Julian Swain noted that it was left out of the Olivier version:

Imagine the chaos this scene might have created in England in 1944. Suspicion would have run high in the military ranks, and innocent men, suspected of being spies and traitors, would probably have been imprisoned or killed.

Some students discussed the flashbacks and Falstaffian characters to illustrate the moral dimensions of Hal's character. Cynthia Moore wrote,

Harry did not prevent Bardolph from being hanged. This symbolizes the fact that Harry had chosen his path of life, and that his past had become exactly that—his past.

Jon Kril wrote on how, as a schoolboy, he had been asked by his teacher to help grade papers and how he had succumbed to his best friend's requests to "change his wrong answers and make his grade higher." He used this incident to lead into a discussion of Henry's moral dilemma with respect to Falstaff and, later, Bardolph.

Several students elected to compare "the enemy" in the two films. Eladio Sanchez:

The most obvious contrast in both productions was the depiction of the French, portrayed as formidable opponents who had the one weakness of overconfidence. Contrarily, in the 1944 version, the French king, presented as idiotic, stupid, and weak, could barely stand up without help. A possible reason for portraying the French king as silly may have been to poke fun at France's Vichy government, which was under Nazi control.

Elissa Dido wrote her entire paper comparing the set of male French characters in the Olivier and Branagh versions:

Even at the end of the film, the Olivier king appears as a much weaker person. He is shown as somewhat senile with the way the queen has to nudge him every time it's his turn to speak, as if he can't think for himself. . . . In the 1989 movie the French King is much more confident, secure, and even seems more intelligent. . . . In both movies the herald Mountjoy is very respectful to the English king; however, in the 1989 movie, there is more of a representation of his emotions and personality. In the 1989 movie, he's not so much of a stick figure. There are more close-up shots of his face that show a kindness in his eyes.

Many students made important comparisons between the battles in the two versions. Irwin Price wrote,

> Probably the most exciting and exhilarating scene in the 1989 version was the Battle of Agincourt. The battle was depicted very realistically, with horror and pain magnified. The fear of the English was emphasized by the deep expressions on their faces. In the 1989 version, certain parts of the battle scene were shown in slow motion, which served to enhance the atrocities and agony of war. Furthermore, the music added a touch of melodrama. It was especially disturbing to see the horses slip and fall, bringing down the men on them. Unlike the 1944 version, this version had more than one swarm of arrows being shot into the heart of the battle by the English soldiers, arrows which not only killed French soldiers, but the English as well, a concept commonly known as friendly fire.

Luis Cirado addressed the killing of the prisoners:

> One scene omitted by Branagh was also cut from Olivier's film: the slaying of the French prisoners. This is understandable seeing as how both directors are English. Even Shakespeare covered up that scene by introducing a new one, a scene where French knights raid the unguarded camp and slay the baggage boys. This scene *was* included in both films.

This is very powerful literary analysis for a first-year student. The student, a business major, demonstrated a sophisticated understanding not only of Shakespeare, but also of how a work of art can be interpreted in different ways to suit differing historical contexts.

I counted this assignment a great success and would recommend it to anyone wishing to teach Shakespeare's history plays as part of a writing course. The screenings of the films do take a considerable period of time, but if punctuated with the kind of discussion I have outlined here, they never become boring or monotonous. Perhaps the greatest reward of this assignment for me was not the excellent essays I received as a result, but my perception that my students had gained a sophisticated facility in understanding how history informs and conditions the "reality" of stage and screen.

References

Berger, Thomas L. 1985. "The Disappearance of Macmorris in Shakespeare's *Henry V.*" *Renaissance Papers:* 13–26.

Branagh, Kenneth. 1988. "*Henry V.*" In *Players of Shakespeare II: Further Essays in Shakespearean Performance by Players with the Royal Shakespeare Company,* edited by Russell Jackson and Robert Smallwood. New York: Cambridge University Press.

———, director. 1989. *Henry V.* The Samuel Goldwyn Company and Renaissance Films.

Cartelli, Thomas. 1986. "Ideology and Subversion in the Shakespearean Set Speech." *English Literary History* 53 (Spring): 1–25.

Forbes, Jill. 1989. "*Henry V.*" *Sight and Sound* 58 (Autumn): 258–59.

Holderness, Graham. 1984. "Agincourt 1944: Readings in the Shakespearean Myth." *Literature and History* 10 (Spring): 24–45.

Keegan, John. 1976. *The Face of Battle: A Study of Agincourt, Waterloo, and the Somme.* New York: Vintage.

Manheim, Michael. 1983. "Olivier's *Henry V* and the Elizabethan World Picture." *Literature/Film Quarterly* 11: 179–84.

Olivier, Laurence, director. 1944. *Henry V.* Rank Pictures: Two Cities Production. Distributed in the United States by Paramount Pictures.

Shakespeare, William. 1974. *Henry V.* In *The Riverside Shakespeare,* edited by G. Blakemore Evans. Boston: Houghton Mifflin.

Taylor, Mark. 1986. "Imitation and Perspective in *Henry V.*" *Clio: A Journal of Literature, History, and the Philosophy of History* 16 (Fall): 35–47.

Wilcox, Lance. 1985. "Katherine of France as Victim and Bride." *Shakespeare Studies* 17: 61–76.

17 Picturing Shakespeare: Using Film in the Classroom to Turn Text into Theater

James Hirsh
Georgia State University

Shakespeare designed his plays to be experienced by playgoers rather than by readers. As a result, reading one of Shakespeare's plays requires a different set of skills than reading a work that was designed to be experienced as a text. In order to appreciate many features of Shakespeare's art, readers need to imagine the events of the play as taking place not merely in a fictional setting, but on a stage. They need to imagine not merely characters, but actors. They need to transform their reading experience into a theatrical experience, much as when a musician looks at a score and imagines the sound of the music. Nevertheless, this imaginative process requires experience, and unfortunately, many students have never attended a live performance by a professional theater company.

Since it is not often possible to take a class to such a performance, a practical way to help students develop the skills necessary to imagine a performance when they read a Shakespeare play is to show and discuss in detail a film version. Although film is a different medium than theater, the set of differences between these two media is different from the set of differences between reading and live performance. Showing a film can thus bring to the foreground the complex array of differences among reading, playgoing, and filmgoing and thereby help students better understand each of the media through which they might experience drama.

Before showing a Shakespeare film to a class, I attempt by means of questions to elicit articulations of some of these differences from the students themselves. In reading a play, because our immediate experience is of words on a page, we are particularly aware of language; we must exercise our imagination to turn those words into characters and actions. Indeed, as readers, we have a great deal of freedom: we can pause at any time to consider the implications of a passage we just read, and we can even go back and reread an earlier passage in light of a later one.

At a theatrical performance of a play, however, our immediate experience is of live actors, whose facial expressions, gestures, and physical actions provide a particularized context for the words that are all a reader encounters. The word *excursions*, which barely registers on most readers, might be manifested in performance by several minutes of vivid activity. Because the director, actors, costume designer, set designer, choreographer, fight master, and other members of the company have exercised their imaginations, the demands on a playgoer's imagination are less than those on a reader's. Consequently, a playgoer also suffers a loss of freedom. Playgoers are discouraged from interrupting a performance to request time to consider the implications of a dramatized incident or to request that the actors reperform an earlier episode. And the interpretive choices made by the performing company may differ from those the playgoer might have made in reading the play. Charles Lamb, among others, resented the loss of interpretive freedom one suffers in attending any live performance.

In contrast to the usually solitary reading experience, our participation as a playgoer at a live performance is a social experience. An exchange of dialogue that might make a reader smile might, in a crowded theater, prompt a wave of contagious laughter. Or an audible hush might occur at a moment of intense suspense and give playgoers goose bumps. If playgoers laugh heartily at the early jokes in a comedy, the performers are likely to act with increasing confidence and energy, whereas if, at a different performance of the same play, the same jokes fall flat, the actors may lose confidence and energy, and the result might be an increasingly dull and lifeless performance. A live performance involves interaction among playgoers, among performers, and between playgoers and performers. For this reason, a live performance, despite numerous rehearsals, is to some extent unpredictable, risky, and spontaneous.

An experience of a film version of a play differs from both a reading experience and a theatrical experience. A film lacks the spontaneity and the potential for interaction between actors and playgoers at a live production. Nevertheless, a film may be visually overwhelming and varied in ways beyond the capabilities of even the most elaborate stage presentations. Indeed, because the visual images are literally larger than life and can change so rapidly and frequently, it is easy for a filmgoer to become passive, to become a mere eyeball. And a filmgoer has even less room to exercise imagination than a theatergoer, even less opportunity to exercise freedom. For example, at a stage production, playgoers usually have some choice about where to focus attention. Most often, one looks at whichever actor is speaking, but experienced playgoers occasionally look at other actors to see how the characters portrayed by those actors are responding to the speaker. At many times in a film, however, such choices are made by the director or editor. When what appears on screen is a close-up of one character's face, the filmgoer cannot choose to look at another character. Students and I also discuss how even the experience of watching a videotape on a television monitor differs from the experience of watching supposedly the same film on a large screen in a theater. After we explicitly discuss many such differences among media, students are better able to appreciate the distinctiveness of each medium, to recognize its opportunities and limitations. In particular, students are better able to make the adjustments necessary to imagine a performance when they read a text.

Another theoretical issue I discuss before I show a film is the unfaithfulness of the filmmaker to Shakespeare's play. Because students and I have already explored differences between live theater and film as media, students realize that any good film of a play will necessarily be an adaptation of the play. For example, because the visual component so important to film as a medium takes up a considerable amount of screen time, and because Shakespeare's plays are long, considerably longer than most contemporary plays, most good films based on Shakespeare's plays cut the scripts severely. Some might argue that if a good film necessarily adapts the play, it might be preferable, for pedagogic purposes, to show a less successful but more "faithful" film. I believe this would be a mistake. A film that is faithful to the letter of *Romeo and Juliet* and yet manages to be dull is somehow unfaithful to the spirit of the original, because *Romeo and Juliet* is not a dull play. In showing an unimaginative film that seems on the surface to be extremely faithful to the play, an instructor runs the risk of inadvertently giving students the impression that Shakespeare's *Romeo and Juliet* is a dull play. I also point out to students that almost all of Shakespeare's own works are adaptations of earlier works; he altered his sources to produce new works of art. We should not deny to later artists the artistic freedom we admire in Shakespeare. Even if a filmmaker's *Hamlet* is not as good as Shakespeare's, an imperfectly faithful new creation that is a work of art in its own right is better than a dead copy of a masterpiece. Furthermore, differences between a film version and Shakespeare's script can have at least as much pedagogic value as similarities. Students are made aware that each re-enactment of a Shakespeare play—whether on stage, on screen, or in the imagination of a reader—is a re-creation, a result of creative interaction with the text.

I do not show a film until after we have discussed the play in some detail, and I ask students to pay particular attention to those ways in which the film differs from the play as they imagined it during the reading process and as we discussed it. I also provide them in advance with a system for categorizing these differences; this system sets up a format for our ex post facto discussion. Some differences, for instance, are the result of interpretation. More than most texts, Shakespeare's scripts allow for a variety of interpretive choices. For example, in the text (or, rather, in both texts) of *King Lear,* Kent is banished and returns in disguise as Caius, but the exact features of his disguise are not specified. In the film of *Lear* directed by Michael Elliott, Kent disguises himself, in part, by shaving the beard he had worn earlier. This example of disguise by removal reinforces the implicit parallel between Kent and Edgar, whose disguise as Poor Tom consists mainly of stripping away his clothes. While not specified in the text, and hence a creation of this particular production, the manner of Kent's disguise in the film is arguably in keeping with the spirit of the play.

Some differences are adaptations rather than interpretations. One kind of adaptation involves cutting the script, as in the complete disappearance of the character of Fortinbras from the film of *Hamlet* directed by Laurence Olivier. As a result of this particular cut, the film is more streamlined and narrowly focused than the play; but the political issues are diminished in importance, and the film lacks the resonance provided by the explicit and implicit comparisons between Fortinbras and Hamlet. Another kind of adaptation is an interpolation, the insertion of a piece of dialogue or an incident not found in the play at all. Very early in Olivier's *Hamlet* occur the following words, spoken in voice-over narration by Olivier: "This is a tragedy of a man who could not make up his mind." Even if this were an accurate commentary, it still would be a major departure from the play in making explicit for filmgoers what the play left up to their judgment. Roman Polanski's *Macbeth* ends with the arrival of Donalbain at the same locale in which Macbeth had met the witches; the pessimistic implications are that Donalbain shares Macbeth's murderous ambition and that the whole process will be repeated. There is no textual basis for this specific incident. A third kind of adaptation is a demonstrable alteration of an incident found in the source. In Polanski's *Macbeth,* as in Shakespeare's, Lady Macbeth walks in her sleep. In the film, however, Francesca Annis is nude, whereas in the Elizabethan theater, where women's roles were played by boys, this would not have been an option. Even though the nudity may remind a filmgoer of Lady Macbeth's earlier sexual manipulation of Macbeth while stressing her vulnerability at the moment the incident occurs, the film version of the episode is nevertheless a departure from the original.

Some students who do not participate regularly in class discussions do participate actively in discussions after a film showing. Perhaps they feel more confident in describing what they have observed on a television monitor than in describing what they have read in a text. But whether they realize it or not, the comparative basis of our discussion leads them to talk about both experiences.

I usually begin our discussion after a film by eliciting overall evaluations and general impressions. But we quickly move to a close comparison of details of the film with details of the text. I ask students to supply examples of aspects of the film that fall into each of the aforementioned categories. These categories are not always clear-cut, and our attempts to categorize a particular feature of the film can sometimes provoke lively debate in class. When students cannot come up with any more comparisons on their own, I consult my own list and supply brief reminders of parts of the play or film that prompt students' recognition of further ways in which the film interprets or adapts the text. In the case of each comparison, we discuss the possible significance of the difference between the play and the film. After making a great many individual comparisons, we try to draw conclusions about the overall implications of the collection of differences we have catalogued. This comparative analysis gives students finely delineated impressions of both the play and the film. It also provides them with an inductive methodology that they can apply in other circumstances.

Because of the time required to show a film and to compare it with a play in detail, I do not show more than one film per term. But one option on a subsequent paper assignment is for a student to do a similar comparative analysis of another Shakespeare film.

I have used over a dozen different videotaped films in my courses, and most have worked well. One that has worked particularly well is the 1969 version of *A Midsummer Night's Dream*, directed by Peter Hall, with an impressive cast drawn from the Royal Shakespeare Company. In the following pages, I will present some conclusions that can be elicited from students during a detailed classroom analysis of the ways in which this film interprets and adapts Shakespeare's play.

Some of Hall's interpretations and adaptations resemble those that might occur in a theatrical production; others are required by or only possible in a film. One moment that is cinematic rather than theatrical occurs when Hermia (Helen Mirren), who is pursued by Demetrius (Michael Jayston), halts in the middle of a stream, turns on him, and pushes him down. Rather than immediately rising, Demetrius, who is so intent on convincing Hermia of his love and sincerity that he is oblivious to the rest of his situation, continues to plead with her from his position, sitting in the stream. A stream, of course, could not have been brought on stage in the Elizabethan theater; in contrast, in a film such a naturalistic setting is not only possible, it is almost required. But in this case, instead of using that setting merely as an inert background, Hall integrates it into the action.

Some other differences between the film and a stage production are less obvious. After Puck (Ian Holm) puts each of the lovers to sleep (at the moment corresponding to the end of III.ii of the text), he casually—half mischievously, half considerately—covers each with a blanket of leaves and small branches. Such props could be employed on a stage, but they would, except in the context of a very elaborate set, call attention to themselves as props (an effect that would not necessarily be out of place in a play that repeatedly calls attention to itself as a play). In the context of the vivid natural setting of the film, however, this action by Puck seems very fitting, almost inevitable (at least after it occurs). In other words, what would seem to be the same bit of business could be effective in both a stage production and a film, but it would nevertheless have different implications because of the difference in media.

Hall also found cinematic means to emphasize particular issues that are explicitly or implicitly raised by the text. The mutability of nature is developed in the text in such passages as Titania's speech on the disruptions of nature caused by the quarrel between herself and Oberon (II.i.81–117) and in such incidents as the various metamorphoses enacted by Puck. Titania's speech and Puck's actions suggest that, in at least some respects, the fairies represent the sometimes capricious forces of nature. In the film, the opening credits are accompanied by a series of natural images and sounds: a lake, a meadow, rain, flowing water, birds, snow, trees, frogs, crickets, thunder, sunlight, more rain. These images and sounds suggest both the fertility and the mutability of nature. The most common element in the sequence of images and sounds is water, which undergoes various metamorphoses. We are occasionally given glimpses of a country house, but the emphasis is on the natural landscape in which the human construction is set. This opening sequence is followed by a contrasting outdoor image: that of human figures on a perfectly straight walkway on an immensely long, manicured lawn. Here the diversity and mutability of nature have been brought under the control of a geometrical orderliness. The filmgoer now hears civilized sounds. A bell chimes the hours—a machine regulates time. We do hear the sound of an animal, but it is the cry of a domesticated peacock. In the text, the human attempt to bring nature under control is developed not only in Egeus's attempt to dictate his daughter's object of affection, but also in the eventual marriages.

In contrast to the tendency of Victorian theater to domesticate the fairies and thereby to convey an image of a domesticated nature, Hall's film exemplifies the twentieth-century tendency to emphasize the otherness of the fairies. Hall's fairies thus have green skin to match their habitat. Their unkempt hair, mud-splattered faces, and foliage-like or, in the case of Titania (Judi Dench), nearly nonexistent costumes suggest that, as representatives of natural forces, they understandably have a different attitude toward cleanliness and attire than most humans. On occasion, Puck sticks out his tongue and pants like a dog; although dogs are domesticated animals, such an action in a human-looking being distances rather than domesticates the character. And, as in Shakespeare's play, Puck does regard the humans as members of a different species: "The man shall have his mare again" (III.ii.463).

Moreover, Hall's film uses techniques not available to a stage production to establish the fairies as a distinct species. For example, Puck has the power of instantaneous appearance and disappearance, created by editing. The most imaginative instance of editing occurs when Oberon (Ian Richardson) gives Puck a series of commands (corresponding to II.i.148–74). As Oberon completes his first command, Puck disappears from his location on the screen and is presumably in transit, but as Oberson continues to speak without a pause, Puck appears instantaneously at another place on the screen to hear Oberon's next command. This process is repeated two more times. Such an effect could not have been produced on the Elizabethan stage, but

Puck's behavior in the film is, well, Puckish. At another moment (corresponding to III.ii.396), by means of a special effect unlikely to be reproducible on any stage, Puck emits a fog from his mouth that encompasses Demetrius and Lysander (David Warner). And Puck's imitation of the voices of the two Athenians is more uncanny in the film than it could be on stage because we see a close-up of Holm moving his lips, but we hear, by means of dubbing, the voices of Jayston and Warner.

Although Shakespeare's play and Hall's film do establish the otherness of the fairies and of nature, both works of art also suggest that culture and nature do not form a simple dichotomy. Human beings are a part of nature, and nature is inside human beings. Thus, Bottom, in the play and as performed by Paul Rogers in the film, adapts rather readily to his transformation; his presumably unnatural reabsorption into nature seems natural. Similarly, the lovers in the film, so engrossed in the confusions of their personal relationships, become, like the fairies, generally oblivious to their increasingly mud-splattered and bedraggled appearances. In this sense they too are being reabsorbed into nature. Conversely, Puck's condescension to humans, "Lord, what fools these mortals be!" (III.ii.115), belies his own capacity for foolishness. Both Shakespeare and Hall play with the distinction between human culture and nature.

Shakespeare and Hall also play with the distinction between waking reality and dream. In accordance with their common title, both works are dreamlike. The costumes in Hall's film, for example, have a dreamlike inconsistency. Helena (Diana Rigg) wears a miniskirt, circa 1969, whereas Hippolyta (Barbara Jefford) wears an outfit vaguely suggesting ancient Greece. And it is not only the different characters who wear historically incompatible garments; even the attire of individual characters is inconsistent. Lysander wears a polyester leisure suit with an Elizabethan collar. At one point, Theseus (Derek Godfrey) wears a similar combination, along with part of a toga. These mixtures of incompatible costume elements correspond to an important feature of the play itself. Shakespeare's *Dream* mixes elements from several widely divergent contexts: Theseus and Hippolyta from Greek mythology, the young lovers from romance, the craftsmen from Elizabethan daily life, the fairies from folklore. The mixture of these seemingly incompatible elements is one technique that makes Shakespeare's *Dream* a dream. Just as Shakespeare includes anachronistic references to the daily life of his own time in a play set ostensibly in ancient Greece, Hall includes, in the same spirit, anachronistic references to our own time.

Yet Hall's film is dreamlike in some ways that a stage production could not be. The film often uses editing to make time seem more flexible than it does in our usual waking experience. Titania's long speech on the disruption of nature, mentioned above, is delivered without pause in a wide variety of settings and under a variety of lighting effects. Such editing does not occur just in the forest scenes. Helena delivers her plaintive soliloquy (I.i.226–51) in at least four different locales without pause: near the house, by a tree, by an obelisk, and by a lake. This suggests that Helena's thoughts are obsessive; they both recur in different locales and make Helena oblivious to her surroundings. Obsession may thus make waking reality dreamlike.

The film also undermines the dichotomy between dream and waking reality during the speech in which Demetrius praises Helena as "goddess, nymph, perfect, divine!" (III.ii.137–44). Demetrius delivers the first few lines of this speech with his eyes still closed; presumably, he is dreaming about Helena. He then opens his eyes to discover the real Helena by his side and continues the speech. That he does not miss a beat has a comic effect. Unlike Madeline in Keats's "The Eve of St. Agnes," who is at first disappointed when she awakens to see the real Porphyro after she has just been dreaming of him, Demetrius inhabits a world in which reality is so dreamlike that the transition from one state to the other is either not noticeable or not worth noting. The same effect in this case would be hard to achieve on stage. Demetrius's awakening would have to be conveyed by broader means than by his simply opening his eyes, but these broader means would emphasize rather than undermine the distinction between dreaming and waking.

A notable feature of Shakespeare's play is its self-referentiality, most apparent in its inclusion of a play-within-a-play, which raises the issue of the relationship between art and life. One of the elements of Hall's film that makes it more than a perfunctory record of a theatrical performance is its imaginative extension of the art-within-art motif. Just as Shakespeare calls attention to his play as a play, Hall calls attention to his film as a film. The examples already cited of the use of editing and other film tricks to produce dreamlike effects tend to foreground the cinematic medium. Even though Shakespeare could not have anticipated the invention of motion pictures, a film version of his play that calls attention to itself as a film is arguably more in keeping with the spirit of a play that calls attention to itself as a play than a film version that is not cinematically self-referential. Hall even finds cinematic equivalent for some of the nuances of Shakespeare's self-referentiality. For instance, Shakespeare establishes implicit contrasts between his own play and the so-called play-within-the-play. Actually, "Pyramus and Thisby" is a very-amateurish-play-within-a-very-sophisticated-play. Similarly, Hall's film contains implicit comparisons between different modes of film. Of the film practices already discussed, some are very arty, whereas some derive from slapstick comedy. In one episode, Demetrius flees from Helena and seems successfully to have left her behind; yet he soon runs into Helena again, well-rested and seemingly waiting for him to catch up with her. This episode seems to be a homage of sorts to animated cartoons. Later in the same encounter with Demetrius, and before we get to see the craftsmen overact in their play, Helena puts the back of her hand to her forehead and emotes in a manner conventional in silent films.

Hall not only calls attention to his film as a film, he calls attention to his film-based-on-a-theatrical-work as a film-based-on-a-theatrical-work. As soon as they see the transformed Bottom, all but one of the other craftsmen immediately run away. Instead of fleeing, the slow-witted Snout (Bill Travers) glances down at his script of "Pyramus and Thisby." Presumably he is looking to see if Bottom's appearance with an ass's head is a part of the play the craftsmen are rehearsing. Not until he realizes that the other craftsmen have fled does he himself take flight. The joke-within-the-joke is that just as Bottom's transformation is not in the script of "Pyramus and Thisby," the series of psychological transformations undergone on screen by Snout are not in the script of Shakespeare's play. By thus turning Shakespeare's *Dream* into a play-within-the-film, Hall recreates the play as a film.

Hall's film has so many imaginative and suggestive details that it nearly always provokes lively and thoughtful responses from students. Other films that have prompted similar responses from my classes include Olivier's *Hamlet*, *Henry V*, and *Richard III*, Polanski's *Macbeth*, Elliott's *King Lear*, Peter Brook's *King Lear*, Jane Howell's *Richard III* and *The Winter's Tale* (among the most successful of the BBC-TV Shakespeare series), Desmond Davis's *Measure for Measure* (also in the BBC-TV series), and Zeffirelli's *Romeo and Juliet*. In each case, rather than replacing Shakespeare's play, the film provides the basis for an illuminating comparison.

References

Hall, Peter, director. 1969. *A Midsummer Night's Dream.* With Judi Dench, Ian Holm, Helen Mirren, Ian Richardson, Diana Rigg, Paul Rogers, and David Warner. Filmways.

Olivier, Laurence, director. 1948. *Hamlet.* With Olivier and Jean Simmons. Two Cities.

Shakespeare, William. 1974. *The Riverside Shakespeare.* Edited by G. Blakemore Evans. Boston: Houghton Mifflin.

18 Shakespeare Enters the Electronic Age

Roy Flannagan
Ohio University

He is already in the mainstream media, with Kevin Kline and Mel Gibson adding to his popularity on television and in the movies. But Shakespeare is also Shakespeare on Disk, Shakespeare on CD-ROM, and SHAKSPER on electronic mail. This latest media transformation is significant: in making the transition onto the dits and dahs of binary digitized data, Shakespeare's texts supply power to the people.

Let me explain: for not much money (in most cases), students and professors alike can own and play with Shakespeare's texts. They (or their English departments or libraries) can purchase the complete plays and poems, and then, with the ubiquitous and speedy computer, search good texts of the plays and poems for anything a reader might need. For a study of aspiration or ambition in Shakespeare, a new historicist scholar could search the whole canon for instances of *can* or *would* in close proximity to a noun like *power* or verbs like *rise* or *aspire*. A feminist scholar might want to locate all feminine personal pronominal adjectives in order to find out how Shakespeare's world was gendered. A drama professor, or anyone wanting to stage a scene of Shakespeare, might extrapolate all the lines spoken by any character in a play from an electronic text and pass that quickly generated script on to an actor.

When the texts enter the computer, becoming part of a database or what is sometimes now called a knowledge base, several marvelous things can occur. Through the logical or serendipitous links of hypertext, words can be linked to other words, as in a concordance; they can be linked to historical definitions, like those preserved in the *Oxford English Dictionary*; they can be linked to other texts, like sources or works a text might allude to; or they can be linked to visual or auditory representations of words or images. My own ideal for Shakespeare's texts would be for the student or teacher or scholar to be able to read the text of a play on a high-resolution, flicker-free color screen, and, when puzzled by an archaism, ask what a word means and get a definition—the best of historical definitions—instantaneously. When one comes upon a passage that sounds biblical, one could search for allusions and draw up pages of passages from the Old and New Testaments, and the Apocrypha and the pseudepigrapha, if necessary. Likewise, hypertext links might lead one to Shakespeare's source material in Cinthio, Ariosto, Spenser, Ovid, Holinshed, Hall, or Stow. The ideal is not farfetched. Already there are word processing add-ons like *Nota Bene's* "N. B. Lingua" that can call up, with several keystrokes, the Bible in three languages. And there are programs like Intellimation's *Shakespeare's Life and Times* that mix images with informative text on HyperCard stacks for the Macintosh computer, so that one can see a bust of Henry VII while reading background material on the history plays. One can also write such a HyperCard stack for one's own class using *Intermedia 3.0*, available from the IRIS project at Brown University.

In fact, one scholar at Florida Atlantic University in Boca Raton, Tom Horton, has even been working on a software program that automates, to some extent, the process of searching for image clusters in Shakespeare. Put Tom together with the electronic version of *The Riverside Shakespeare,* and he can find connections between *nets, sheets,* and *death,* metaphorically speaking, using the principles of searching outlined in Edward A. Armstrong's *Shakespeare's Imagination* (Lincoln: University of Nebraska Press, 1963).

The idea of hypertext also allows for hypermedia, or linked and clever mixing of media. When that imagined reader I was envisioning came to a song, for instance, I would like for him or her to be able to click on an icon that would bring up an image of a page of music and then have the computer play the music on the page, well-synthesized to sound like a Steinway or a Bosendorfer, through a pair of high-quality speakers attached to a sound card in the computer. One click more might bring up the image of the character Feste, with a lute and in full period dress, skillfully performing the music.

There is no end to the uses of the computer and hypertext for teaching, combining for the student all the excitement of playing *Dungeons & Dragons* with much of the excitement of seeing a live performance of Shakespeare. Already there exist videotapes of plays in German and movies in Spanish or Japanese with English subtitles that are linked with the text; a student watching a performance can thus go from moving image to still image to text, or read and watch the drama at the same time. With hypertext, the wonderful principle of serendipity is constantly at work; when one clicks on an unfamiliar icon, one never knows exactly what is to be found. Students may have the delight of discovering something they did not even know they were looking for. The larger the knowledge base (the more memory the computer or mainframe has available for text and images), the more nearly limitless the exploration open to the individual mind. The French government, for instance, has mounted an enormous hypertext program for eighteenth-century history, literature, and art on the Macintosh. The Perseus Project at Harvard has combined the best of ancient Greek texts of plays and histories with pictorial representations of the most current discoveries in archaeology, again using the Mac. And hypertext experts at Oxford are trying to recreate the world of an Anglo-Saxon poem, *The Seafarer,* from ship and shield design to the agriculture that produced the foods on board.

One computer, the NeXT, brain-child of Apple Computer's founder Steven Jobs, comes with the Oxford modern-spelling texts for all the plays of Shakespeare collected on its hard drive; thus, if one buys the computer, one buys Shakespeare. Other bundled packages of software and hardware, as sold by DAK Corporation and CompuAdd, come with internal CD-ROM drives and discs with libraries of literature that sometimes include the complete works of Shakespeare.

So, the computer, in clever combination with the media already available to it, can divulge whole libraries of words and images from within its own memory, or that of a CD-ROM. And the reader or viewer can interact with the text or the images or the sounds emanating from the computer and make exciting discoveries. The whole process is a game, but at its best the process of education is itself a clever game, enticing and opening the mind of the student. One could play *Scrabble* using Shakespeare's vocabulary, for instance, or trace Tolkien's monsters through their progenitors in *Beowulf* and English folklore to parodies of them in *Monty Python and the Holy Grail.* Learning just might be fun again.

E-mail versus Snail-mail

There is one other important part of the electronic revolution that is coming to be very much a part of Shakespeare studies: electronic mail. I have been lucky enough to have had access to electronic mail service through my university for about two years now, so I have lived through the exciting age of the pioneers in the medium. For instance, an e-mail pal at the University of Waterloo in Canada (whom I have never met face-to-face but still like very much) and I have discussed the very strange phenomenon of an electronic text of Milton's *Samson Agonistes* flying in magnetized particles over the Atlantic, landing at the Oxford Text Archive, where it was to be stored, only ten seconds or so after it took off from North America. And we have both entered significant amounts of original texts on the computer, reduced those texts to their simplest encoding, and traded them, like school-kids trading baseball cards or marbles. Through the phenomenon of electronic mail, moving those texts—or the bad quartos of Shakespeare, for that matter—around the airwaves is almost incredibly easy and fast. Indeed, snobbish e-mailers now refer to the service of the United States Post Office as "snail-mail."

Again, through my university (most universities and some high schools with computer centers support electronic mail for their faculties), I have access to electronic file-servers, bulletin boards, and symposia such as SHAKSPER at the University of Toronto (run by an enterprising and well-informed graduate student named Ken Steele); HUMANIST at Brown University, a list of about one thousand worldwide humanists (run by Elaine Brennan and Alan Renear); and FICINO, a Renaissance-everything symposium (run by Willard McCarty, an affable gentleman housed at the Centre for Computing in the Humanities at the University of Toronto). And these are just the special-interest lists that have something to do with Shakespeare. There is also a list dealing with the teaching of rhetoric (PURTOPOI at Purdue) and another dealing with rare-book librarians (EX-LIBRIS at Rutgers)—just a few of the file-servers that a Shakespeare scholar might be interested in.

Electronic mail symposia are an extraordinary source of information and a valuable resource for teaching, among other things. Students, graduate and undergraduate, are included on the entirely democratic rosters for each list, so we have feedback from all ages and all points of view. We also make queries. I once asked about the references to women in medieval and Renaissance medical practice on HUMANIST and received about fifty answers to my query—some of which provided extensive bibliographies on the subject—from people all over the world, specialists I never knew existed, living in Haifa or Tubingen or Tromso. I also once posted a final exam for a Shakespeare histories course and received feedback even before the exam was given out (no, none of my students listened in to the preview).

Combine the idea of e-mail symposia with teaching and with generation of texts, and you have all sorts of exciting possibilities. Ken

Steele generates and collects texts of even the most obscure and corrupt quartos, and people in FICINO have been talking lately about the possibility of making their own anthologies of Renaissance literature, compiled from texts they themselves would keyboard in and send to FICINO as a central clearinghouse. One glorious thing about such texts is that unlike published texts, they would be correctable by anyone using them. Once an error is detected, reported back to the librarian at FICINO, and then entered on a master document, the text would be improved from that day on. In that case, committee work really would significantly improve the texts. And anyone who had the time and love for the texts might enter them, in a process not unlike that described in Ray Bradbury's *Farenheit 451.* The more texts, the more choices for the Renaissance anthologies. The larger the number of Renaissance or Restoration or Enlightenment collections, the more valid any critical generalization about any one text. If one wants to say that Milton uses the pronoun *I* more than any other Renaissance epic writer, one would be able to test the supposition against the epic works of Boiardo, Trissino, Ariosto, and Tasso, almost instantly, if one has collected a Renaissance knowledge base. If one has the electronic *OED,* one can easily find a definition for an unusual word or a word first coined by Shakespeare, such as *shog* (meaning "get along quickly," or, in modern slang, "buzz off") in *Henry V.*

Textbases and CD-ROMS

A commercial firm based in Cambridge, England, Chadwyck-Healey, has recently announced plans for an English poetry full-text database that will include the works of 1,350 poets from the years 600 to 1900, a total of about 4,500 books. The collection will be made available in machine-readable form on CD-ROM or magnetic tape, but will most likely be purchased only by major universities, since the total cost for three CDs will be over $30,000. Nevertheless, representatives from Chadwyck-Healey estimate that libraries will be paying only about $9 per book for books that would ordinarily be hard to find and expensive to purchase. Libraries considering the enormous expense will have to measure both the cost of the rare books and the savings in shelf space (three CDs versus 4,500 books).

Another CD-ROM repository of texts is the *Library of the Future,* a collection of texts from Aristotle and Aeschylus through Edgar Allan Poe. Shakespeare's plays and poems seem to all be there, but the documentation is on the order of "One wedding turns into three" as the plot of *A Midsummer Night's Dream*. Still, if one wanted to compare all of Shakespeare's work with all that of Arthur Conan Doyle, this would be the place to do it. What the publishers have done is to reprint what are in most cases out-of-copyright editions of major authors. The collection is a bit eccentric, and it is expensive at an asking price of $695, but it comes "free" with some computer packages from DAK Corporation.

Text-manipulating Software

WordCruncher is perhaps the best-known text-retrieval and indexing software, since it has been endorsed by the powerful Modern Language Association. It can be used to cruise easily through *The Riverside Shakespeare* or *The Library of America*, both available on CD-ROM from Electronic Text Corporation, or you can load the complete works on your hard drive, space permitting. *Folio Views* is another excellent all-purpose program and is used by one of the purveyors of electronic texts, InteLex, a small firm specializing in e-texts of philosophers such as Descartes and Spinoza. There is even an excellent text-massager published free from the University of Toronto, TACT, the product of the Centre for Computing in the Humanities (where FICINO and SHAKSPER originate). It comes with texts of Chaucer (J. H. Fisher's edition), Shakespeare (the tragedies, in old-spelling texts edited by Ken Steele), and Milton (my old-spelling texts of the English poetry)—a huge bargain, considering that it can be ordered for the cost of the discs alone.

All these electronic uses of text and hypermedia are tied together. On various electronic mail services, we discuss scholars' ideal computerized workstations, we devise methods to test students or help them with their writing (as with sending them e-mail messages or allowing them to submit drafts to us via the campus mainframe), and we query the scholarly community to see if what we think is right or to find out what we do not know. Indeed, as we learn more and compile more and more varied data, our judgments will no longer be the guesses of visionaries, but the well-informed opinions of authorities. With electronic mail services, we can pool our individual knowledge and experience together, expanding both what we know and have access to knowing. We can, for instance, compile lists of the best Shakespeare videos or record firsthand impressions of great lecturers like Northrop Frye or Umberto Eco. We can even voice our opinions instantly to British civil servants over exactly how the Rose or Globe or Swan theaters might be preserved (I know; I have done just that). There is virtually no limit to what we can do electronically to improve both our own understanding and that of our students.

Resources for Electronic Text Retrieval, Text-manipulating Software, Hypertext Access, and Electronic Mail

Chadwyck-Healey Inc., 1101 King Street, Alexandria, VA 22314. Telephone 703-683-4890; toll-free 800-752-0515; FAX 703-683-7589.

FICINO is an electronic seminar devoted to the discussion of Renaissance literature, art, and history; it is located at the University of Toronto and operated with a genial sense of humor by Willard McCarty, who can be reached via e-mail at Ficino@UTorepas.

Thomas B. Horton, Department of Computer Science, Florida Atlantic University, Boca Raton, FL 33431. BITNET address: HortonT@servax.

HUMANIST is an electronic seminar devoted to the subject of computing in the humanities and includes over one thousand members from all over the world who have disciplines as varied as lexicography and archaeology; it is run by Elaine Brennan and Alan Renear at Brown University. BITNET address: editors@Brownvm.

InteLex Corporation, Route 2, Box 383, Pittsboro, NC 27312. Telephone 919-542-4411. Or contact Mark Rooks via e-mail at Rooks@cs.unc.edu.

"Intellimation Library for the Macintosh" catalogue is available free from PO Box 1922, Santa Barbara, CA 93166-1922. Telephone 800-346-8355.

IRIS Intermedia 3.0 is available from the Institute for Research in Information and Scholarship (IRIS), Brown University, 155 George Street, Providence, RI 02912. Telephone 401-863-2001. With *Intermedia,* students and teachers can write their own interactive HyperStack programs.

Library of the Future, Series First Edition, advertised as "The Complete Text of 450 Historical, Classical and Cultural Titles on CD-ROM," was published in 1990 by World Library, Inc., 12914 Haster Street, Garden Grove, CA 92640. It is packaged as part of a computer/CD-ROM collection by DAK Corporation, the mail-order company whose glossy brochures are in nearly everybody's mailbox. Telephone (for *Library of the Future*) 800-443-0238 or 714-748-7197; FAX 714-748-7197.

"N. B. Lingua," an add-on to the academic word processor *Nota Bene,* is available for about $150, plus an additional fee for each biblical text, from Dragonfly Software, 285 West Broadway, Suite 600, New York, NY 10013. Telephone 212-334-0445. *Nota Bene* can view and print text in a number of languages.

Oxford University's Centre for Textual Studies, part of the Computers in Teaching Initiative, is developing a model for the study of Anglo-Saxon culture on HyperCard called *Seafarer.* For information, contact Marilyn Deegan, Centre for Textual Studies, Oxford University, 13 Banbury Road, Oxford OX2 6NN, United Kingdom; Professor Deegan's e-mail address is Marilyn@vax.Oxford.ac.uk.

Oxford University Press has an Oxford Electronic Text division, which offers the complete Oxford texts of Shakespeare on disc and also publishes the CD-ROM version of the *Oxford English Dictionary* (but wait until the second edition of the CD-ROM version is out, since it will incorporate the new version of the *OED*). The OET can be reached c/o Oxford University Press, Walton Street, Oxford OX2 6DP, United Kingdom. Telefax 0865 56646. Or send e-mail messages to Ruth Glynn, whose e-mail address is RGlynn@vax.Oxford.ac.uk. The Oxford Text Archive is a repository of donated texts maintained by Lou Burnard (Lou@vax.Oxford.ac.uk).

The Renaissance Knowledge Base is an airy scheme devised by Roy Flannagan and Ian Lancashire of the University of Toronto to collect all significant literary texts of the English Renaissance, everything published from about 1465 to about 1680. For further information, Ian's e-mail address is Ian@utorepas; Roy's is Flannaga@ouaccvmb.

Shakespeare on Disk, Hollow Road, PO Box 299, Clinton Corners, NY 12514. Sam Reifler is president of this small company, and his wife Willofer is his partner in the enterprise; one or the other is apt to answer the telephone. Telephone 800-446-2089 or 914-266-5705.

SHAKSPER is an electronic seminar for those interested in talking about, teaching, or viewing the plays of Shakespeare, or the nondramatic works, for that matter. It is run by a graduate student with considerable experience in entering the lesser-known texts: Ken Steele, whose e-mail address is KSteele@utorepas.

TACT is made available through a grant from IBM Corporation by the Centre for Computing in the Humanities, Robarts Library, 14th Floor, University of Toronto, Toronto, Ontario M5S 1A1, Canada. Ian Lancashire, head of the CCH, is the prime mover for the project, but he works closely with programmers John Bradley and Lidio Presutti.

WordCruncher version 4.40 (manufactured by Electronic Text Corporation) is marketed by Johnston & Co., PO Box 446, American Fork, UT 84003. Telephone 801-756-1111. *WordCruncher* is the software bibliographic and indexing program that allows manipulation of texts like *The Riverside Shakespeare*, available on disc or on CD-ROM as part of ''The WordCruncher Disc, Volume 1'' (price to nonprofit or academic customers about $160). For ETC customer support, call 801-226-0616 between 9 a.m. and 5 p.m. mountain time.

IV Difficult Situations

19 Shakespeare Is Not Just for Eggheads: An Interview with Two Successful Teachers

Linda Johnson
Highlands High School, Fort Thomas, Kentucky

Jim and his friends were watching Tony change the tire on his old '67 Chevy when Jim, obviously bored, blurted out, "Hey, fellas, listen up." When it became apparent that he had everyone's attention, Jim cleared his throat and began: "Out, damned spot! Out, I say!—One; two; why, then 'tis time to do't.—Hell is murky!—Fie, my lord, fie! a soldier, and afeard? What need we fear who knows it, when none can call our power to account?—Yet who would have thought the old man to have had so much blood in him?"

"What're you talkin' about, man? What kinda talk is that?" asked Tony.

"I'm talkin' Shakespeare. This is old Lady Macbeth after her husband's killed someone. She's havin' a hard time. Walks in her sleep; tries to wash her hands of blood."

"Kling, you're crazy, goin' around readin' Shakespeare. Nobody does that."

"But listen, man, this story's cool. It's all about a guy who wants to be king, and he kills off all the people who stand in his way. His wife, this Lady Macbeth, wants to be queen, and she's all for helpin' him, any way she can; sorta thinks of him as being wimpy at times."

An unthinkable scene? Not when kids are turned on to the language of Shakespeare, and two northern Kentucky teachers of English are doing just that. "You have to make Shakespeare very exciting if you are going to interest them," says Dan Davies, a teacher at Bellevue High School. "You have to pull Shakespeare down off the pedestal and help students know that Shakespeare is not just for 'eggheads.' "

Letting students know that Shakespeare is not just for "eggheads" is what Norman Yonce, a teacher at Highlands High School, does as well. He says, "I try to bring Shakespeare down from that ethereal level on which most people have placed him. I do a good deal of background on why Shakespeare wrote *Macbeth*. After King James revamped the troop of players and writers of which Shakespeare was a part and placed them on a regular salary, Shakespeare wrote the play to publicly thank the king. He includes all sorts of ideas on witchcraft and the divinity of kings, which James expounded upon in his books *News from Scotland, Daemonologie,* and *Basilikon Doron.* I try to assure students that Shakespeare was, like most writers, trying to make a living. He was as mercenary as any other writer."

Before beginning any reference to Shakespeare or *Macbeth* at all, Yonce does an "anticipatory" lesson with a general discussion of politicians, asking such questions as "What are your prevailing attitudes toward politicians?" and "How much do you trust politicians?" and "How far do you think a politician would be willing to go to fulfill his political ambitions?" (You can imagine the negative responses to these questions.) Then he leads into a discussion of the intoxicating and corrupting effects of power. After a lively discussion, he begins to tell the story of "someone" who wanted a political post very badly, particularly because some people who seemed to have special foresight predicted he would one day have it. This "someone" became so obsessed with the idea that he eventually killed to get the post. Then paranoia led him to kill others who became suspicious. Once the students are caught up in this tale, Yonce reveals that he is talking about Macbeth and starts the play.

One way that Yonce immediately gets his students involved in understanding the language of the play is through paraphrasing. "I really try to have students paraphrase most of the play. They can easily understand Shakespeare once they get the language into their own," he says.

Davies also tries to "pull all the kids into the play at the beginning of the class by putting it into modern language." His method, however, is somewhat different from Yonce's. Davies approaches Shakespeare from a dramatist's point of view. His avocation is acting and directing in community theater, and when he teaches Shakespeare, he acts out every part: "I play every character; I tried having students read the parts, and they just can't do it. They have tremendous trouble with the language. Kids need to hear the language read well. Even when they have heard it read correctly, they have a difficult time with plot and the beauty of what is being said. When kids read the passages aloud, the other students will ask the teacher to explain what is being said. When kids read, they don't know how to pause at the right place; they don't get the rhythm; they don't get the sense of what they are saying; and they don't know how to use vocal inflection to make the text easy to understand."

For Davies, "our main problem is getting the students to appreciate and understand the language of Shakespeare." Still, he laments that "about the time we get them acclimated to the language, we have completed the play. I think it would be wonderful to have the opportunity to teach an extended class in Shakespeare for a semester. Then the students could become very fluent and be able to understand the text as well as the language and performance elements of the play."

Yonce agrees: "For a couple of semesters, when we were on the phase elective kick, I did teach a semester course. And Dan is right. The students became proficient in reading, interpreting, and understanding Shakespeare. We were also able to appreciate the full range of Shakespeare, since we could cover tragedy, history, and comedy."

Although Davies cannot get that "ideal setting," he does try to get his students to think about Shakespeare from a dramatic point of view. He says that this "makes it easier for the students to understand blank verse and then easier for them to understand the context of the passage. I try to make it like conversation."

Davies does think that high school kids can learn how to use the language and their voices to do Shakespeare; but he also believes that it takes much more time to teach Shakespeare with this type of involvement than he has available during the regular school year. "Kids can learn to do more than just memorizing the passages; they can bring it to life with a lot of training and pushing. However, you must have time to do this, and the regular school set-up does not provide this time," he says.

Yonce also reads the play aloud to students. However, instead of emphasizing the play as drama, he approaches it from a structural analysis point of view. He says that "in structural analysis, we examine the components of literature as presented in the drama and try to conclude how the author's choices have contributed to producing an artistic whole. I ask students to pick out vivid images and discuss the effectiveness of those choices. We look at significant diction and unusual syntax. I have students read single lines to practice tone. We look at mood, especially how the first scene of *Macbeth* establishes the mood for the entire play. We examine recurring images or motifs, such as sleep, garments, blood, and birds, and discuss how they enhance the writing. We examine organization. We study symbolism and devices such as contrast and parallel situations. Structural analysis looks at, simply, *how* the writer's choices in structuring the work have all worked together to produce an artistic and aesthetically pleasing literary work."

One of the ways that Davies gets students involved in the language of Shakespeare is through playing games. For example, when he works with motifs, he has students find lines that illustrate a motif such as the use of the words *fair* and *foul,* in *Macbeth.* Students looking for this motif might find the line "Fair is foul, and foul is fair," which they might explain as Lady Macbeth looking like an innocent flower while all the time she is a serpent underneath. This motif is also carried out at the end of the play when all the prophecies that at one time looked so fair to Macbeth turn out to have in fact predicted his doom; to Macbeth at least, such prophecies are certainly foul. Conversely, Malcolm is shown as being fair but looking foul. Students might also look at a recurrent image, such as death or sleep. For instance, Malcolm asks Macduff, "What's going on?" Macduff replies, "Your father is dead / Shake off the downy cover of sleep, death's counterfeit / And look on death itself." In *Macbeth,* Shakespeare is always playing with sleep and death. At any rate, Davies notes that "when students can take these motifs, find them, and explain their meaning, they are beginning to have a good understanding of the language of the play."

Yonce does a similar activity with his students as he tries to help them see the intricacies of the writing itself. He interests his students through cross-referencing. He may, for example, have them trace recurring images like sleep, garments, and birds in *Macbeth* or weeds, cosmetics, disease, and decomposition in *Hamlet.* Or, with some students, he might present generalized ideas and have the students find specific examples to support those generalizations. For example, Yonce might assert that Hamlet is an idealist who, because of the evil surrounding him, retreats into madness in order to survive. He then has the students define what an idealist is. They search out separate examples of idealism and reclusion. In doing so, they familiarize themselves with the play. Yonce notes, "By having students select five or six generalizations, they get to know the play very well."

Shakespeare's language is rich in puns, and students can have a lot of fun once they learn how to understand these puns. For instance, Davies says that in *Julius Caesar,* the use of puns in the opening lines is not funny to students today because the language is so unfamiliar. Thus, to prepare students for the study of Shakespeare, he begins the year "by giving students a handout making puns of their names. Then, throughout the year, we look for puns, matching definitions to examples." When he begins *Julius Caesar,* he explains all of the words to the class—shoemaker, shoe repairman, awl: "I play around with these words, and then I talk about some of the puns—'I am a surgeon to old shoes.' After doing this a few times, I tell the kids, 'You catch them for me.'" He also tells the students that puns do not always have to be funny. They can be poignant as well. He points out that Brutus's line "It is not Caesar who has falling sickness, it is we" is a good example. Davies also finds that kids like to "catch" the puns for him, and that after their study of Shakespeare, they will continue to point out puns as they occur in other situations.

"We also discuss puns," Yonce adds, "and Shakespeare's uncontrollable urge to use them, even in very serious moments, such as Donalbain asking, when roused out of bed on the night his father is murdered, 'What is amiss?' And Macbeth answers, 'You are, and do not know't.' In other words, you are *missing* a father. The students always appropriately groan."

For Yonce, "It is also fun to play with the idea of and examples of chiasmus used by Shakespeare, phrases such as 'Fair is foul, and foul is fair' and 'Fathered he is, and yet he's fatherless.' Since students are usually familiar with Kennedy's 'Ask not what your country can do for you, but what you can do for your country,' they can come up with others."

Davies also has students study the structure of tragedy. He likes to see them deal with the turning points, those fatal moments upon which a play hinges. And as Yonce has his students study structure, Davies has them "search for character motivation": "We discuss the idea that the point where character and plot come together produces motivation, and then we look at examples—what is taking place, how the character reacts, and what has produced the motivation."

Moreover, Davies tries "to get students to understand why Shakespeare would insert a soliloquy." He says, "I might pose the question 'Why does Macbeth or Hamlet do this?' Then we can discuss the skills of the playwright in creating this scene to develop how the plot works. I also try to get them to see the difference between an aside and a soliloquy. I ask, 'What is the purpose of this aside? Why is it effective?' For example, Banquo, in an aside, begins to become suspicious of Macbeth. This is the first indication that anyone is catching on."

Davies also wants the students to understand the "illusion of the fourth wall." That is, in a soliloquy, the speaker is not talking to the audience; he is on the stage trying to create the illusion of a different space. If he did speak to the audience, he would be breaking the "illusion of the fourth wall." This is a technique used by modern playwrights as well. Davies explains to his students that sometimes playwrights want to break this illusion and thus do have the characters address the audience, a technique that Shakespeare also uses.

Finally, Davies asks his students to think about the play and determine where they feel the climax should be. He asks them to relate the character's tragic flaw to the climax, and then he has the students discuss and analyze the particular weaknesses that bring about the character's doom. And, in calling upon his experience as an actor to play all the roles, Davies is able to show his students how actors performed female roles during Shakespeare's time.

Although Yonce does not teach Shakespeare from the dramatist's point of view, he does have his students think about how the play should be staged. He asks, "How would you present this part on stage?" Then the students come up with ideas of how they would interpret a particular character. Like Davies, he is especially interested in the intonation of a character's lines. He asks, "How would you instruct the actor to deliver Hamlet's line 'I never gave you aught' when Ophelia returns his gifts?" He says, "If the *I* in the sentence is emphasized, it could mean that Hamlet is admitting that he is not the same person who gave her these gifts, having been changed so much by the events that have occurred in Denmark. If the *you* is stressed, the line could mean that he believes Ophelia is not the same person he once loved, since she is now allowing herself to be manipulated by her father and the king. The inflection of the line definitely changes the meaning."

Yonce emphasizes the poetic power of the plays: "I talk about the ability of poetry to lift the commonplace and the ordinary to a sublime level. I try to take several passages and show the beauty of the language. I also stress the use of metaphors and similes and how they say so much more than a straightforward account."

Davies and Yonce both try to lure students into reading Shakespeare by talking about the bawdiness of his language. Davies says that when he gets down to the nitty-gritty, he doesn't try to hide the bawdiness. "In fact," he says, "I try to make a point of telling the students about the colorful scenes. I also point out the scenes that have been cut out of textbooks, and I tell them when I am offended that a scene has been cut. I try to get them to know that they can have a good time with Shakespeare. Once these students get the idea that someone has censored Shakespeare, their ears perk up, and they are intrigued with what he wrote, and many will go to the original source to find those missing sections." Yonce also draws his students into their study: "I make students aware of the book *Shakespeare's Bawdy,* by Eric Partridge, which is a scholarly, fully documented examination of the sexual allusions in Shakespeare and an explanation of the slang of the Elizabethan period. Students are amazed—and a bit titillated—by what Shakespeare *really* is saying."

As both of these teachers demystify Shakespeare and lead their students into an appreciation of the richness and variety of his language, they are able to instill in many of their students the idea that studying Shakespeare is indeed "cool."

20 Teaching Shakespeare against the Grain

Ronald Strickland
Illinois State University

By identifying the sociocultural coordinates from which Shakespeare is variously appropriated or resisted by groups within the academy and in society at large, we can encourage our students to develop what Jerry Herron (1988, 117–29) has described as a sort of "critical" literacy: a contingent set of terms and rhetorical practices that enable us to openly and self-consciously engage in the (often masked or suppressed) ideological conflicts through which social values are established.

Take *Macbeth*, for instance. A traditional approach, attending to Aristotle's prescriptions for great tragedy or following the influential model of A. C. Bradley's *Shakespearean Tragedy*, might focus on the character of Macbeth. One might emphasize Macbeth's personal struggle with ambition or his susceptibility to Lady Macbeth's influence. This sort of reading makes a certain kind of sense for us, and some version of it would, no doubt, have been available to Shakespeare's original audience as well. But there are other operative frameworks of meaning for *Macbeth*. A historicized perspective would note that the play also served an ideological function in legitimating the Stuart accession. As Richard III had embodied all the evils of the Yorks in one person against whose villainy Queen Elizabeth and her Tudor predecessors could appear in heroic glory, Macbeth did the same for King James. Recognizing this ideological function enables a certain kind of critique of individualism to emerge; we can see how political propagandists may simplistically "demonize" a particular individual in order to mobilize public opinion in favor of some particular program or cause or to divert public attention away from some pressing crisis.

As students may notice, this is essentially what happened on American television during the Persian Gulf War. Saddam Hussein was demonized; President Bush, on the other hand, was apotheosized. The United States' less than altruistic interests in the Persian Gulf were forgotten, as were domestic problems such as the recession and the savings and loan crisis. We are not accustomed, perhaps, to thinking either of Shakespeare or of our television news media as propagandists. Nonetheless, each of these discourses—Shakespeare and the nightly news—have at times performed propagandistic functions. Teaching our students how to "read" such functions across different discourses and in various contexts is, in my view, one of the most urgent missions of a college education.

Shakespeare as Cultural Capital

A pedagogy focused on critical literacy would reveal "Shakespeare" as a body of knowledge shaped and constructed by critical and pedagogical apparatuses, rather than as a distinct and substantial subject that exists independently of our work as scholars, teachers, and students. As Gerald Graff (1987, 247–62) has reminded us, the familiar subjects and methodologies of our curricula are themselves products of historical conflicts that have been systematically forgotten. What the teacher can do in this situation is to acknowledge his or her implication in the institutional assumptions and conceptual frames that produce our particular constructions of "knowledge." This acknowledgment in turn calls for a questioning of those intellectual boundaries and opens up the possibility for alternative knowledges produced in other cultural sites, knowledges that contest the social values implicit in the institutionally supported curriculum.

The "indoctrination" model of literary study—like what Paulo Freire (1974) has called the "banking" model of education—assumes that students come into the university as blank slates waiting to be stamped with a set of values. In fact, of course, students enter our classrooms as subjects situated within complex networks of sociopolitical power. Students, that is, are always already indoctrinated; they are "organic intellectuals," in the Gramscian (1971) sense, who already have a stake in the political struggles that shape our society. In this context, literary study presents itself to the progressive intellectual as one of several important sites of ideology production available for political struggle. Other sites include the entertainment industry (especially popular music and cinema), news media (ostensibly "objective" newspaper and broadcast journalism as well as the subjective discourse of television pundits, newspaper columnists, and other commentators), and the radio and television call-in programs that blur the lines between entertainment, education, and journalism. These various discursive arenas each present different opportunities and obstacles for critical analysis, but the literature classroom, I would argue, offers the greatest potential for a sustained, articulate debate on sociocultural values. We simply have more time and space and shared commitment to devote to the project of critical literacy than do the editorial writers, movie makers, and talk-show hosts.

Classroom Strategies

In an oppositional classroom, Shakespearean texts can become the subject of ideological critique—a practice that reconstructs the historical conditions in which the texts were and are (re)produced and that places the Shakespearean text in relation to other contextual and "countertextual" texts. I introduce the issue of the ideological effects of literary study with one or more assigned readings—usually Louis Althusser's essay "Ideology and Ideological State Apparatuses" (1971) and Terry Eagleton's "The Subject of Literature" (1985–86)—at the beginning of each semester. These essays—particularly Althusser's— are difficult for students. Students find them difficult not so much because they are written in high academic style, or because the ideas set forth are particularly complex, but because the arguments made are relatively unfamiliar to them. Both Althusser and Eagleton argue that education often serves to limit one's personal freedom as much as to expand it. This thought makes some students uncomfortable; nevertheless, their discomfort can lead to productive discussion and debate.

In the core curriculum or general education Shakespeare course, we often teach students—business majors, science majors, and other students pursuing technical and explicitly vocational degrees—who are merely fulfilling a graduation requirement and who have no particular interest in Shakespeare. As teachers, we may fall into the uncomfortable habit of trying to cajole such students into enjoying Shakespeare's plays. A much better strategy, however, is to acknowledge and critique this discomfort as a symptom of the conflicting agendas I mentioned earlier: the concern that students be indoctrinated with traditional values, on the one hand, and the need for a streamlined technical training, unencumbered by a critical encounter with culture, on the other. One implication of Althusser's and Eagleton's view is that the general education Shakespeare course may function as a sort of values-indoctrination for vocationally oriented students. If this implication is considered, students' resistance to Shakespeare takes on more urgent significance and can become an important issue for class discussion.

After addressing the general problem of the place of literary study and "Shakespeare" in the academy and in the larger social formation, I next raise the question "Who is Shakespeare?" Students find this question both surprising and fascinating. I usually assign a general theoretical reading on the problem of authorship and intention—such as Michel Foucault's essay "What Is an Author?" (1977)—in conjunction with other readings specifically focused on the Shakespeare authorship question. The first chapter of Marjorie Garber's book *Shakespeare's Ghost Writers* (1987) gives a colorfully written account of the principal nineteenth- and twentieth-century debates over whether William Shakespeare of Stratford or some other mysterious person or persons actually wrote the plays. These debates are often quite entertaining in their own right, but they also open up opportunities to raise key theoretical questions concerning the plays. Does the meaning of *King Lear* change, for example, if the play was actually written by the aristocratic Earl of Oxford, as Charlton Ogburn thinks, instead of the middle-class Shakespeare?

I often use a transcript of a program entitled "The Shakespeare Mystery" (1989) from the Public Broadcasting System's "Frontline" series. In the statements of scholars and interested partisans interviewed for this program, students can identify several distinctively different "Shakespeares." Charles Burford, a descendent of the Earl of Oxford, observes that only a cultivated, educated aristocrat such as his ancestor could have written the plays. Enoch Powell, a retired cabinet minister, argues that the author of the works known as Shakespeare's must have been someone with a firsthand experience of governing. Charlton Ogburn is moved to tears as he spins a sentimental, romantic tale of Oxford as a great man tragically unrecognized. And scholars such as A. L. Rowse and Samuel Shoenbaum haughtily dismiss the Shakespeare-Oxford authorship controversy as a tempest in a teapot cooked up by "ignorant" and presumptuous amateurs.

What the authorship controversy illustrates most clearly is that there is real cultural power at stake in the Shakespeare "industry." If students gain an understanding of how and why "Shakespeare" can be claimed as a "member" of one group or another—liberals or conservatives, pragmatists or idealists—then the function of "Shakespeare" as a sort of cultural capital produced and disseminated in the university can be explored. Perhaps the most famous modern instance of this sort of appropriation of "Shakespeare" for a propagandistic use is Laurence Olivier's 1945 film version of *Henry V.* But Margot Heinemann (1985) gives an interesting account of a more recent instance in an essay entitled "How Brecht Read Shakespeare." Heinemann analyzes an interview with Nigel Lawson, then Chancellor of the Exchequer, in which the conversation turns on Ulysses' speech on chaos and social hierarchy from *Troilus and Cressida:* "Take but degree away, untune that string, / And hark what discord follows." To the interviewer's query of why he likes those lines, Lawson responds,

> The fact of differences, and the need for some kind of hierarchy, both these facts, are expressed more powerfully there than anywhere I know in literature.

"So," the interviewer asks, "Shakespeare was a good Tory?" And Lawson replies, "Shakespeare was a Tory, without any doubt."

There is an especial irony involved in this particular appropriation of "Shakespeare," because it flouts the conventional ironic interpretation of that passage from *Troilus and Cressida.* "It's interesting," as Heinemann goes on to observe, that

> to make his point Mr. Lawson has to remember his examples so wholly out of dramatic context, disregarding entirely the conflicts of values and actions that surround them in the plays. Ulysses may talk about the sacredness of hierarchy and order, but the setting shows him as a cunning politician whose behaviour undercuts what he says here, as indeed does the whole play. (1985, 203)

One sometimes hears the criticism that introducing historical or political contexts into the study of Shakespeare results in "reductive" readings of the plays. Perhaps this may occur if the teacher focuses on a single issue. But an emphasis on poetic excellence or plot structure can be just as reductive, and such issues are more likely to seem merely irrelevant. In using texts and strategies such as those I have described above, I aim to make visible the social, institutional, and historical contexts in which the class is reading Shakespeare. Having begun to develop these kinds of contextual frames for reading the plays, students can make connections and critical comparisons between the knowledge and values produced in the Shakespeare course and in other areas of their social and academic experience.

In addition to introducing supplementary texts that raise larger institutional questions about literary study, Shakespeare's plays can be "expanded" in ways that enable larger political and philosophical questions to be raised around them. In this way, we can engage our students in issues that are more important to them (and to us, perhaps, more often than not) than esoteric and unconnected questions of history and aesthetics. With the goals of critical engagement and significance in mind, I never teach a play as an isolated text. Instead, I teach Shakespeare's plays as parts of ensembles or clusters of texts that implicitly or explicitly problematize some reading of the play (or vice versa). For example, I often teach the *Cliffs Notes* or *Monarch Notes* for a play alongside the play itself. This produces several interesting effects. Since many students see these study guides as aids for cheating, they are surprised to find them on my syllabus, and this can lead to productive considerations of what it means to "read" or to "know" literature. As condensed (and often reductive and formulaic) readings of literary texts packaged for student-consumers who are "too busy" to read for themselves, the study guides promote the most pernicious aspects of the "cultural literacy" approach to education; they encourage readers to memorize disjointed facts at the expense of critical thinking, and they present a body of mostly centrist-to-conservative values and opinions as the authoritative interpretations of literary texts. But they are useful as teaching tools precisely because of these shortcomings. By reading various study guides in conjunction with the plays themselves, students can gain an understanding of how the meanings of social texts (such as the plays) are mediated and negotiated through other texts, and of the transformations in meaning that may result from this process.

Along with the commercial study guides, I use film adaptations and parodies of the plays, advertisements, music videos, newspaper reviews, scholarly journal articles, and introductions to literary textbooks as "contextual" texts available for critical and oppositional readings by students. Often I introduce accounts of provocative modern productions of the plays. When teaching *Romeo and Juliet,* for instance, I have students read a *New York Times* article ("In Cornerstone's Shakespeare, Romeo Raps," 7 May 1989, 2:5–6) in which reporter Nita Lelyveld describes the Cornerstone Theater Company's 1989 production of the play in Port Gibson, Mississippi. The Cornerstone Theater Company is a traveling troupe that goes into small rural communities and performs classic plays with the help of local residents. In this way, Cornerstone brings art into some out-of-the-way places, and, more often than not, they bring out unrecognized individual talents and unexpected displays of community spirit among the local residents. In the Port Gibson production, the play was adapted slightly, with some of the language updated, and the cast featured a black Romeo and a white Juliet. According to the *Times* article, the resulting script for *Romeo and Juliet* was both very much in the spirit of the original play and a critique of Southern society and racism. Lord Capulet, for example, became Mamaw, Juliet's grandmother and a harsh and unbending Southern matriarch. Tybalt, played by a company actor, Ashby Semple, was a racist young woman full of hatred for blacks. Friar Lawrence, played by a company actor, Peter Howard, became Father Lawrence, a Catholic priest forced by Romeo to put into action the liberal beliefs he espouses. (7 May 1989, 5)

This scenario, and the passionate scenes between the two leading characters, at first caused some apprehension among local members of the cast. But the end result seems to have been worth the risk. In a forum held after the production closed, townspeople and Cornerstone staff had an open and enlightening discussion on such issues as "the de facto segregation in area schools" (*New York Times*, 7 May 1989, 5).

This article raises several interesting theoretical questions. To begin with, Is this Shakespeare? At what point does an adaptation of a Shakespeare play cease to be the "real thing"? Is this adaptation better or worse, in some way, than a traditional production? By what critical standards can such a judgment be made? Does the aesthetic value of Shakespeare's play suffer from Cornerstone's politicized production? How is the issue of racism altered when it is presented through an adaptation of *Romeo and Juliet*? How students answer these questions is less important to me than for them to develop the habits and skills to engage in thoughtful, critical discussions of such questions.

In another critical textual juxtaposition that is particularly popular among my students, I provide brief excerpts from a version of *Romeo and Juliet* in a high school textbook for comparison with the play as we read it. For many students who have studied *Romeo and Juliet* in high school, this comparison produces a startling revelation. They often remark that they didn't like the play in high school, that it seemed boring, or that it didn't make much sense. Now they understand why. The editors of the high school textbook version have silently "bowdlerized" the play, cutting out most of the language containing sexual puns and innuendo. Students are amazed to see how much difference it makes to read an uncut version of the play. More importantly, introducing the bowdlerized text raises a variety of crucial issues, such as censorship, aesthetic integrity, the question of how aesthetic appreciation is produced, and the role of literature in education.

A similar instance in which we discuss the teaching of Shakespeare in high schools focuses on an incident reported in the winter

1987 issue of the *Shakespeare Newsletter.* The teaching of *The Merchant of Venice* was prohibited in a Waterloo, Ontario, high school after parents became concerned that the play was fostering anti-Semitism among students. When I teach *The Merchant of Venice,* I devote a considerable body of time at the beginning to a lecture on the history of anti-Semitism in Europe and America and to the characteristics of Christian-Jewish relations in various historical contexts accessed by the play as we will encounter it: Renaissance Venice and London and modern England, America, and Canada. After developing these contexts at some length, I give students copies of the *Shakespeare Newsletter* article, which describes incidents of anti-Semitism among students and reports arguments in school board meetings from parents and teachers on both sides of the controversy. I ask my students to take up positions on the quesiton of whether *The Merchant of Venice* should be taught in high school, and we debate the issue.

Often it is precisely the peripheral material associated with a literary text that provides the loose thread that will unravel an ideologically oppressive construction of the work. For example, when the British Broadcasting Company's Shakespeare plays were aired on the Public Broadcasting System, several of the plays were accompanied by short introductions and closing interviews featuring executive producer Jonathan Miller and, occasionally, one of the actors from the production (John Cleese, who played Petruchio in *The Taming of the Shrew,* and Warren Mitchell, who played Shylock in *The Merchant of Venice*). Miller's comments on the controversial plays reveal a concern to forestall criticism of Shakespeare as sexist, racist, or anti-Semitic. Miller (1980) acknowledges, for example, that modern viewers may be offended by the apparent sexism of *The Taming of the Shrew,* but he urges us to bear in mind the historical context of the play. In the case of *Othello,* Miller (1981) opines that the key element of the tragedy is Othello's jealousy, not his race, and that the play could be produced with a white actor portraying a white character with no loss of tragic power. In an interview with Warren Mitchell on the BBC's *The Merchant of Venice,* Miller (1980) fends off an anticipated charge of anti-Semitism with a preemptive reversal, noting that the production is unique in that it had a Jewish producer (Miller), a Jewish director (Jack Gold), and a Jewish actor (Mitchell) playing Shylock and expressing a passing concern that the play may be taken as *anti-Christian.* I provide transcripts of these introductions and interviews for students to respond to in position papers, and I focus paper topics and class discussions on the issues of sexism, racism, and anti-Semitism in relation to the BBC productions and Miller's comments.

I require students in my classes to produce several one- to two-page critical response/position papers on key issues raised in the course. Each week I reproduce a packet of eight or ten of these student-generated texts, along with position papers that I write against some of them, for distribution to the entire class. In this manner, a considerably larger proportion of the class discourse is textualized than would be the case in a traditional lecture/discussion course. The position papers produced in the class become part of the general text to be studied, decentering the institutionally authorized content of the course and producing alternative centers of meaning (on the margins of the discipline) where readers situated differently in relation to class, race, gender, and other culturally significant discursive categories can engage the "official" texts of a Shakespeare course. Through this practice of publishing the texts of both students and teacher, positions are occupied in a way that makes them much more accessible for critique than in traditional classroom discussion.

Increased textualization also produces some welcome and practical side effects. For one thing, it encourages students to give more carefully considered thought to their responses to the issues raised in the course. Though many teachers use reading journals to achieve this purpose, I think the response/position paper has considerable advantages over the journal. As an ostensibly "private" mode of writing, the journal is unavailable as a source of knowledge and as a target of criticism for other participants in the class. Thus, the journal cannot contribute directly to the productive conflict that I seek. Another useful side effect results from the attention focused on students whose papers are circulated to the entire class. This attention, I have observed, is inevitably perceived as a mark of distinction, even when the students' positions are subjected to the critical attacks of the teacher and other students. Thus, the response/position paper functions as a sort of reward, allowing a relatively large proportion of the work produced in the course to remain outside the institutional sphere of the grading system.

I can imagine several kinds of objections to the somewhat unorthodox approach to teaching Shakespeare that I have described in this essay; I have felt some of them myself. For example, it does take some extra effort to assemble the extracanonical materials I use to produce contextual clusters around the various plays. For several years now I have been collecting these items, saving newspaper reviews of the plays, haunting garage sales and secondhand bookstores for *Monarch Notes* and *Cliffs Notes,* keeping track of controversial scholarly articles, and noting instances of Shakespeareana in popular culture. It does take some time, but the extracanonical material is extremely useful as a way of bridging the gap between students' reference frameworks and the reference framework of Shakespearean scholarship. Further, in the juxtaposition of these different frameworks, or discourses, each of the knowledge and value systems may be problematized, or thrown into relief, in ways that enable students to see the values and limitations of different discursive positions with increased clarity.

It may be objected that the kind of critical pedagogy I have described for the general education Shakespeare course does a disservice to the plays themselves. With all of this extra reading and discussion going, the reader may wonder, when does one have time to read the plays themselves? It is certainly true that we spend less time on close, line-by-line readings of the plays in my classes than on other projects, and it is also true that we read fewer plays (usually only five or six per semester) than we might if I merely focused on close reading of the plays. But I would argue that it is more important for students to gain a critical, contextual understanding of "Shakespeare" as a social and ideological phenomenon than to read several plays with the goal of merely developing an understanding and appreciation of Shakespeare. This appreciation may not happen, at any rate, if students are not able to see any way in which the plays relate to their lives. And, while I do not think the inculcation of taste and "appreciation" should be primary goals of any university literature course, nonetheless, in my experience, students are just as likely to develop a fondness and appreciation for Shakespeare after reading the works in relation to problematic contexts as they are after reading the works as isolated aesthetic masterpieces.

Finally, some may ask, "What is wrong with the goal of producing students as members of a cultivated audience who can appreciate Shakespeare?" The very fact that such an audience has to be produced—that it will not just be found—begs the question, Why produce it? What interests are served by its production? As this mission is generally understood, I think, it means producing an audience that will acquiesce in subjection to a conservative historical reverence that supports an oppressive status quo. It is not surprising that students resist this kind of subjection. Producing this sort of faithful "appreciation" of literature is not a proper goal for a college course.

References

Althusser, Louis. 1971. "Ideology and Ideological State Apparatuses." In *Lenin and Philosophy, and Other Essays,* translated by Ben Brewster, 127–86. London: New Left Books.

Eagleton, Terry. 1985–1986. "The Subject of Literature." *Cultural Critique* 2 (Winter): 95–104.

Foucault, Michel. 1977. "What Is an Author?" In *Language, Counter-Memory, Practice: Selected Essays and Interviews,* edited by Donald F. Bouchard and translated by Donald F. Bouchard and Sherry Simon, 113–38. Ithaca: Cornell University Press.

Freire, Paulo. 1974. *Pedagogy of the Oppressed.* Translated by Myra Bergman Ramos. New York: Seabury Press.

Garber, Marjorie. 1987. *Shakespeare's Ghost Writers: Literature as Uncanny Causality.* London: Methuen.

Graff, Gerald. 1987. *Professing Literature: An Institutional History.* Chicago: University of Chicago Press.

Gramsci, Antonio. 1971. *Selections from the Prison Notebooks.* Edited and translated by Quentin Hoare and Geoffrey Nowell-Smith. New York: International Publishers.

Heinemann, Margot. 1985. "How Brecht Read Shakespeare." In *Political Shakespeare: New Essays in Cultural Materialism,* edited by Jonathan Dollimore and Alan Sinfield, 202–30. Ithaca: Cornell University Press.

Herron, Jerry. 1988. *Universities and the Myth of Cultural Decline.* Detroit: Wayne State University Press.

"*The Merchant of Venice* Banned in 9th and 10th Grades in Waterloo, Canada." 1987. *Shakespeare Newsletter* 37.4 (Winter): 47–48.

Miller, Jonathan. 1980. "Introduction and Interview with Warren Mitchell." *The Merchant of Venice* (BBC). PBS, 23 February.

———. 1980. "Introduction and Interview with John Cleese." *The Taming of the Shrew* (BBC). PBS, 16 January.

———. 1981. "Introduction." *Othello* (BBC). PBS, 12 October. "The Shakespeare Mystery." 1989. *Frontline.* PBS, 14 February.

21 Shakespeare and the At-Risk Student

David B. Gleaves, Patricia A. Slagle, and Kay E. Twaryonas
Seneca High School, Louisville, Kentucky

During the winter of 1990, a small group of teachers from the English Department at Seneca High School met informally to explore a collaborative venture focusing on the study of Shakespeare with regular program students. The impetus of this discussion was to rethink the exploration of Shakespeare with students often excluded from programs, assemblies, and projects involving upper-track students. This core of English teachers wanted to more actively involve these at-risk students, both with Shakespeare and each other.

Regular program is the third track in our district high schools, following the advanced and honors programs. Regular program students are working at or below grade level on test-measured reading and writing skills. Furthermore, many of these students may be enrolled in more than one English class to make up credit for previously failed classes. Regular program is not considered a college preparation track, and many regular program students attend vocational schools for half the school day. At best, attendance is sporadic, as many of these students are not academically motivated.

The choice of Shakespeare as a project focus was made simply because most students would have a common base of knowledge, if only vague familiarity, to draw upon, as at least three years in our high school curriculum include the study of Shakespeare. Furthermore, many teachers had attended the Teachers' Institute sponsored by the Kentucky Shakespeare Festival and had gathered ideas for classroom use. Additionally, Shakespeare's birthday offered an occasion for a celebration theme.

We wanted the students to have an experience that would entice them beyond typical classroom instruction and activity. Furthermore, we hoped that as active participants in this adventure, their self-esteem would grow. We also desired to demonstrate that at-risk students could not only present and perform, but be appropriate audience members as well.

Thus the Shakespeare Celebration at Seneca High School was born. Now we have had two Shakespeare Celebrations that have received kudos from students, administrators, PTSA leaders, and other teachers. We are certain that this type of project provides valuable cognitive and affective learning experiences for students perceived, both by the public and by many educators, as at-risk.

The Shakespeare Celebration

The Shakespeare Celebration is a culmination of classroom activity and instruction. In order for a class to participate in the event, it must agree to mount a display, make a presentation, and compose appropriate letters of thanks. These guidelines are intentionally general, allowing classroom activity to be tailored to the students' interests and abilities as well as to each teacher's particular style. Nevertheless, the impending Shakespeare Celebration, as the situation and setting in which students demonstrate their efforts, acts to guide decision making in individual classrooms.

Our Shakespeare Celebration is held in a multipurpose room that does not have an elevated staging area but that is furnished for an audience with folding chairs on risers. Flat, freestanding panels normally used for room dividers are borrowed and placed side by side to form a "backdrop" where students exhibit their drawings, posters, and visual projects. In addition, the room is lined with cafeteria tables where students arrange such display items as costume-clad dolls, student-decorated T-shirts, bloody daggers, even a model of a decapitated head. *All* projects produced by students are displayed, giving every participating student ownership in the event.

Each class has approximately ten minutes for its presentation. Individual teachers use various methods to determine what presentation will be given by their class. For instance, some teachers require students to participate in individual or group presentation projects, after which the class votes on which will represent it at the celebration. Other classes give presentations such as choral readings that involve the entire class. Julius Caesar may be assassinated more than once, but no one minds. Participating teachers agree to brainstorm for project ideas with their students and pool the results. Suggestions include dramatizations, skits, videos, and reenactments. Original poems read to Elizabethan music as well as Shakespeare raps are popular. The only limitation is in the students' imaginations. As a result of student brainstorming, one group developed a takeoff of *The Arsenio Hall*

Show, with "Arsenio" telling Shakespeare jokes in the opening monologue and featuring as guests two "actresses" who portray Kate and Bianca in a forthcoming film of *The Taming of the Shrew.* The "actresses" even performed a "clip" of a fight between the two sisters.

The day prior to the celebration, each participating class meets in the performance and display space. The performers rehearse while other students hang and arrange displays. Initially, this plan was built into the model to minimize school disruption, but we later realized that spending further time preparing in the performance space would tax our students' interest.

Arrangements are made with the school media center to videotape the celebration. This video document proves to be a valuable aspect of the experience, as it provides the students with a vehicle for self-evaluation. In addition, the students thoroughly enjoy seeing themselves and their classmates on video, and their responses indicate that this activity does much to promote self-esteem.

The second year of our celebration, we secured funds that allowed us to invite two professional actors to present scenes from four of Shakespeare's plays after the students had given their presentations. In addition, we hired a professional actor to appear as the Bard and to be the master of ceremonies. This added a degree of festivity to the occasion, but it was not crucial for our celebration's success.

The framework of our Shakespeare Celebration remains fluid. Each year it has assumed a somewhat different look and feel, accommodating creative changes based on student choices. This flexibility keeps the event fresh, exciting, and enticing so that it does not become a static repetition of the previous year. This feature also allows for some of the same students to participate in subsequent years with a similar degree of motivation to that of their first year of involvement.

Shared Beliefs

In planning our second year, we continued to assume that all of our students can understand and appreciate the works of William Shakespeare. We also agreed that the studying and performing Shakespeare can and should be fun. And we again integrated the language arts—reading, writing, speaking, listening, viewing, and thinking—to generate the most effective student response and learning.

Collaboration was also important, because as teachers, we feel that collaborative learning is a powerful classroom experience. We thus took several opportunities to weave collaborative techniques into our celebration plans. From the beginning, we teachers modeled for our students the collaborative process at work. For instance, we often mentioned in our own classrooms the ideas and processes that other teachers were using with their students. And as students began their work, several teachers visited their colleagues' classrooms to offer ideas, share plans with students, compliment student work, and elicit ideas and suggestions for celebration preparation.

The value of our celebration is hard to measure in a traditional sense because students benefited in many ways that go beyond objective measurement. For instance, students improved their attitudes toward their responsibilities, gained renewed or new-found confidence as learners, and enhanced their self-esteem. Students who had rarely participated previously worked on their celebration projects in class and at home. Celebration participants made or selected costumes, wrote scripts, invented props, and directed their celebration presentations. Many students who seldom visited the library made use of its resources for their projects. Some students who frequently missed class improved their attendance during the project period. Students who seldom kept classwork eagerly requested personal copies of the videotape of the Shakespeare Celebration. During and after the celebration, students enjoyed Shakespeare, each other, and public attention.

Patti's Story: Sophomores

The first year of our Shakespeare Celebration, I introduced my sophomores to *The Taming of the Shrew*. Unlike some of Shakespeare's plays often studied in high school, it offers rich possibilities for female as well as male students. The play also includes considerable action that provides opportunities for engaging projects. My students became quite enthusiastic about the play and expressed enjoyment of its themes and characters.

We began by viewing Zeffirelli's film of the play, starring Elizabeth Taylor and Richard Burton. Mental images in place, the students worked in study groups examining and exploring the act of the play that they would be responsible for teaching to the rest of the class. Each group received scripts and resources that I had available, including audiovisual materials from our media center. Working in their groups, the students were required to write a scene-by-scene summary of their act to copy and distribute to each of the other groups. In addition, they wrote descriptions of the characters in their act, produced a visual plot outline for display, rewrote one of the scenes in their act in modern English and one in slang, and prepared a dramatization of one incident from their act. This dramatization could be presented either in Shakespeare's language or in another language style. As might be expected, some groups chose to present their scene rewritten in the latest slang. Others chose to perform a skit, recite a choral reading, or compose an epic poem. Some groups chose to alter the setting to the Wild West, a Mafia family, or a soap opera. These dramatizations were presented to the class with the opportunity for constructive critique. The entire class thus assisted with polishing the performances for presentation at the Shakespeare Celebration. The class also wrote narration that was read between each scene to give the audience background information from the play. To conclude our study, each group took a collaborative test over the entire play, and the class viewed the *Moonlighting* spoof.

Each student was required to keep a daily work log verified by the group leader they had chosen. Individual groups determined the division of responsibilities, thus allowing students uncomfortable with performing to contribute in another aspect of the project—art, for instance.

I felt this approach was successful. Students assumed responsibility within their group, helped and supported one another, worked independently from my supervision, were enthusiastic about their endeavors, and had fun. This assessment should not imply that everything went smoothly all of the time. As with any venture, there were glitches and snags along the way, but these provided students with problems to solve. For the most part, students were actively learning independent of my overriding instruction. I was facilitator and coach, having fun and learning right along with my students.

Patti's Story: Juniors

The second year of our Shakespeare Celebration, I taught juniors, some of whom I had taught the previous year. In exploring which Shakespeare play to pursue, I realized that most were familiar with *Romeo and Juliet*; some had studied *The Taming of the Shrew,* and others *Julius Caesar.* So I decided to do a review of those three plays as well as the new Zeffirelli *Hamlet.* I initially arrived at this approach because my juniors wanted to participate in the Shakespeare Celebration even though Shakespeare's works are not included in the eleventh-grade curriculum. Our Shakespeare review reinforced previously studied material and explored familiar, and thus less intimidating, plays.

In reviewing each play, we read a synopsis, viewed a filmstrip retelling the story, studied a scene-by-scene summary, wrote character poems, improvised incidents, and responded to characters, plots, and themes in journal writing. Due to popular demand, we also viewed the *Moonlighting* spoof of *The Taming of the Shrew.*

Improvising incidents proved a highlight of our exploration, leading directly to performance projects. I learned from previous experience that presenting complete scenes is too unwieldy for at-risk students. So instead, working together, we identified incidents within scenes for improvisation using students' own language and dialects. Such incidents included Calpurnia talking Caesar into staying home from the Senate, Petruchio and Katharina meeting for the first time, Benvolio and Romeo discussing Romeo's love life, and Horatio and Hamlet talking about the ghost of Hamlet's father. These manageable incidents provided students with increased success.

After our review, students were ready to make project choices. Each student completed one visual or performance project, individually or with a group. They also had the option of pursuing a second project for bonus credit. Each project needed to demonstrate understanding of the plot, characters, or theme of a play. At this point, though, we simply brainstormed for possibilities. Then the students made decisions about their projects: what to do, with whom to work, and whether or not to do a second project. At this stage, students assumed control of their learning activity. Each student or group turned in a planning sheet listing necessary supplies and materials, tasks, and a work plan.

Half of the students' grade was based on their progress in developing their project and half was based on the completed project. I felt their grade should reflect attainable working behaviors more than aesthetic or artistic quality assessments.

Since due day was rainy, some students were dismayed by wet projects. Yet students who rarely worked in class had worked at home and felt pride in their accomplishment. Even damp efforts were of interest to us all. Andrea, who had done little more than sleep and write notes in class, had laboriously made *Julius Caesar* and *Romeo and Juliet* doll costumes from illustrations in a library book. Paul, Nathan, and Suke produced a videotaped spoof of Mel Gibson as Hamlet, while Matt and Lee did a Shakespeare *Jeopardy!* takeoff.

One of the most inspiring projects for me was performed by former "sleepers" Lamont and Darmetrius, who teamed with Lashenta, a budding actress from last year's celebration who lacked self-discipline. These two quiet young men came to life as Petruchio and Baptista scheming to tame Lashenta's Kate. They were delightful—and knew it. The rest of the year their renewed classroom interest earned respectable grades instead of the familiar failures. In fact, when we later studied *The Glass Menagerie*, they were two of our best actors.

In post-project journal responses, students expressed their feelings about their part in the Shakespeare Celebration. I also asked them to reflect on its value. Their responses were enthusiastically positive. The one that touched me the most was from Lamont, who wrote, "I wish I could have you for English next year, so I could do this Shakespeare thing again."

David's Story: Seniors

A major problem confronting teachers ambitious enough to acquaint at-risk students with Shakespeare is getting these reluctant learners to sense a connection between themselves and what the Bard has to offer. One way to solve this problem is to help these students become familiar with Shakespeare, his audience, and Elizabethan customs, beliefs, and family life. Students soon become fascinated with the similarities and differences between themselves and their Elizabethan counterparts.

The source that spurred my students' interest in Shakespeare's culture was Joseph Papp and Elizabeth Kirkland's engaging *Shakespeare Alive!* (1988). The authors' presentation of Elizabethan life generated interest and aroused the curiosity of my students.

I felt the best way to get my classes involved with Shakespeare was first to let several students choose a chapter in *Shakespeare Alive!* and then form groups to present the chapter's contents. If anyone had a question about a chapter, I briefly discussed its subject matter. We solved the problem of several groups wanting the same chapter by a coin flip; happily, the "losers" soon became interested in another chapter in the book. After the various chapters were assigned, students read their sections considering the following criteria:

1. If you were the teacher, what five things from your chapter would you want your students to know?
2. What are your reasons for selecting these items?

The following school day each group met and selected the ideas they felt were the most important, culled from the lists of all group members. During this selection process, I met with each group to help them compile their "final" list. I served only as an advisor; each group had the final say for the ultimate makeup of its list.

Group presentations were next. This activity convinced me that my students were learning and were eager to display their newly acquired knowledge of Shakespeare and Elizabethan life. For instance, students enthusiastically designed their own posters, selected costumes, made props, created special effects, and wrote their own scripts. All of these activities were accomplished by group collaboration with a minimum of disharmony.

By the end of the introductory study of Shakespeare, my students were noticeably proud of their status as "experts" on at least one segment of Elizabethan life. They were eager to present their new-found knowledge at the Shakespeare Celebration. During our two-week unit, attendance improved; all of us, it seemed, enjoyed the experience.

Papp and Kirkland's book can be used with any of Shakespeare's works. The book's contents and fluid style helped make my at-risk students willing, curious readers of Shakespeare.

Kay's Story: Seniors

Before preparing for the Shakespeare Celebration, we read and studied *Macbeth* and saw the Gibson-Close film version of *Hamlet*. Students liked both plays. They responded to characters and events in the works and drew personal parallels. They were entranced by the mean-spirited Macbeth and King Claudius, the colorful machinations of the witches and their apparitions, and the naivete of King Duncan. The love story between Hamlet and Ophelia and Hamlet's relationship with his mother generated unique, individual responses. Of course, the fighting and violence in each play drew much attention. Suddenly my students were enthusiastic about swords and daggers, newt's eyes and adder's forks, cauldrons and motives for murder. For the celebration, student interests directed our preparation for exhibits and presentations. I wanted to find some way that most students could work collaboratively on a presentation. A few years before, at a Kentucky Shakespeare Festival workshop, I had acquired choral readings based on scenes or speeches from several plays. Because they were fun and active, I hoped my students might choose them for their class presentations at the Shakespeare Celebration. Fortunately, they liked the readings because they were different from the usual skits.

One reading was based on the witches' scene from *Macbeth*; the other was a shortened version of *Hamlet*'s "To be or not to be" speech, with sound effects and solo and small group parts. My smaller class presented the witches' scene, whereas my larger class participated in the "To be or not to be" reading.

The collaborative aspects of the choral readings suited our purposes well. The students, eager to make changes in the original versions of the readings, altered the pacing and added gestures, such as grasping small, cardboard daggers when they spoke the lines "To be, or not to be . . ." The three young men who played the witches in *Macbeth* decided on all black costumes with sunglasses. The sound effects crew wore masks representing wind, howling dogs, and thunder.

These presentations united the students in a shared goal. On the final practice day, as nerves began to show, one very quiet girl, Trina, grew restless with the seeming disorganization of the practice. She walked before the chorus and declared, "We're going to do this right tomorrow, and I guess I'm going to lead." The next day, Trina directed her classmates impressively during the *Hamlet* choral reading. After the celebration, students performed a final time, recording audio tapes for future classes to use as models. These examples offer clear evidence of how the celebration's activities revealed leadership and reflected pride in self, group, and performance, not often experienced by at-risk students.

The exhibits for the Shakespeare Celebration were individual and group efforts. I made suggestions, students elaborated on them, and I offered consultation and encouragement. Several students made "wanted" posters. Heather, who seldom exhibited much enthusiasm in class, made a unique poster of Macbeth in a carefully drawn, surreal style. Other students made models of swords and daggers using the library for research on Elizabethan weaponry and fencing techniques. And some students made unusual projects, including a model of the bloody head of the slain Macbeth and a poster depicting the ingredients of the witches' cauldron.

I encouraged students to develop interactive exhibits. Beth wanted to portray Lady Macbeth. She finally coerced Larry to dress as the king, and they developed "quotation sticks," searching the text of *Macbeth* for dialogue between the two characters. Then they cut cardboard quotation "bubbles" modeled after those in comics and inserted sticks between them, thus producing dialogue from the play. Strolling the celebration as Shakespearean characters come alive, they looked authentic and were a popular attraction.

Three other students decided to portray *Macbeth*'s apparitions. They thus created the armored head of Macduff; the bloody child Macduff, "untimely ripped from his Mother's womb"; and a crowned Malcolm with a branch in his hand.

One interactive exhibit involved the audience in voting to elect the "most heinous criminal": Macbeth or King Claudius. With campaign posters and printed ballots, Clint and Deanna staffed the voting table urging students to vote. Macbeth won the dubious distinction by a narrow margin.

These interactive exhibits were collaborations for success. Enthusiastic students were involved in learning, proud of their creative efforts and successful results. My students learned that by hard work, perseverance, and responsibility, they could engineer a successful celebration. Leaving the celebration, several students commented, "You know, Ms. T., this was really fun. Thanks for letting us do it."

Recommendations

As we have indicated, flexibility is the key to a successful Shakespeare Celebration such as ours. But we also feel that there are some guidelines that do promote success. Teacher preparation should be voluntary, with requirements for commitment clearly defined. Within individual classrooms, structure activity so that every student has ample opportunity for success. Furthermore, do not forget that students, particularly at-risk students, have a limited attention span. Do not drag activity out for so long that students peak in the classroom before they ever get to the Shakespeare Celebration experience.

In designing your Shakespeare Celebration, keep it relatively simple; getting too elaborate can be deadly. Also, remember to remain flexible with your program design, because anything can happen. For instance, one celebration day a student who was to portray Julius Caesar landed in in-school suspension! Plan your celebration to cause minimal disruption for teachers not involved in the program. This small gesture will build goodwill for your program.

A key to appropriate audience behavior is to make sure that every student who attends the Shakespeare Celebration has ownership in the event: art or project on display, participation in presentation, master of ceremonies' responsibilities, stage manager duties, whatever. Display all student art and projects, even if you think some may not be of very high quality or may reflect minimal effort. Students' eyes may see them differently than yours do. Besides, knowing that the project will be displayed motivates students in the classroom preparation portion of this endeavor. Do not expect perfection in the student performances. Remember that the students are performing for each other, not for a critic. If possible, videotape your Shakespeare Celebration; students like to view the results.

Above all, tailor your festival to your needs and situation. What we have presented is merely a blueprint for many possibilities.

22 Decentering the Instructor in Large Classes

Robert Carl Johnson
Miami University

Every year I teach one section of an undergraduate Shakespeare course to some fifty students. Ten years ago the same course enrolled no more than thirty-five students, but since the course meets a requirement for an increasing number of majors, and since it is an elective course for students outside the department, enrollment pressures have made it increasingly difficult to keep to the active discussion format with heavy student involvement that had characterized all sections of the course in the past. With an enrollment of fifty students, discussions tend to be dominated by a vocal few, and some are increasingly able to treat the class like a lecture course: listening but not participating, simply copying down what they perceive as the salient points in preparation for their eventual reading of the play and the upcoming exam.

The main goal for my course has remained the same for the last few years. If the class has been successful, the students will leave with confidence in their ability to read and interpret an unfamiliar Shakespeare play. A second goal is to create students who find Shakespeare relevant to their lives today and who see the class as the beginning of a long-standing study and appreciation of Shakespeare. At the end of the term, I ask the students to rate their own ability to read and understand an unfamiliar play. This past semester, forty of the forty-two students responding to this question rated their ability as above average or excellent, the top two categories on a five-category scale. Now I will admit that these self-ratings may reflect a false confidence, but they also reflect the fact that I consciously attempt to decenter the instructor throughout the course, so that by the end of the term the students are completely responsible for interpretations of the final play. If I am successful, when we read the last play, I will supply no answers; I simply raise questions. For some students, this process can be frustrating. I remember a year ago a student expressed her frustration in class: "If you aren't going to tell us the correct response, what will we do on the final exam?" But I have found that response to be an atypical one, and most students relish their freedom and empowerment. Too often students enter the class with fears about their abilities to read and understand Shakespeare. They believe he is that monumental author to be respected and revered, but that the task of understanding his work will be a formidable one and that there will be a limited sense of enjoyment.

To make the students first see themselves as fellow participants and learners, I try to discourage the idea of the student as notetaker. I suggest that they not fill their notebooks with my comments, but instead jot their own comments and reactions in the margins of the text. I remind them that they are not going back to their notebooks years from now, but if the class is successful, they will return to their texts, and their marginalia will be both an interesting memory and a source of comparison with their new reactions and interpretations.

I have found that an adaptation of the one-minute paper at the end of class can be an effective way of engaging a wide variety of students. The original idea of the one-minute paper was to have students write about what confused them or what unanswered questions they still had. Yet I now prefer to ask them to react to a question over material we have not yet discussed or to offer an interpretation of a scene or character from a play we have just started to read. These short papers are ungraded, of course, but by reviewing them before the next class, I have a good idea of how to focus the discussion, and I am able to use the work of several students as contrasting interpretations or as springboards to get class discussion going. Indeed, when students have committed themselves to an idea in writing, they are much more willing to defend, discuss, and modify their position. The fact that the brief essays are ungraded allows the students to experiment, to take an individual position without any risk. These short papers can also give me a good indication of how well a particular session has gone. For example, after finishing *The Taming of the Shrew,* I asked the students to comment on Kate's last speech. It was obvious from the papers that my impression that they had understood the cultural context in which the speech occurs was wrong. Plans for the next class changed immediately, and instead of moving on to the next play, we returned for two more sessions on Kate and women in the Renaissance. What my students and I attempt to keep in mind is that finishing everything on the syllabus is not a goal of the course, but having a complete confidence about what we do finish is.

The Folger Shakespeare Library has recently released the film *Teaching Shakespeare: New Approaches from the Folger Shakespeare Library.* I strongly recommend this film and its strong emphasis on involving the students in acting out various interpretations of individual scenes. I have long been a proponent of performance-based criticism, and I have found that involving students in often humorous and amateurish role playing enhances both their understanding of the play and their interaction with their fellow learners. Some students, to be sure, are reluctant at first to participate, but in every play there are scenes in which even the most reluctant student can participate successfully. Some questions do not even demand that the student read the lines. How does Volumnia act as she enters Rome after saving the city from the attack of her son? How is the initial part of the fight between Tybalt and Mercutio to be staged? How effectively does Falstaff fight before he runs away at Gadshill?

There are other ways to reduce the anxiety that students may feel about such active participation. By dividing the class into groups of six or seven to discuss the interpretation or staging of a particular scene, the groups can return to the class with several different interpretations, arguing the merits of each, picking and choosing the best from each one. Dividing into small groups has another distinct advantage: I am able to join one or more of the groups, usually just listening, but occasionally asking a question or contributing just like any other member of the group. Moreover, within the small groups, all students are willing and able to participate, and through the semester a greater camaraderie develops among the students.

As the students struggle with their varied interpretations of a scene, they quickly understand the complexities of the characters and the variety of responses that any scene presents. To explore and develop further their capacity as critics, I use videotaped or film versions of the plays. Under the best circumstances, there will be a live Shakespeare production somewhere in the area. One semester I was extremely fortunate, as there was a performance of *The Taming of the Shrew* in a nearby city and a performance of *Romeo and Juliet* on campus. The students were able to compare these live performances with other versions of the play available in the school library. Students are not only quick to recognize differences in the versions, but also become extremely confident in defending the version they prefer. For instance, the director of *The Taming of the Shrew* chose to set the play in the 1990s and to have Kate fall in love with Petruchio at their first meeting. Their relationship throughout the rest of the play was based on the premise that they were together playing a joke on the others and that they were equal in the marriage from the start. The last speech by Kate, then, which I had thought might be dropped or changed drastically, seemed completely out of place as the actress delivered it seriously, in a manner wholly devoid of irony. For me, the play was disappointing, but for many of my students, especially for a number of women in the class, it was an entirely successful experiment. One student commented that it was only after seeing that version that she could understand and appreciate the play. For her, the play had a new relevancy and meaning, which she embraced completely and confidently as she and others defended their position against both the teacher and those who had not liked this particular version.

Of course, one cannot always be so fortunate to have a live performance for comparison, nor is a new version of *Hamlet* available every semester. But even when there are not such resources available, there are now enough versions of Shakespeare's plays available on videotape that both full-length and scene-by-scene comparisons are possible. The student who has seen two or more versions of, say, the play-within-the-play scene in *Hamlet* not only has a greater understanding of the complexity of the scene, but is also willing to criticize the various choices and suggest his or her own choices. It is important to remember that if one's goal is to empower the student, then it is always necessary to confront the student with alternatives and options. There are serious problems with having students view one performance of a play. Too often students will accept that version as a definitive version. But the exact opposite occurs when the student sees two or three versions of the same scene.

To return to the play-within-the-play scene, I start with a simple question: What does Hamlet wish to accomplish through the performance of his play and how successful is he in proving the veracity of the ghost? But I also ask the students to pretend that they are someone other than Hamlet at the performance (Gertrude, Claudius, Rosencrantz, Guildenstern, Ophelia, a simple courtier). Then I ask that they explain from that point of view what is happening in the scene. The class will divide into groups depending on which charcter they have chosen, and they will discuss what their character is doing or thinking at each moment in the scene. Very soon we reach a level of confusion. Often the students struggle with the lines between Hamlet and Ophelia, especially the exchange between the two of them immediately before the entrance of the murderer. Where is Hamlet at that point? One student who has chosen to be Claudius asks if he hears those lines. Another who is trying to be Horatio does not understand what Hamlet is doing and feels that Hamlet has forgotten his real purpose. I then offer the Olivier, Jacobi, and Gibson versions of this scene. Basil Sydney in Olivier's version is quickly rejected by those who have chosen to be Claudius. For many, he becomes a caricature, too weak an opponent. Patrick Stewart's Claudius confronts them with a completely different problem, as he violates their basic assumption that Hamlet does cause the king to leave the play in anger and fright. Since neither version is completely satisfactory, neither supporting or validating its own interpretation, students can return to their own interpretations with an increased confidence in their insights. Is it possible to use that exchange between Hamlet and Ophelia? One student said the exchange cannot possibly work if Hamlet is standing between the players and is not even close to Ophelia. Another suggested keeping Hamlet by Ophelia but focusing on a sardonic and aloof Hamlet who is confident that the play is having the desired effect. The students quickly understand that the possibilities are endless, that each decision has other ramifications, that each student has different and often equally valid insights, and that my interpretation is but one of several and by no means the definitive answer.

By the time we have reached the end of the term, these various activities have decentered the instructor and given the students a sense that they can understand or interpret Shakespeare on their own. For one of the final plays (this year it was *Macbeth*), I completely removed myself from the discussion. To focus the direction of the class, I asked the students to form into groups of four or five and answer a series of questions I supplied. They had to reach a consensus within their group and then try to convince any disagreeing group of the validity of their interpretation. After supplying the questions (I offer below the questions for Macbeth and Lady Macbeth for the first two acts of the play), I simply moderated the debates.

Questions for Macbeth (keyed to lines)

I.iii.51	Explain your startled reaction to the witches.
I.iii.135	What is the horrid image you imagine?
I.iii.153	Are you being honest with Banquo?
I.v.11	You refer to Lady Macbeth as your "dearest partner of greatness." Do you consider her your equal?

I.v.66	Your face is like a book. What "strange matters" may men read there?
I.vii.1–2	What do you mean?
I.vii.29	Why did you leave the dining chamber?
I.vii.46	What actions "become a man"?
I.vii.48	When did you "break this enterprise" to Lady Macbeth?
I.vii.60ff	Do you think Lady Macbeth's plan to kill Duncan is a foolproof scheme?
II.ii.14ff	What would have happened to you here without Lady Macbeth?
II.iii.91–6	Explain what you mean here.
II.iii.106	Why did you kill the grooms? Did you tell Lady Macbeth?
II.iii.109ff	Do you think your explanation for your actions is effective or convincing?

Questions for Lady Macbeth

I.v.17	Is it wrong to be full of the milk of human kindness?
I.v.18–25	Have you and Macbeth earlier discussed his becoming king?
I.v.31	Why is the servant mad to say the king is coming here tonight?
I.v.40ff	Why do you wish to be unsexed?
I.vii.55	Could you dash that babe's brains out?
I.vii.60ff	Have you considered that the grooms might deny they killed Duncan?
II.ii.1	Why have you been drinking?
II.ii.30–1	Have you been able to avoid thinking of the deed and do you plan not to think of it?
II.ii.60ff	Is it easy to get Macbeth to your chambers and get washed and changed?
II.iii.88	Since I assume that you had a chance to think of what you might say when you hear that Duncan is dead, can you explain why you said this?
II.iii.106	What do you think of Macbeth's killing of the grooms?
II.iii.118	Why do you collapse?

By the time we have reached the last act, the students are raising questions themselves and answering them effectively and confidently.

Trying to decenter the teacher can be risky, and I find myself at times wishing to go back to a more structured approach, to assure that all of the material is covered and that the students understand the impact of new historicism on our study of Shakespeare. But I have finally decided that such study can wait for a later date (perhaps graduate school). And when a student writes the following on the final course evaluation, I think the approach is working: "The instructor opened up a whole new world for me. I never liked Shakespeare; now I plan to keep my text and read it again and again throughout my life."

23 Where There's A "Will," There's A Way!

Mary T. Christel and Ann Legore Christiansen
Adlai E. Stevenson High School, Prairie View, Illinois

Since teachers are always looking for fresh and stimulating ideas to generate enthusiasm for Shakespeare, here are some suggestions of what works for teachers in the Communication Arts Department at Stevenson High School. Another source for ideas was Professor Andrew McLean at the University of Wisconsin–Parkside. His National Endowment for the Humanities summer seminar on Shakespeare's Henriad contributed valuable insights into the use of film. The various strategies presented here have been used and refined in the classroom in order to promote a sense of enjoyment as well as an understanding of difficult material. As English teachers, our love for Shakespeare is sometimes too intellectual, and we forget that Shakespeare's purpose was to entertain. Plays were written to be performed and experienced, and various techniques involving the media or performance are needed to fulfill these original intentions. The more students are involved, the more enthusiastic and receptive they will be. They will hopefully present you with fewer complaints, and everyone will be happier studying Shakespeare.

"Going Hollywood"

Read and View

Using film versions of Shakespeare's plays—especially *Romeo and Juliet, Hamlet,* and *Macbeth*—to help students understand and enjoy them is nothing new. Yet most teachers tend to use a film to "cap off" a unit after the play has been read, possibly even after the students have been tested. This strategy, however, does not always make most effective use of the virtues of film. Sometimes real understanding of a play's character and plot comes when students explore a visual presentation while they are studying the play. The use of film to promote understanding is usually "wasted" by presenting it after the play has been read in its entirety.

A different strategy for using a film version is to present a segment of it that corresponds with each act of the play. Students can thus immediately benefit from the visual impact of period costumes, staging, and actors' interpretation of their roles. The reinforcement of the text in small increments is especially important to the understanding and enjoyment of the text for students of lesser ability. And the actual implementation of this technique provides a great deal of incentive for students to get through the reading and discussion of the text in order to "see" what happens next. The only drawback to the technique is the changes directors make in the text, location of scenes, and interpretations of characterization.

Nevertheless, for average and above-average students who are not struggling to understand the text, these changes can provide the springboard for a discussion of how effective the changes actually are. Different film versions of a particular scene or soliloquy might thus be interesting to compare. One interesting comparison would be to look at the witches' scene from *Macbeth* using Roman Polanski's, Orson Welles's, and Maurice Evans's versions of that play. Students can comment on the different moods and the effectiveness of each treatment. Another interesting comparison would be to look at Hamlet's "To be or not to be" speech as done by Derek Jacobi, Laurence Olivier, and Mel Gibson, among others available on videotape.

Companion Films

In order to broaden the students' experience of literature and film, especially in honors and advanced placement courses, a teacher should consider the variety of companion films available on videotape and laser disc, especially if students are capable of understanding and appreciating a play without the need for visual reinforcement. This strategy allows students to explore the universal nature of Shakespeare's themes and characters as they have been adapted by contemporary filmmakers from various cultures. Here are a few suggestions.

Romeo and Juliet

The most obvious use of a companion film would be pairing *Romeo and Juliet* with the film version of the musical *West Side Story*. This could be accomplished at the end of the unit even if the Zeffirelli film version of Shakespeare's text is shown in act-length increments.

Macbeth

In addition to the various adaptations of Shakespeare's play in English, Japanese director Akira Kurosawa crafted a cross-cultural version of *Macbeth* called *Throne of Blood.* Kurosawa sets the tragedy in medieval Japan, blending elements of classical Noh plays with Shakespeare's basic plot elements. David Cook (1981), in *The History of the Narrative Film,* calls Kurosawa's adaptation "perhaps the greatest version of Shakespeare on film" (582).

A film from 1991, *Men of Respect,* places the Macbeth tragedy in a contemporary gangster setting. Due to the graphic violence, it would not be suitable to screen in its entirety; but it would provide interesting excerpts to compare to scenes from a traditional version of the play.

King Lear

Two very different choices exist to partner with *King Lear.* Kurosawa again provides a feudal Japanese version with his masterwork, *Ran,* and Peter Yates's *The Dresser* offers a traveling company of actors performing *King Lear* in war-torn Britain. Little of the actual play is depicted in *The Dresser,* but of interest is the relationship between the actor-manager and his dresser, which approximates the relationship between Lear and his fool. Students can experience the tragedy of Lear's fate either transplanted to another culture or to a more contemporary context. Either case illustrates the universal nature of the tragedy.

The Tempest

A traditional choice to pair with *The Tempest* is the science fiction classic *Forbidden Planet,* which borrows liberally from Shakespeare in terms of plot, characterization, and theme. Paul Mazursky's *Tempest* updates the fanciful tale with Prospero and Miranda (as played by John Cassavettes and Molly Ringwald) escaping the pressures and chaos of civilization for life on a secluded Greek isle. The film runs over two hours and makes its thematic point early on, but students would benefit from viewing key scenes that retain elements of characterization and ideology representative of Shakespeare's original text. Especially entertaining is the treatment of Caliban (as played by Raul Julia).

"Enquiring Minds Want to Know"

Act and scene summaries are fairly standard assignments for promoting students' understanding of Shakespeare's plays. Yet a creative twist can be applied that would still promote understanding and critical thinking skills. Why not assign each student a character from the play, either major or minor, and have the student summarize the scenes from that character's point of view? The trick in this kind of summary activity is to coach students both into creating the voice of the character and knowing how this character would be privy to the information. For example, if a student were using Portia's point of view, she could receive intelligence of the conspiracy from a "spy" or perhaps from idle ladies' gossip. Students using Caesar's point of view could have fun with his ghost discovering all the intrigue after his death. With this kind of summary activity, students develop an understanding of a particular character as well as basic plot points.

"Imitating Will"

Probably the most sophisticated test of a student's understanding of a Shakespearean play is imitation or parody. Those students who might have the skill or desire to knock off a bit of iambic pentameter could write scenes or soliloquies that they would like to see included in the play, especially since so many key events take place offstage. Or perhaps they could begin a sequel. Of course, parodies of Shakespeare's great tragic works provide the most fun for students, and the most irreverent parodies seem to work the best. What about bringing together Lear's three daughters on *The Oprah Winfrey Show* to discuss sibling rivalry? Artistic students could create a comic strip using well-known characters. Good ol' wishy-washy Charlie Brown could portray the vacillating Hamlet. Sometimes drawing a famous character in an appropriate costume is a sufficient parody.

Quoting the Bard

Teachers of Shakespeare usually lament that their students have no appreciation of the play's poetic language. Here is a creative approach for examining the famous and not so famous lines from the tragedies and comedies. Get out the scissors, paste, construction paper, and old magazines. Have students cut out magazine pictures that illustrate a quotation in a serious, humorous, or absurd fashion. Then have them mount the pictures on construction paper with the quotation and a citation that indicates the speaker, act, scene, and line numbers. Some examples from *Julius Caesar* include Jim Palmer in his Jockey shorts paired with "Give me my robe, for I will go" (II.ii.107), two high school basketball players embracing in obvious defeat teamed with "And we, like friends, will straightway go together" (II.ii.128), and a man taking a photograph standing next to a sign saying "Send Money" with "By any indirection, I did send / To you for gold to pay my legions / which you denied me. Was that done like Cassius?" (IV.iii.75–77). This activity forces students to comb the text to find quotations that suit the pictures they select. Or the teacher can preview this activity early in the unit so that students can jot down memorable lines that might be useful later. And the resulting mounted pictures make great decorations for bulletin boards!

Hitting the Highlights

Use only selected high-interest, key scenes from a play to teach character and plot development. For years English teachers have thought students needed to read every word for understanding. Yet contributing actions can be summarized in a paragraph or two on a handout. As a result, students will not become bogged down in minor details or actions. Also, students, especially lower-level students, can focus more easily on the main conflict.

The key for this activity has to be a conscious focus by the teacher so that the line of plot or character development to be followed is absolutely clear. For example, in the tragedy *Macbeth*, I.iii begins with the witches' scene and eventually leads to the prediction that Macbeth will become Thane of Cawdor and "King hereafter." This begins Macbeth's intrigue with power. It is very easy to set the previous scene in a few sentences, summarizing the battle fought and Macbeth's valor. One can also summarize scene I.iv, with the exception of Macbeth's short speech about how he must deal with Malcolm being named as the heir apparent. Some teachers may want to have students read scene I.v in detail because of the intervention at this point by Lady Macbeth; however, scene I.vii develops this circumstance in more detail, so both scene I.v and scene I.vi could be summarized.

This technique presents no difficulty for students attempting to understand the play if the teacher carefully chooses the passages. Indeed, students already use commercial study guides to abridge the text. Summarizing scenes thus circumvents student objections to reading a long and difficult text while still getting them to read the author's words and not a paraphrase.

Acting Up

Students enjoy acting out scenes that contain physical action or high emotion. Give students a list of possible scenes from which they can choose. Scenes that contain several characters work best because students can work in groups and get more ideas. They also feel less self-conscious and become more free in groups of four or five. Two suggestions are III.i of *Romeo and Juliet* and IV.i of *Macbeth.* The *Macbeth* scene has three witches, Hecate, Macbeth, First Apparition, Second Apparition, Third Apparition, and Lennox. Speeches are not long, and with a few practice sessions, students can present their scene from memory.

A writing assignment asking students to explain why the scene is important can also be included. The writing details action leading up to the scene and continues by summarizing the action that occurs as a result of the scene. This technique also makes a nice review for students because they must go back over the text for the information.

An old technique is to have students memorize lines. This activity has fallen from favor over the years but can be revitalized in a nonthreatening format. The students choose a number of lines set by the teacher and memorize them. Each student is instructed to write out the lines on a sheet of paper. Students break up into groups of four or five and recite the lines to their small group. The members of the group listen and circle words or lines missed. They also write comments about expression used in delivery. Students are very supportive of one another and will act as a coach or prompter, if necessary.

Another activity involving improvisation is to assign a character to each student from a particular scene in the play. The student must determine what the character wants in the scene. For example, in II.v of *Romeo and Juliet*, Juliet wants information from the Nurse. The nurse wants to give her the information but also wants to tease Juliet and prolong the anticipation of the moment. Students can determine these character objectives as they discuss the scene. Then, rather than using the lines in the play, they use improvisation to put Shakespeare's language into the vernacular. Teachers may consult some books on improvisation, specifically Viola Spolin's *Improvisation for the Theater* (1963) for further suggestions of improvisational techniques.

Playing the Part

A writing assignment for a play can be done in a format other than the standard expository form. Ask the students to analyze a character from the play. Students need to know that the audience learns about each character not only from what the character says or does, but also by the words and actions of other characters. For example, in *Macbeth,* the character should be traced through all five acts. Students do not have to focus on Macbeth but could consider Lady Macbeth or Macduff. Have students try writing diary entries from Macbeth's point of view as he looks back over the events or confessions from Lady Macbeth as she regrets her lust for power. Students could also consider how Macduff might have written to his wife telling her to beware of Macbeth. One student's writing assignment follows:

Confessions: The Diary of Lady Macbeth

I feel that my life will soon end. It is because of my greed and selfishness that I am cursed to suffer in such agony. My obsession to be queen was so great, I would stop at nothing to gain that position.

Often I had dreamed of being such a powerful figure. Alas, I never thought I would truly be queen. When I received my husband's letter telling of the witches' prophecy, I knew my chance had come, and I would do everything in my power to make my dreams a reality. And I knew the only way to make it possible was to kill Duncan. I realized it was wrong, but my need for power dominated my sense of morality. How I longed to be Lady Macbeth, Queen of Scotland. I asked the spirits to make my blood thick and fearless to accomplish such a task. That night when my husband returned home, I confronted him with my idea. At first he was skeptical, as I knew he would be. He was afraid of getting caught and ruining his chances of being king. Naturally, I convinced him otherwise. "Only look up clear," I told him. "To alter favor is to fear. Leave all the rest to me."

When my husband completed the task, I felt as if the world were mine. Naturally, I lead on as to be shocked by Duncan's death, although I was truly elated.

We hope these suggestions will help to make Shakespeare both more fun and more accessible to students. For additional ideas or further explanation, a good resource is the seventy-five-minute video *Teaching Shakespeare: New Approaches from the Folger Shakespeare Library.*

References

Cook, David A. 1981. *A History of Narrative Film.* New York: Norton.

Spolin, Viola. 1963. *Improvisation for the Theater: A Handbook of Teaching and Directing Techniques.* Evanston, IL: Northwestern University Press.

Teaching Shakespeare: New Approaches from the Folger Shakespeare Library. 1986. West Tisbury, MA: Vineyard Video Productions.

V Frequently and Not So Frequently Taught Plays

24 Digging into *Julius Caesar* through Character Analysis

Larry R. Johannessen
Saint Xavier University

At the end of an inservice program I recently conducted at a local high school, two young teachers approached me and, in obvious desperation, asked if I had any ideas about what they could do with *Julius Caesar,* which was one of the works they had to teach as part of their tenth-grade curriculum. "I've had it," one of them said. "None of the suggestions in the teacher's guide for the anthology seems to work."

I immediately sympathized with them. I remembered my first two years of teaching and my own nearly futile attempts to get my tenth graders through the play as I tried to follow the suggestions in the teacher's guide for the anthology we used in our tenth-grade curriculum. So I explained to the two teachers that I did have some ideas about what they might do with the play, ideas that might make it an exciting and rewarding experience both for them and their students.

My first suggestion to these two young teachers was that they should throw out the teacher's guide. In fact, I would argue that the primary teaching mechanism presented in most high school texts is at the root of why many students have difficulty with Shakespeare's plays. Yet in order to understand why this is so and what can be done to make teaching plays like *Julius Caesar* an exciting learning experience for students, it is first necessary to examine what is involved in reading and interpreting literature.

In his best selling book, *Cultural Literacy,* E. D. Hirsch (1987) states that reading is a complicated process. He notes,

> The reader's mind is constantly inferring meanings that are not directly stated by the words of the text but are nonetheless part of its essential content. The explicit meanings of a piece of writing are the tip of the iceberg of meaning; the larger part

lies below the surface of the text and is composed of the reader's own relevant knowledge. (34)

Hirsch's solution to helping students learn how to read beyond "the tip of the iceberg" and dig into its bulk is to have them become acquainted with his sixty-three-page list of people, places, terms, texts, and events. Presumably, memorizing the meanings of items such as *irony, symbol, parody, Brutus, Mark Antony, Julius Caesar,* and *King Lear,* just to name a few, provides students with the background knowledge needed to interpret complex texts and become literate Americans.

Yet in an article in *English Journal,* Michael Smith and George Hillocks (1988) argue that while background information is important, depth of understanding is also a critical factor in interpreting literature, something Hirsch neglects in arguing on behalf of breadth (45). As my two young high school teachers discovered, having students memorize Hirsch's list of items, or the similar lists of literary terms that dominate most secondary literature texts, will not go far in helping students learn how to interpret a play such as *Julius Caesar.*

If Smith and Hillocks are correct, then the question becomes, How can instruction be set up so that it will provide students with the depth of understanding that will enable them to interpret and write about the play? Smith and Hillocks cite research that suggests that when students are given extended practice with what they call "conceptual knowledge," their ability to understand texts increases dramatically (46, 48). I would extend their argument and suggest that when students are given extended practice in dealing with a particular interpretive problem, and when that practice includes knowledge of how to turn their interpretations into analytical compositions, their ability to interpret texts and write effectively about their interpretations increases dramatically. In other words, instruction, if it is to be effective, should focus on key interpretive problems in the work, provide students with practice in making appropriate interpretations, and incorporate knowledge about turning their interpretations into written compositions.

One way to accomplish these goals is to focus instruction on analyzing major characters in the play. Secondary students are often drawn to the characters; therefore, focusing instruction on them can potentially generate interest. More important, if students are going to be able to understand—interpret—the play, they need to be able to make inferences about major characters: why they behave the way they do, what their motives are for taking certain actions, even why they speak in certain ways.

The series of activities that follows focuses on analyzing major characters. It illustrates one way to set up instruction that engages students in an interpretive problem, helps them make complex interpretations, and enables them to transform their conclusions into effective literary analysis.

Student Opinionnaire

When I ask teachers what they do to prepare students for reading a play, many tell me that they tell students about the author, about historical background, or a bit about the story. When I ask them why they do these things, they often indicate that the play is so far removed from students' life experiences that they believe doing such things will help students with reading problems and motivate them to read. Yet while E. D. Hirsch might think this is a good idea, Louise Rosenblatt (1968) argues that this approach often puts the students' focus on "much that is irrelevant and distracting" (27). An alternative approach I have used is the opinionnaire activity. This approach is designed to foster what Rosenblatt calls "fruitful . . . transactions between individual readers and individual literary works" (26–27). The opinionnaire activity is based on a simple idea: that students have opinions about various subjects. The opinionnaire thus uses those opinions to create interest in the work and helps with problems students might have in trying to interpret character and understand themes. The Politics, Patriotism, and Protest opinionnaire (see Figure 1) is keyed to two main characters, Brutus and Mark Antony, and the issues they face in the play. (This opinionnaire is adapted from Kahn, Walter, and Johannessen 1984, 25.)

The first step in using the opinionnaire is to hand it out to the class, perhaps the day before they start reading. Have students mark whether they agree or disagree with each of the eleven statements. Then, lead a class discussion focusing on each statement, encouraging students to express their opinions and challenge the views of others. Most often, a lively discussion ensues. In fact, even students who are reluctant to speak up in class become actively involved in the discussion, because the activity encourages them to express their opinions.

This activity encourages discussion and helps students prepare for reading the play in another way as well. In marking their answers, students, without realizing it, often contradict themselves. For example, some students agree with statements 1 and 3. As the discussion develops, however, students often realize (on their own or as a result

---

Politics, Patriotism, and Protest

Directions: In the space provided, mark whether you agree or disagree with each statement.

Agree or Disagree

1. It is never right to kill another person. _____

2. Political leaders usually act in the best interest of their countries. _____

3. If a political leader has done something wrong, it is all right to get rid of him or her by whatever means necessary. _____

4. "Power corrupts, and absolute power corrupts absolutely." _____

5. In certain situations, it may be justified for a political leader to bend or break the law for the good of the country. _____

6. People should never compromise their ideals or beliefs. _____

7. "My country right or wrong" is not just a slogan; it is every citizen's patriotic duty. _____

8. "Cowards die many times before their deaths; the valiant taste of death but once." _____

9. "The evil that men do lives after them; the good, is [often buried] with their bones." _____

10. No cause, political or otherwise, is worth dying for. _____

11. "Ask not what your country can do for you, but what you can do for your country."

Figure 1. Patriotism, Politics, and Protest Opinionnaire

of their classmates pointing it out) that they have some contradictory thoughts. It is not uncommon for one student to tell another, "How can you say it is all right to kill an evil political leader when you just got through saying it is wrong to kill another person!"

Once students have discussed all the statements, point out that they deal with aspects of major characters in the play and that they should keep them in mind as they read. In fact, statement 3, "If a political leader has done something wrong, it is all right to get rid of him or her by whatever means necessary," is keyed to the character of Brutus and his killing of Caesar for the good of Rome. In a like manner, statement 4, "Power corrupts, and absolute power corrupts absolutely," is related to Mark Antony's desire for power. In later discussions of the play, you can refer back to how students responded on the opinionnaire and compare their responses to what they actually find in their reading.

This activity links student attitudes and opinions to the ideas and characters in the play by providing a context—a place to start—for understanding the characters, their actions, and their motivations. According to Smagorinsky (1989) and Smagorinsky, McCann, and Kern (1987), this kind of activity establishes a cognitive map that provides a framework for the understanding that is critical to comprehension.

What If Brutus . . . ? Questionnaire

While the Politics, Patriotism, and Protest opinionnaire provides the framework for helping students analyze characters, the next activity is of crucial importance in helping students begin to delve more deeply into the major characters. Once students are fairly well into reading the play, they are ready for the What If Brutus . . . ? character questionnaire (see Figure 2). Adapted from Kahn, Walter, and Johannessen (1984, 29), this activity is designed to give students practice in making inferences about a character, gathering and selecting evidence, and explaining how this evidence supports a conclusion about a major character. In other words, in this activity, students practice orally the skills involved in analyzing and writing about a character in a literary work.

Don't let the format of the activity—multiple-choice questions—deceive you. It is not a test. Rather, the questions are designed to focus on the character of Brutus and take him out of the context of the play and put him in new situations. The catch is, as the directions state, students must use evidence from the text to support their interpretations.

Have students complete the questionnaire on the basis of their understanding of the character. Then, divide the class into small groups and have them try to reach a consensus on their answers. This will usually not be a simple task, since the multiple-choice questions are not designed in a typical fashion. No *one* answer is the correct answer for a given question. For most questions, several of the possible answers might be reasonably defended. The questions are deliberately designed to create disagreement so that the students must actively engage in making inferences, gathering and selecting evidence, and explaining evidence as they argue their choices.

For example, question 3 usually creates considerable debate.

What If Brutus...?

Directions: Read each of the following statements and circle the letter that best completes the statement in terms of what you think would fit the character of Brutus. Be prepared to defend your answers with reasoning based on evidence from the play.

1. If Brutus had been a general in Adolf Hitler's Secret Service, he would have
   A. waited until the right opportunity and then shot Hitler.
   B. hired someone to assassinate Hitler.
   C. worked to overthrow Hitler.
   D. praised Hitler.

2. If Brutus were at a baseball game, he would be
   A. a pitcher.
   B. an umpire.
   C. a fan who sits quietly and enjoys the game.
   D. a fan who harasses players, coaches, and umpires.

3. If people started a campaign today to elect Brutus president, he would
   A. pretend that he didn't want to run.
   B. try to talk them into running a better candidate.
   C. make deals with other political leaders to make sure that he won the election.
   D. refuse to run.

4. If Brutus were at a large family picnic today, he would most likely
   A. go off by himself, sit under a tree, and read a book.
   B. organize and participate in contests and games.
   C. stand around and sulk until someone asked him to participate in the activities.
   D. have long talks with anyone who might give the family a bad name.

5. Brutus would most admire
   A. George Washington.
   B. General H. Norman Schwarzkopf.
   C. Jack the Ripper.
   D. the Beatles.

6. In school, Brutus's favorite course would be
   A. philosophy.
   B. English.
   C. political science.
   D. speech.

7. If Brutus were alive today, he would most likely live
   A. in a mansion.
   B. in a monastery.
   C. in an apartment.
   D. on a farm.

8. Brutus would probably most enjoy a social gathering of
   A. close friends.
   B. family.
   C. Hollywood film stars.
   D. college professors.

9. Today, Brutus's favorite hobby would most likely be
   A. listening to music.
   B. playing cards.
   C. driving race cars.
   D. reading.

10. If Brutus took a vacation today, he would most likely travel to
    A. Washington, D.C.
    B. the Amazon jungles.
    C. Alaska.
    D. Miami Beach.

11. If Brutus were alive today, he would probably be
    A. a computer programmer.
    B. a used car salesman.
    C. a sports announcer.
    D. a lawyer or judge.

12. Brutus's favorite television program would be
    A. a detective show.
    B. a soap opera.
    C. a game show.
    D. a situation comedy.

Figure 2. What If Brutus . . . ? Character Questionnaire

Some students argue that Brutus would try to talk them into running a better candidate, citing his honesty about his own shortcomings and his statements about Caesar's many leadership qualities. Others argue that he would refuse to run for president for the same reason and because he would say others could lead the country much better than he could. Still others say that he is so easily manipulated by others like Mark Antony that he would end up making deals to ensure that he won the election, which unfortunately would lead to his downfall.

At the conclusion of the small-group discussion, have the students reconvene as an entire class. As they discuss each question, disagreements often arise; as they debate back and forth, let them draw conclusions based on evidence from the play. One of the strengths of this activity is that the questions take students outside the experience of the play, and they are encouraged to explore, defend, and elaborate their unique ideas. In addition, for many students, the characters come alive as they make connections between characters in the play and historical figures named in various questions.

As a follow-up writing activity, have students select one of the questions and write a paragraph explaining which of the answers would best fit Brutus and why. I would encourage students to use evidence from the text to support their conclusions. In this way, students are making inferences about character, drawing conclusions from those inferences, and turning their conclusions into written analyses.

Obviously, with minor modifications, similar questionnaires might be constructed for other characters in the play. One interesting variation is to have the students make up questions, or perhaps even whole questionnaires, for other characters.

Values Profile

The next activity I have students do builds on the inferential skills they have practiced in the What If Brutus . . . ? questionnaire. It thus requires increasing sophistication on the part of the students. In the What If Brutus . . . ? questionnaire, students practice making initial inferences, and each question is designed to focus on a single aspect of character. In the Values Profile activity (see Figure 3), students are given a list of twenty-two values that they must rank for two major characters, Brutus and Mark Antony (adapted from Kahn, Walter, and Johannessen 1984, 30–31). They must decide what each character values most and what each character values least. Making this ranking

---

Values Profile

Values

1. Acceptance (approval from others)	8. Health	16. Pleasure
2. Achievement	9. Honesty	17. Power
3. Beauty	10. Justice	18. Recognition
4. Altruism	11. Knowledge	19. Religious faith
5. Independence	12. Love	20. Self-respect
6. Companionship (friendship)	13. Loyalty	21. Skill
7. Creativity	14. Morality	22. Wealth
	15. Physical appearance	

Characters Analyzed _____   _____

	First Character	**Second Character**
What does the character value *most?* List his or her top three values *in order.*	1. _____ 2. _____ 3. _____	1. _____ 2. _____ 3. _____
What does the character value *least?* List his or bottom three values *in order.*	20. _____ 21. _____ 22. _____	20. _____ 21. _____ 22. _____

Be prepared to present *reasons* and *evidence* for your choices.

Figure 3. Values Profile

requires students to make complex inferences. They must consider and weigh many possibilities. And in making their choices and later arguing with peers, students also practice supporting and explaining their conclusions with evidence from the play.

When I hand this activity out to students, I spend a few minutes going over the definitions of terms listed on the sheet. Then I have the students decide which values each character considers most important and which each character considers least important. After they have completed their individual rankings, I put students in small groups and have them try to reach a consensus. As students discuss their rankings in small groups, they make some interesting discoveries. For example, some students think altruism is what Brutus values most, citing his decision to kill Caesar for the good of Rome. Others select morality. After all, they argue, he is the man who will never compromise his standards of what he considers right and wrong. Power, wealth, and justice often appear in the top of Antony's list. At any rate, students soon discover that Brutus and Mark Antony are motivated by very different values. In addition, students often discover that the values they regard as most important to Brutus are very often those they saw as least important to Antony, and vice versa. Most significant, though, is that in discussing their rankings, students find specific and concrete ways to talk about the actions and motives of a character, and they are practicing making and supporting conclusions. And as students debate possible values, they reach a fuller understanding of the character.

Once students reach a consensus in their small groups, I have them debate their ideas in a whole-class discussion. I usually begin by writing the characters' names on the board and under each name writing "1. _____, 2. _____, 3. _____" for possible top values and "20. _____, 21. _____, 22. _____" for possible bottom values. I then go from group to group and ask for their top three and bottom three values for each character. As the groups report, I write in their rankings. While many of the groups have similar values in the top and bottom three rankings, there is never complete agreement.

We then debate the students' ideas in a whole-class discussion. As the groups compare answers and discuss why they ranked a character's values the way they did, the discussion is at a high level because of their previous work. One of the most exciting aspects of the activity is that in order to argue that one value is more important than another, students must look to the text in order to support their interpretations.

Once the class has discussed the values of both characters, we then examine the differences between them. Here students see that it is their different values that at least in part brings Brutus and Antony into conflict. The activity also helps students make inferences about these characters, how they are different, and why they are in conflict. Ultimately, it helps them understand the meaning of the play.

In this activity, students have progressed from making their own independent decisions to refining those ideas and challenging others in small groups to finally debating their conclusions with the whole class. In addition, the discussions help students clarify their interpretations. Hearing what others have to say often helps students refine or change their own interpretations. And comparing the values of the two major characters helps students to make insights about the structure and meaning of the play. Finally, this activity is set up so that students are orally practicing the skills that will help them in writing a character analysis essay.

Sometimes the discussion concludes with most or all of the

students agreeing on rankings for one or both characters. More often than not, however, there is still some disagreement. This disagreement provides an excellent opportunity for students to do a short follow-up writing assignment in which they explain why one value, such as power, is more or less important than another value, such as wealth or justice, to the character of Mark Antony.

Character Analysis Composition

At this point, most students are ready for a more independent activity in which they must use what they have learned in previous activities. One possible culminating writing assignment is to have students compare and contrast the values of Brutus and Mark Antony to determine which would make the better leader and why. This assignment challenges students to apply in an independent and new writing situation the analytical and writing strategies that have been the focus of this series of activities.

Another possible assignment is to have students write a composition focusing on the values of a single character. They might thus determine what Brutus or Mark Antony values most early in the play and then decide what their character values most at or near the end of the play. If a character's values do change, the students might give reasons and evidence for the cause of this change.

The quality of student writing with these assignments is usually quite high. They tend to write some fairly sophisticated analyses of the character or characters. The student compositions also generally use evidence effectively to support their viewpoints. In analyzing the character or characters, many students come upon insights into the central meaning of the play. In short, their essays show how using a series of activities like those I have described enables students to dig deeply into a play. They also show how such a series can provide students with the extended practice that Smith and Hillocks (1988) say is necessary if students are to have the "in-depth knowledge of concepts . . . and discourse conventions" that will enable them "to mature as readers" (48), and, as I argue, as writers.

References

Hirsch, E. D., Jr. 1987. *Cultural Literacy: What Every American Needs to Know.* Boston: Houghton Mifflin.

Kahn, Elizabeth A., Carolyn Calhoun Walter, and Larry R. Johannessen. 1984. *Writing about Literature.* Urbana, IL: ERIC/NCTE.

Rosenblatt, Louise M. 1968. *Literature as Exploration.* Revised edition. New York: Noble and Noble.

Smagorinsky, Peter. 1989. "Small Groups: A New Dimension in Learning." *English Journal* 78 (February): 67–70.

Smagorinsky, Peter, Tom McCann, and Stephen Kern. 1987. *Explorations: Introductory Activities for Literature and Composition, 7–12.* Urbana, IL: ERIC/NCTE.

Smith, Michael W., and George Hillocks, Jr. 1988. "Sensible Sequencing: Developing Knowledge about Literature Text by Text." *English Journal* 77 (October): 44–49.

25 A Whole Language Approach to *Romeo and Juliet*

John Wilson Swope
University of Northern Iowa

Like many high school students, I began my study of Shakespeare with *Romeo and Juliet* in the ninth grade. Although I have forgotten most of what happened in the classroom with thirty-two other students that spring, I realize that I am one of the lucky few who have come to love Shakespeare.

Because *Romeo and Juliet* is usually the first experience that high school students have with Shakespeare, how we as teachers present this particular play affects more than what our students learn about the feud between the Capulets and the Montagues. The students' experience with *Romeo and Juliet* determines how receptive they will be to *Julius Caesar, Macbeth,* and *Hamlet* in subsequent years.

Those of us who have taught *Romeo and Juliet* know how difficult it is for our students to understand the words in the contexts in which Shakespeare uses them. Our students need to make sense of what they have read—to comprehend what they have read—before we can help them understand either the characters or the beauty of the poetry. Although authors and editors of textbooks frequently footnote, providing students with definitions of words and explanations of allusions and concepts, the problem of readability goes beyond the words to the prior knowledge students must bring to reading the play. As Vaughan and Estes (1986) point out, "successful comprehension depends upon one's ability to relate prior knowledge to the information in a reading selection. In fact, comprehension of anything, books included, occurs because the reader can relate concepts to one another, particularly known concepts to new concepts" (107).

As teachers, we know that students have more in common with Romeo and Juliet than they realize. Although the students may know little about Elizabethan verse or Renaissance Italy, they have experienced the pain of adolescence. They know what it is like to maintain a grudge, to love for the first time, or to have parents forbid them to see their friends. When we help students either to recall and organize their prior experiences or to create their own speculative experiences in ways that relate to *Romeo and Juliet,* their comprehension of the Elizabethan verse will improve.

Helping students improve their reading comprehension of the play is the first step. Like all of Shakespeare's plays, however, *Romeo and Juliet* is meant to be performed. Students need to participate in the play. They need to experience the literature as fully as possible. A whole language approach to *Romeo and Juliet* actively involves students in the play. According to Brown and Cambourne (1990), whole language teaching begins with the view that language is not fragmented into the traditional strands of reading, writing, speaking, and listening. Instead, language is viewed "as a single, unitary process, manifesting itself through a range of different, but essentially parallel forms" (23). As a result, using reading, writing, speaking, listening, and viewing in combination fosters overall language growth. In short, a whole language approach expects students not only to read Shakespeare, but to write, talk, listen, and think about the literature as well. The end result is that students achieve a fuller experience with the literature and become active participants in the play, sharing responsibility for learning with the teacher.

Just as we have come to recognize and teach writing as a process, we need to recognize that reading is also a teachable process if we use a whole language approach. Prereading activities help students assess and organize information or personal experiences that relate to what they will read. These activities connect students' prior knowledge to the text. They also assist students in anticipating what may happen next in the play. During-reading activities permit students to actively comprehend what they are reading and to explore the literature. These activities encourage students to take more responsibility for their own learning. Postreading activities allow students to resolve problems they have with the literature and to develop further understanding of the play. Finally, extending activities encourage students to apply what they have learned about the literature to alternative situations. Both postreading and extending activities can assess student learning without using traditional testing.

The following whole language activities are based upon the assumption that a positive experience with literature begins with student response. Indeed, Parsons (1990) argues for the inclusion of students' responses as the beginning of their understanding of literature:

> Students need to be persuaded that the search for meaning starts with their own feelings and experiences. They need to chart and explore those beginnings and then to "step back" and analyze them. They need to see the study of literature as an opportunity to learn more about themselves and the world around them. The study of literature has often been considered an end in itself; we need to convince our students that it's actually a powerful and liberating "means." At the heart of that understanding lies the concept of *personal response*. (11–12)

Nevertheless, these activities are only a sampling of the many that teachers can choose from when students are allowed to become actively involved with the play.

Prereading Activities

I use prereading activities to meet two related goals for *Romeo and Juliet*. The first is to help students assess, organize, and focus their prior knowledge in order to apply it to the scene that they will read. The second is to give students an overall understanding of the action of the play.

Focusing activities can take various forms. I may ask students to improvise a scene, use exploratory writing or speaking, engage in small- or large-group discussions, or view a videotaped version of a scene to help them anticipate what they will read. I generally use only one of these activities for each scene, but I like to have a repertoire of several to call upon. Students like variety in their classroom activities, so the one I use depends on what we may have done in the preceding class period and the type of postreading activity I want to use after we have read for the day. I generally do not use the same activity for both focusing and postreading activities during the same class period.

Improvisations

Asking students to act out an improvisation helps them to connect their personal experience with the action of the play. Consider the following scenario, presented prior to reading the prologue and first scene of *Romeo and Juliet*:

Scene: The school cafeteria or commons area before
             school, at lunch, or immediately after school.
Characters: Pat and Leslie, Jamie and Kim.

Action: Pat and Leslie are good friends and hold a grudge against Jamie and Kim. Pat and Leslie see the other two and want to provoke a fight, yet want to make the administrators and teachers in the area believe that the others started it.

Having four students perform in front of the class requires only a few minutes of preparation. To perform, the students have to draw upon their independent backgrounds, briefly discuss what they would do, and then act out the scene.

For this improvisation, I have had students call each other names, hurl insults, and make threatening gestures. Students have even asked me if they could cuss or make obscene gestures. Although I have had to tell them no, I recognize that they are closer to the action of the play than they realize, for biting one's thumb does have a modern counterpart.

After students become more familiar with the play and its characters, improvisations draw more upon the characters, settings, and situations of the play. For example, this improvisation could precede the students' reading of the scene in which Romeo and Juliet's Nurse meet (II.iv):

Scene: A street in the middle of Verona, Sunday morning.

Characters: Romeo and Juliet's Nurse.

Action: Juliet has sent her Nurse to find out what Romeo's plans are. What does Romeo tell her? How does the Nurse, who wants Juliet to be happy, reply?

Speculations

Another focusing activity is to have students speculate in writing for a few minutes and then share and discuss their responses with either a small group or the class prior to reading a scene. For example, prior to reading the scene in which Romeo and Juliet meet for the first time at the Capulets' ball (I.iii), I present the students with these prompts:

As Romeo, a seventeen-year-old boy, you have just seen and fallen in love with Juliet. Describe the situation and your feelings as you might in a personal diary or journal.

or

As Juliet, a fourteen-year-old girl, you have just seen and fallen in love with Romeo. Describe the situation and your feelings as you might in a personal diary or journal.

Small-Group Discussion

Another focusing activity is to have students discuss specifically prepared questions as a small-group activity. For example, these questions could precede the reading of the scene in which Mercutio and Tybalt die (III.i):

> At the end of Act II, Friar Laurence marries Romeo and Juliet, hoping to end the feud between the Capulets and Montagues. So, what seems to be a happy ending has occurred prior to the middle of the play. Yet let's review lines 5–8 from the prologue:
>
> > From forth the fatal loins of these two foes,
> > A pair of star-crossed lovers take their life:
> > whose misadventured piteous overthrows
> > Doth with their death bury their parents' strife.
>
> From these lines, what do you think will happen to Romeo and Juliet? Whom do you think will be involved to bring about the unhappy ending that the prologue predicts?

Viewing Videotape

Instead of waiting to view *Romeo and Juliet* after the students have completed the play, show students a scene from either a movie or television production of the play prior to reading it. Follow the viewing with a brief discussion and then proceed to read the scene. This activity helps students to focus and better understand the scene they are going to read. And since reading all scenes may not be beneficial with some groups, various scenes might be viewed rather than read.

Prose Summaries

To further meet the second goal for prereading activities, I provide students with a prose summary of the scene that they are about to read. Because Shakespeare's plays have complex plots and numerous literary allusions that students may not understand on the first reading, these summaries serve as "road maps." While many texts do provide a one- or two-line synopsis of each scene, these rarely help students when they get lost in the middle of a scene. Thus, I make sure that my own summaries contain enough detail to cover both the overall action of the scene as well as the digressions that may occur. For example, before reading I.iv, which contains one of *Romeo and Juliet's* greatest digressions, Mercutio's "Queen Mab" speech, I provide students with the following summary:

> *Act I, scene iv.* Later that evening in the street, Romeo and his friends, Benvolio and Mercutio, a cousin of the prince, have

put on masks to crash the Capulets' party. Mercutio delivers the "Queen Mab" speech. Queen Mab is the fairy queen that Mercutio describes as coming to bewitch men in her tiny carriage made of a hazelnut shell, a carriage with a cover of grasshoppers' wings and wagon spokes of spiders' legs, all drawn by motes driven by a liveried gnat. Romeo, before leaving for the party, states that he fears some serious events will result from this evening.

These brief summaries assist students in two ways. First, they enhance students' understanding of the particular scene. Second, they keep the students interested in reading further.

During-Reading Activities

While prereading activities help set up the reading for the students, during-reading activities allow students to test the presumptions, speculations, and assumptions they make while they read. These activities actively engage students in comprehending and exploring the play.

Organization of Group Reading

Like many teachers, I prefer to have students read parts of *Romeo and Juliet* aloud in class. Even though their reading will be halting and awkward, having students hear the language as well as read it promotes better understanding. Yet rather than have this oral reading occur as a whole class activity, I divide the class into groups of six to eight students and have each group read aloud simultaneously. Although the play has twenty-five speaking parts, I have found that when we have read it as a whole class, only a few students actively participate. Dividing the class into smaller groups involves all of the students.

Prior to reading specific scenes for a given class period, I review them and identify the number of characters necessary for each scene. I then assign parts to particular readers, combining several smaller roles for some readers while assigning major roles to others. In determining who reads what part, I avoid having any one student read two parts that speak directly to each other. Because there are few women's roles in any Shakespearean play, I assign male roles to female students. From day to day, I also vary the students who read the major roles, so that all students get involved. Here is a sample role assignment chart for the play's prologue and first scene that requires only six readers:

Reader	Roles
Steve	Sampson, Lord Capulet
Tanya	Gregory, Citizens, Lady Capulet
Sanjay	Abraham, Lord Montague
Krista	Chorus, Benvolio
Joanna	Tybalt, Lady Montague
Hector	Officer, Prince Escalus, Romeo

While students are reading, I encourage them to pause and reflect upon what they read as they read it. This allows them to discuss the presumptions, speculations, and assumptions they made prior to reading the particular scene. If their predictions turn out to have been wrong, they can always take the new information, attach it to their previous predictions, and form new ones. If their predictions were correct, then the brief discussion further enhances their understanding of the play.

We also need to encourage students to read with pencils in hand. With Shakespeare, the student is reading a foreign dialect, if not a foreign language. As a variation upon Vaughn and Estes's (1986, 136–41) INSERT strategy, have students use hard lead pencils and place light check marks in the margin of sections that they understand and question marks beside those that they do not. Plus signs in the margins signify confirmation of prereading predictions, while minus signs indicate contradictions. Whatever the strategy, students must be writing and discussing intermittently while they read—comprehending, reacting, and questioning.

Response Journals

The response journal, which is based upon Bleich's (1975) subjective criticism, provides a place for students to use language to make sense of what they are reading or have just read. The emotional response allows the students to rant and rave, to be affected emotionally by the text. The associative response permits them to make a connection between what they have read and their own lives. Responding to features lets students dwell on language that attracts their attention for some reason and provides opportunities for better understanding of particular scenes. And the problem section allows students to record questions or note troubles that they are having while they read.

When I begin using a response journal with students, I give them the following directions:

Response Journal Assignment

Although we often read silently, reading is an active process. As we run our eyes across a line of text, we transform the letters and words into mental images. Moreover, words have the power to affect us in many ways. The purpose of a response journal is to help you as a reader verbalize several different types of responses immediately after you've read and to assist you in recalling the experiences prior to a discussion.

Your response journal is a personal place for you to react to the play. You may wish to do it as you read or immediately upon finishing a reading assignment. It won't be nearly as effective if you put it off! There are four types of responses you should make each time. None of these needs to be more than a brief paragraph.

1. How does the play make you feel at this point? Record your reactions in a few sentences and then explore each for a few minutes, trying to figure out why you feel as you do.

2. What persons, places, or ideas from your own experiences came to your mind while you were reading this portion of the play? Try to list three to five associations. Don't worry about trying to figure out why they came to mind, just accept that they occur.

3. What portions of Shakespeare's language attracts your attention? These might be individual words, phrases, lines, scenes, or images. Try to select the particular features that you feel are most important to the meaning of the play. Speculate for a few minutes about what you think they might mean and why they are important.

4. Make note of any portion of the play, either in its language or in its events, that seems to cause you problems. Note any questions that you might ask.

Here is a sample journal for the scene in which Lady Capulet first mentions the idea of marriage to Juliet (I.iii):

1. The Nurse certainly does like to hear herself talk! Small wonder Lady Capulet becomes impatient. Juliet here doesn't seem to know very much. She seems uninterested in the idea of love. I like the honesty of Juliet's wait-and-see attitude. I want to read on.

2. I get impatient when my sister monopolizes the conversation. I've taken a wait-and-see attitude when presented with meeting new people. When the Nurse talks about her daughter playing with Juliet, I remember watching the children in my neighborhood play together. My great aunt used to talk for hours about nothing.

3. At the end of the scene, Lady Capulet asks Juliet, "Speak briefly, can you like of Paris' love?" Juliet replies, "I'll look to like, if looking liking move." I like the way the meaning

shifts with each form of *look* and *like*. Juliet seems to say, "I'll try, Mom. I'll look at Paris to see if I like him."

4. What does the Nurse mean when she says that "women grow by men"?

Postreading Activities

Postreading activities help students make sense of their explorations of the play and come to an overall understanding of it. In a teacher-centered classroom, either teacher-led whole group discussions or teacher-prepared lectures on the "real meaning" of the text have been common. Often the primary means of assessing students' comprehension and understanding is a test or quiz composed of multiple-choice or other "objective" test items. Yet full comprehension does not occur immediately for all students. Instead, most need help making sense of the literature. Using a student-centered whole language approach, a teacher can determine whether students understand what they have read without relying upon objective quizzes.

One way of doing this is for the teacher to skim through the students' response journals, paying particular attention to the students' associations with the text and the important features that attracted their attention. The teacher also needs to answer any questions that students record about the reading. I respond to each student's journal in some positive way. Because I recognize the response journal as a form of exploratory writing-to-learn, I ignore all errors in grammar, usage, and mechanics (GUM). I usually write my responses in the margin and keep them as brief as possible. After reading the students' response journals, I know which students are having problems, what areas of the play need more attention in class, and which parts of the play the students clearly understand.

Another means to assess students' comprehension is to allow them to improvise, using their own language, the action of particular scenes. As the student actors get stuck, I allow other students either to side-coach the actors or to replace them at a particular moment. When questions arise, I direct the students back to the text to resolve the problem. This activity not only allows me to assess where the students are in their understanding of the play, but also helps the students immediately increase that understanding.

Probably the most common postreading activity is to provide students with specific discussion questions and have them answer them in either small or large groups. Christenbury and Kelly's (1983) approach to questioning focuses the discussion upon a single dense questions, the only one that students need to have presented to them in writing. They encourage the teacher to develop this question after examining the interactions between the text, the students' personal experiences, and world/other literature. These interactions should produce six other questions that the teacher can use to assist the students in their explorations of the dense question.

To illustrate, I have developed the following questions for use after the students have finished reading Act III, which begins with the slayings of Mercutio and Tybalt and ends with Lord Capulet's threat to throw Juliet out of the house if she does not marry Paris:

> Dense question: If Juliet were a friend of yours today, what advice would you give her at this point?

Questions to help students explore the dense question:

1. Compare Juliet's reactions in both I.iii and III.v to her parents' news that she will marry Paris. How do you account for the differences in Juliet's responses?

2. In other works of literature that you've read, how have the characters sought revenge against others?

3. When have you acted to maintain your reputation or to keep up appearance rather than simply stating how you felt?

4. To what extent do you think Mercutio's and Tybalt's fighting is motivated by revenge and to what extent do you think it is motivated by their desires to maintain their reputations as excellent swordsmen?

5. When you act to maintain a reputation or receive attention, how do your peers react? How do adults that may observe your actions react?

6. If you lived in a society in which you were totally dependent upon your parents, as Juliet does, what circumstances would cause you to risk being thrown out of the house and have society scorn you as an ungrateful child?

Extending Activities

Once students have developed their understanding of the play through prereading, during-reading, and postreading activities, extending activities encourage students to apply their learning to alternative situations. Students can complete these activities individually or in groups. No matter how they are used, though, these activities should be fun for the students. Extending activities also provide the teacher with an alternative to a unit test as a means to assess students' learning.

Improvisation

Throughout this essay, I have included improvisation as both a predictive reading strategy and a means to check comprehension. When using improvisation as an extending activity, I urge students to apply their understanding from the play to a new situation. Here are a few sample situations that students might try:

1. Suppose you are a guidance counselor, Ms. Laurence. How do you suppose you would counsel Romeo about his problems in II.iii, II.vi, III.iii, and V.i?

2. What would the apothecary who sold the illegal poison to Romeo say to his wife when he returned from being awakened?

3. It's after the party at the Capulets'. Tybalt is still angry about Romeo and his friends crashing the party. He calls the young men of the Capulet household together and convinces them to seek revenge. What does he say?

Puppets and Masks

Although students enjoy acting out scenes on their own, some often feel that they need to have costumes and props. While this is possible when the teacher has his or her own classroom, it is not feasible for those teachers who move from room to room. An alternative, then, might be for students to use puppets and masks. Indeed, using puppets and masks often makes students more comfortable during classroom performances, as the student actor literally has something to hide behind, something to use to become someone else. Even the most reluctant students get involved when they can use puppets or masks.

Students can make simple puppets from paper bags. Any sized brown paper bag that has a flat bottom can serve. Using any type of stiff drawing paper, have students draw and cut out the head and upper face of the puppet and mount it on the flat bottom of the bag. The mouth and lower part of the face, as well as the body of the puppet, are mounted on the side of the bag over which the bottom folds. Insert a hand into the bag, keeping the bag partially folded, and move the upper part of the hand to make the puppet talk. Turning a table on its side makes an adequate stage for the puppets. And placing the table in front of a bulletin board or blank wall makes an ideal place to hang a mural if the students feel the need for a backdrop.

Students can make simple masks from large white paper plates. Simply have them cut two eyeholes, draw on the plates with markers or crayons, and decorate them with yarn or paper hair. The students can then attach strings to tie on the masks or mount them on dowels to hold in front of them while performing.

Writing Assignments

Writing assignments as postreading activities are not new. In a whole language classroom where students have been introduced to *Romeo and Juliet* for the first time, writing assignments tend not to be literary analyses. Instead, writing tasks provide students with opportunities to incorporate their new understanding of the play into a piece of writing. The following examples are starting points for process writing instruction and permit students to demonstrate their understanding of the play:

1. Based on your understanding of the play, write a letter as one of the characters listed below to a cousin living in Venice, another Italian city-state. Relate the events of the play and your response to them.

   Escalus, Prince of Verona   Lord Montague
   Lord Capulet   Benvolio
   Friar Laurence   Balthasar
   Juliet's Nurse   Lady Capulet
   Peter, the Nurse's servant

2. Early in the play, Romeo tells Friar Laurence that he has fallen in love with Rosaline but that he is out of favor with her. Write both a note from Romeo to Rosaline and her answer to it.

Romeo and Juliet is often students' introduction to Shakespeare. Although the play is difficult to read, the experience is worth the trouble. To become actively engaged in the experience of the play, students need to use all of their linguistic abilities to understand it. Whole language activities permit students to read, write, listen, speak, and view in response to the play. Providing these activities to students also enhances their understanding of the Elizabethan verse. With guidance and patience from the teacher, students take on more responsibility for their own learning and come to better understand the play. And when students experience success with *Romeo and Juliet*, they become more receptive to other plays as well.

References

Bleich, David. 1975. *Readings and Feelings: An Introduction to Subjective Criticism.* Urbana, IL: NCTE.

Brown, Hazel, and Brian Cambourne. 1990. *Read and Retell: A Strategy for the Whole-Language/Natural Learning Classroom.* Portsmouth, NH: Heinemann.

Christenbury, Leila, and Patricia P. Kelly. 1983. *Questioning: A Path to Critical Thinking.* ERIC/RCS Theory and Research into Practice (TRIP) Monograph Series. Urbana, IL: ERIC/NCTE.

Parsons, Les. 1990. *Response Journals.* Portsmouth, NH: Heinemann; Markham, Ontario: Pembroke.

Shakespeare, William. 1959. *The Tragedy of Romeo and Juliet.* Edited by Virginia A. LaMar and Louis B. Wright. The Folger Library General Reader's Shakespeare. New York: Washington Square Press.

Vaughn, Joseph L., and Thomas H. Estes. 1986. *Reading and Reasoning beyond the Primary Grades.* Boston: Allyn and Bacon.

26 "Sleep that knits up the raveled sleave of care": Responding to *Macbeth* through Metaphorical Character Journals

Gregory L. Rubano
Toll Gate High School, Warwick, Rhode Island

Philip M. Anderson
Queens College-CUNY

The importance of reader-response theory to the improvement of literature study in the schools is not tied solely to contemporary literature. Reader-response activities are a necessary part of the literature curriculum, and we must apply them to what remains the core of that curriculum: Shakespeare's plays.

The most common activity for promoting literary response is the use of classroom journals. Journals used during the reading of the text normally allow students to record personal responses or, in some cases, to respond to analytical questions posed by the teacher. Employed in these ways, journals provide a means for affective response and analytical interpretation. When differently employed, however, journals can provide the means for aesthetic response to a literary text as well.

One way to accomplish this aesthetic aim is to require journal writing done in literary frameworks. In fact, we have found that assigning journal writing tasks that require students to come up with their own literary creations is more likely to produce aesthetic responses to the text. This may be so because such responses have a greater affinity with the text: that is, both the student's response and the literary text at hand are in literary language. For this sort of journal assignment, the formality and length of the literary responses are not as important as their poetic form and intention. And, practically, not every journal entry need be in a literary form to promote aesthetic response.

One specific approach to responding through literary form is the metaphor. Especially pertinent in responding to Shakespeare's figurative language, metaphorical writing is a key way of representing aesthetic response. Unfortunately, literary studies frequently treat metaphor as ornamental, as merely a figure of speech. Nevertheless, metaphor is a form of representing experience, a form of representation that lies at the heart of literary cognition. Metaphorical writing directs the attention of the reader to the aesthetic language qualities of the Shakespearean text, which is, after all, verse drama.

Character Journals

One popular type of journal is the character journal—a journal that focuses on a character's developing thoughts and feelings. In the following activities, the students write in metaphorical forms, assuming a character's identity and imagining what sort of thoughts or dreams that character might record in a journal. The students thus use metaphorical constructions to recast in poetic form their understandings of a literary character. In this way, students are writing a poetic text in response to a poetic text.

The metaphorical journal writing below is embedded within various condensed and highly symbolic structures, and often within a dream narrative as well. In all cases, the metaphor's intrinsic operation as an organizing agent is brought to bear. The following activities demonstrate that this organization encompasses a different psychology and function when an aesthetic form of response is used to represent the interiority of a character. The journal writing itself takes two forms: the in-process journal and the final journal.

The In-process Journal

First students are asked to compose journal entries as they read. Not all of these entries are metaphorical; students often choose to write plain description of a character's reactions to the events and situations in the play. Nevertheless, using the structural prompts given by the teacher, the students must also include metaphorical responses that acknowledge the feelings of the character at selected moments in the work. The teacher's role is to generate additional questions and considerations that both capitalize on the metaphor's components and associations and serve as a stimulus for further reflection and reconceptualization. Examples of questions that could be used for such purposes are listed after the specific student examples cited below.

For this activity, then, students are presented with a prompt that includes both a metaphorical context for the writing and a specific moment in the text to apply it to. Following a review of each student's creation, the teacher responds to its implications and introduces a different metaphorical context and another moment.

Prompt

It is the night before the assassination. Macbeth is writing in his journal after having a dream involving a tightrope walker.

Student example

Macbeth speaking: ". . . I dreamed Lady Macbeth was on the other side of a tightrope I was attempting to cross. The rope is covered with a black substance and yet my Lady's feet are clean."

Possible teacher responses

From what platform is Lady Macbeth leaving?

How far across the rope is Macbeth at this point?

Has he ever lost his balance? How did Lady Macbeth keep her balance?

How can you represent this in the analogy?

Where does she go once she has reached this platform?

How does Macbeth's soliloquy at the end of Act I relate to your analogy?

Which of Lady Macbeth's words reveal how she has seemingly traversed the path without touching the rope?

Is it really possible to travel over this black substance and not pick up any "black substance"?

Prompt

Macbeth has a dream the night of Banquo's ghost's visitation. The dream involves the building of a wall.

Student example

Macbeth speaking: "I couldn't do it! With the rain it was impossible to build the wall. When I looked over to Lady Macbeth, I could no longer see her. All I could see was the wall that she had built. Frantically, I sped up my wall building but the rain continued to wash the mortar away. . . .

"Now I've got it. The trick is to build the stone wall around myself. The rain no longer washes the mortar away. The wall grows and I reach the top and join Lady Macbeth. The rain has stopped and the sun appears. The hot beams of the sun begin to make the mortar crack. We take no notice."

Possible teacher responses

What does the rain represent?

Which lines in the play suggest Macbeth's cognizance of such rain?

Which of Macbeth's words indicate to you that he is becoming increasingly immune to the calls of his conscience?

At this point in the play, how would Lady Macbeth interpret this dream?

Is the mortar defective?

What stones are needed to build such a wall?

Why not make the wall freestanding?

Other possible prompts

Macbeth is writing in his journal comparing himself to a gymnast on an apparatus of your choosing. Or use a wall-building metaphor again. Be prepared to discuss at what point in the play this journal entry could have been written.

Student example

"I advance toward the pommel horse. My speed is so important for the vault. I spring toward the horse and vault over it beautifully. I can't remember touching the horse itself. My landing, however, is jarring."

Possible teacher responses

At what exact point in the play is this journal entry written?

What injuries has Macbeth suffered?

How can they be healed?

Student example

"As I sleep my mind plays with my thoughts. I see a pile of blocks next to a wheelbarrel of mortar. Then the blocks float up, as if it were a cartoon, and dip themselves into the mortar. They place themselves one on top of another. Soon a fenced-in area is formed. It is raining out, but I can see that this area is one of many such areas on the edge of a small town. Next, I see the wall take itself apart so that its height is halved. Because there are blocks left over, a larger area is formed. The sun comes out, and I discover that the wall is on top of a hill in the middle of a city with smaller walls around it."

Possible teacher responses

At what point in the play does this "scene" occur?

What forces are at work in this "scene"?

What exists inside the fenced-in area?

What does the rain represent, and how does it affect the mortar?

What is being suggested by the presence of the extra, unused blocks?

Can these unused blocks be made to construct a wall? With the same mortar?

Using specific lines from the play to make your case, discuss what the smaller walls surrounding the city's core represent. For example, when were they built? Are they constructed of the same material as the others?

Another exercise for the in-process journal involves the use of metaphorical couplets. At a point designated by the teacher, the students, *as a class*, are asked to compose a series of first lines that begin with "Once I . . ." These lines are meant to suggest a stage or a feeling that a character has experienced at some point in the play. Then, individually, the students complete the second line, "Now I . . .," and choose one of these couplets to represent what they perceive to be the present condition of the character.

The students are asked to compose a minimum of five such metaphorical couplets and insert them at different points in their journal. The journal entry itself is composed of the actual text lines that the student believes evokes the couplet followed by the couplet itself. Since students share all couplets with partners, and since a "pool" of such creations is collected, they may on occasion select the same or derivative couplets. In fact, it is interesting to see such nuances of response. Some student examples (including the text to which each couplet corresponds) follow.

"When you durst do it, then you were a man; / And to be more than you were, you would / Be so much more the man" (I.vii.49–51).

> Once the wind whistled softly.
> Now it rings in my ears.

"But now I am cabin'd, cribb'd, confin'd, bound in / To saucy doubts and fears" (III.iv.23–24).

> Once I danced in the swaying grass.
> Now I trip on the weeds.

"I have almost forgot the taste of fears. / The time has been, my senses would have cool'd / To hear a night-shriek" (V.v.9–11).

> Once the sun shone brightly on me.
> Now I am cast in shadow.

"And that which should accompany old age, / As honor, love, obedience, troops of friends, / I must not look to have; but in their stead, / Curses, not loud, but deep" (V.iii.24–27).

> Once I gazed at the sparkling stars.
> Now the stars pierce my eyes.

"To-morrow, and to-morrow, and to-morrow, / Creeps in this petty pace from day to day, / To the last syllable of recorded time / . . . / . . . It is a tale / Told by an idiot, full of sound and fury, / Signifying nothing" (V.v.19–28).

> Once I spun about wildly and fell.
> Now I spin infinitely.

"I have no spur / To prick the sides of my intent, but only / Vaulting ambition, which o'erleaps itself, / And falls on th' other—" (I.vii.25–28).

> Once I spun about wildly and fell.
> Now I spin and cannot stop.

"Glamis, and Thane of Cawdor! / The greatest is behind" (I.iii.116–17).

> Once I danced in muddy pools.
> Now the mud dances upon me.

"I cannot fly, / But bear-like I must fight the course. What's he / That was not born of woman? Such a one / Am I to fear, or none" (V.vii.2–4).

> Once I danced in muddy pools.
> Now the mud dances upon me.

"I am settled, and bend up / Each corporeal agent to this terrible feat" (I.vii.79–80).

> Once I swung among the tree tops.
> Now the rope breaks forever.

"I am sick at heart / . . . / I have liv'd long enough; my way of life / Is fall'n into the sear, the yellow leaf" (V.iii.19–23).

> Once I floated in the wind's gust.
> Now the wind sweeps me away.

It is exciting to see the range of metaphorical applications that this exercise elicits. As the examples reveal, the "once-now" couplets seem to add a moral reflection or a concrete, expressionistic portrayal of Macbeth's psychological disposition. We would argue that the drama of these writings is in the language, both Shakespeare's and the students'. It seems almost a transgression for English teachers not to give the students an opportunity to respond from such a poetic vantage.

We do not ask students to defend their couplet or to discourse upon its relationship to the text they have chosen. These images are not meant to illustrate Shakespeare's lines. Of course, their richness and intensity are responses to a most gracious, careful, and obliging host: Shakespeare's language. Nevertheless, the imaging and apprehension of the metaphors are, in fact, "ways of knowing," and the students' metaphors represent their understandings in a distinct way, a way that cannot be rendered in other forms.

The Final Journal

Written after the students have completed their reading of the play, the final journal asks students to review the in-process journal entries that were offered as tentative understandings. As they reread these entries, they are free to delete, expand, or refine their conjectures. They may also add additional entries, including those composed for moments in the play that they may have previously ignored or not fully appreciated. What is *required* is that they return to previously introduced metaphors and "update" and extend them so as to represent the latest conditions—and reflections—of the character.

The final metaphorical journal entries are meant to be consistent responses to questions previously raised. Essentially a rewriting of the in-process journal, the final journal represents the students' polished and formal renderings of their current conclusions. Some examples of student entries follow.

Student A: Wall analogy—Macbeth's dream the night before the assassination

"Huge gray bricks quickly slide across undisturbed earth and position themselves in the shape of a circular wall. They leave a deep gouged path behind themselves and appear menacing and omnipresent. A sky that just moments ago was blue and scattered with a few clouds turns dark and cold, allowing no light to penetrate it. The wall grows higher and higher and eventually stops a few inches above his head."

Wall analogy—after the assassination

"I stand atop a slight hill in an infinitely visible field. Blocks come flying from all around and surround me. The wall grows higher and higher and higher . . ."

Student B: Tightrope walker—Lady Macbeth before the assassination

"There is a large net beneath Lady Macbeth. She is almost to the very end. There is a spotlight; however, it is panning the audience and never shines upon her flaunting silhouette. Her balancing rod is especially long. She seems to be overpowering the rope, forcing it to be stable, to not shake."

Tightrope walker—last act of the play

"The rope is very fragile, almost limp. Asleep, Lady Macbeth is walking backwards. The spotlight blinds her. As she walks along the rope, she continually rubs her hands. Every time she speaks, she almost loses her balance. She finally falls from the rope but lands in the safety net. She climbs out of the net and falls to the ground."

Student C: Tightrope walker—Macbeth following the killing of Banquo

"With a final jump, I have reached the other side of the rope, but as I step upon the platform, the spotlight snaps on, white light pouring down upon my face. The voices of the audience can now be heard. I look back at the rope; it seems thinner than before; it disintegrates. I cannot go back at all.

But, as I look forward, it seems as if a line of tightropes stretches out endlessly before me."

Tightrope walker—following Macbeth's second encounter with the witches

"It is odd how easily my feet glide over the tightropes now. Once my feet stuck firm in the grip of my conscience. Now they slip over the ice that is my soul."

Aesthetic Reading and Response

The approach to Shakespeare presented above draws its theoretical rationale from research and theory in reader response, especially the theories of Louise Rosenblatt (1978). Rosenblatt argues that literary reading is accomplished only by assuming an aesthetic psychological stance toward a text and that aesthetic reading is a necessary element both in learning to read literature and in developing a full range of language functions. Reading literature in a nonaesthetic way not only denies our students literary experience, but hinders their socio-psy-cholinguistic development as well (Anderson and Rubano 1991).

Rosenblatt distinguishes between reading from an *aesthetic* stance—focusing on the "lived-through" experience of the text—and reading from an *efferent* stance—focusing on what the reader carries away from the text (22ff). The efferent/aesthetic relationship represents a continuum, with variable attention to each depending on the text at hand and one's purpose in reading. The psychological stance for reading informational texts, for example, would be toward the efferent end of the scale, while the stance for literary reading would be near the aesthetic end. For the student to achieve an aesthetic stance in a classroom setting, the teacher must structure the reading task to promote the aesthetic end of the continuum; that is, the teacher must provide language activities that promote an aesthetic response.

As we suggested previously, requiring tasks that evoke literary forms of response is a surer way to promote the aesthetic stance than requiring tasks that use nonliterary language. Our reasoning on this issue is framed by the research and theory of James Britton and his colleagues (1975). They have developed a theoretical system describing writing that parallels Rosenblatt's reading theories. The poles of Britton's continuum are *transactional* writing—writing to communicate with an audience or accomplish a task—and *poetic* writing—writing to represent a world view or picture an experience. Transactional discourse normally assumes a known and definable audience, while poetic discourse is addressed to an undefined audience.

Transactional emphasis produces letters and essays; poetic emphasis produces stories and poems. Most school writing, especially in response to literature, is of the transactional variety, especially if the task is perceived as communicating a point of view to a defined audience of "teacher." Given a transactional approach to response, readers are more likely to assume an efferent stance toward the text. Conversely, assigning poetic discourse forms for response would promote an aesthetic stance toward the text.

We are not suggesting that transactional writing necessarily requires an efferent stance toward a text; but as Susan Hynds (1989) and others have discovered in studying English literature classrooms, this is generally the case. Moreover, using expressive writing (what Britton calls writing done for an audience of oneself)—the type of writing normally asked for in journal writing—does not promote an aesthetic stance as much as a subjectivist critical approach. Only the assignment of poetic discourse maintains the psychological focus most appropriate to aesthetic reading and response.

Conclusion

Ideally, Shakespeare's plays and all literary texts would be approached aesthetically, that is, as verbal art. Unfortunately, as Maxine Greene (1981) argues, literature study, though one of the few artistic domains of the traditional academic curriculum, is unlikely to be studied from an aesthetic point of view (116, 118). The limited view of reading and thinking that dominates the schools usually reduces literature study to the traditional formal analysis of texts and the study of historical artifacts.

Reader-response approaches to literature study seek to remedy this situation by promoting aesthetic responses to literary texts. Providing structure so that students assume an aesthetic stance toward a literary work in the classroom means moving beyond our routines and rethinking our notions of writing about literature. Nevertheless, it is one of the responsibilities of the English teacher to provide aesthetic language experience, especially in a school curriculum dominated by functional and analytical reasoning. And, finally, doesn't the most gifted writer in English deserve readers who perceive and respond to the beauty in his works?

References

Anderson, Philip M., and Gregory Rubano. 1991. *Enhancing Aesthetic Reading and Response.* Urbana, IL: NCTE.

Britton, James, et al. 1975. *The Development of Writing Abilities (11–18).* Schools Council Research Studies. London: Macmillan.

Greene, Maxine. 1981. "Aesthetic Literacy in General Education." In *Philosophy and Education,* edited by Kenneth J. Rehage and Jonas F. Soltis, 115–41. 80th Yearbook of the National Society for the Study of Education, Part I. Chicago: University of Chicago Press.

Hynds, Susan. 1989. "Bringing Life to Literature and Literature to Life: Social Constructs and Contexts of Four Adolescent Readers." *Research in the Teaching of English* 23.1 (February): 30–61.

Rosenblatt, Louise M. 1978. *The Reader, the Text, the Poem: The Transactional Theory of the Literary Work.* Carbondale, IL: Southern Illinois University Press.

27 Building a Bridge to Shakespeare's *Macbeth* with Cormier's *The Chocolate War*

Margo A. Figgins
University of Virginia

Alan Smiley
Kent Denver School, Englewood, Colorado

"I think Macbeth's acting just like Archie, thinking he's too cool to ever get burned!" Imagine this moment in the classroom when a student discovers Archie (from *The Chocolate War,* Cormier 1974) at the very heart of Macbeth. Such moments make the teacher's task of guiding students through the intricacies of theme, character, and symbolism feel more exciting and possible. Students have experienced Macbeth's "kind" before, and in a more familiar context. The path of discovery is suddenly lit.

Engineering an enthusiastic encounter with Shakespeare's *Macbeth* or a similarly difficult text for a class of twelfth-grade students is every senior English teacher's annual challenge. Young-adult novels remain a largely untapped pool of literature for meeting such challenges. While many young-adult novels exhibit stylistic excellence, perhaps one of their greatest strengths is their ability to make complex human issues—pride, greed, fear, deceit—more accessible to teenagers. Although many of these works are worthy of independent examination, a careful pairing of quality young-adult literature with traditional and often more difficult works can broaden the range of good literature available to young adults. It can also provide an essential "bridge" (Farrell 1966) into the literary themes and techniques characteristic of canonical works.

We illustrate this pairing process with *The Chocolate War* and *Macbeth*. Our discussion includes elements common to both works, including thematic relationships and selected strategies for evoking student response. It does not include an exhaustive analysis of either work. Rather, our purpose is to sketch a process for providing greater access to a difficult text, a process that can ultimately lead students to a more critical reading of the work at hand.

Introducing *The Chocolate War*

"They murdered him." This simple opening paragraph introduces the protagonist of *The Chocolate War*, Jerry Renault, a freshman at Trinity High School whom the football team and its coach are testing for his toughness. Can he take the abuse? The bigger test, however, lies ahead of him: the candy campaign, organized by the corrupt Brother Leon, a teacher whose decisions serve only his own greed and overwhelming desire for power. In this test, Jerry finds his own standard of measurement; he refuses to sell the fifty boxes of chocolates assigned to him. This brings upon him the heat of the school gang, the Vigils, led by Archie Costello, whom Leon employs to do his dirty work. As Jerry's resolve deepens with each attempt to break him, so does Archie's vengeance, culminating in a climactic boxing match that leaves Jerry both physically and psychologically battered on the same field where his story opened. Jerry's daring attempt to disturb the universe thus dissolves into unmitigated violence, leaving him utterly alone with "the sickness of knowing what he had become, another animal, . . . another violent person in a violent world, . . . not disturbing the universe but damaging it. He had allowed Archie to do this to him."

In beginning study of *The Chocolate War*, and thence into *Macbeth*, we recommend starting with an expressive writing activity that focuses students on the issue of authority figures. By focusing on people who have influence over them—parents, teachers, coaches, peers—and who sometimes coerce or otherwise pressure them to act against their will, students examine the politics of power in their lives. Using Gary Gildner's poem "First Practice" will lend powerful dramatization to the relationship between control and power through the voice of an athletic coach coercing players to perform like hungry men:

> . . . [he] said
> he was Clifford Hill, he was
> a man who believed dogs
> ate dogs, he had once killed
> for his country, and if

there were any girls present
for them to leave now.
                              No one
left. OK, he said, he said I take
that to mean you are hungry
men who hate to lose as much
as I do . . .
(Gildner, in Janeczko 1983)

Students may extend their response by selecting an authority figure in their own lives and, with "First Practice" as a model, by writing their own poems representing how someone exercises power over them. In this way, the poem connects students to the initial conflict in *The Chocolate War,* as experienced by Jerry, and thus helps to establish a reference point for the students' eventual discussion of the way in which Lady Macbeth exerts control over Macbeth's actions.

Considering Shared Themes

With this introduction, students have anticipated a central theme that *The Chocolate War* shares with *Macbeth*: individual will versus institutionalized authority. Much of the novel focuses on those who victimize others to gain social power, enabling students to more readily consider in both the novel and the play the behavior of characters both inside and outside the power structure. From this vantage point, students can more critically view times when they themselves have behaved in similar ways, as well as ferret out character inconsistencies.

A second theme, tyranny, is also fundamental to the comprehension of both works, especially if students are to see possible alternatives to the outcomes in each. The teacher can facilitate students' more critical perceptions by raising these questions:

- What is meant by "tyrant"?
- How does a tyrant exercise authority differently from other types of leaders?
- Who in the novel fits the category of "tyrant"?
- What other models of leadership does Cormier offer?

Once students have arrived at these distinctions, their discussion can extend to more complex issues, such as why characters abuse their power, how these characters are affected by forces stronger than themselves, and why others capitulate to their power. Students might also explore the dichotomies of power by creating a dialogue between the tyrant and the tyrant's victim. In assuming the personas of tyrant and victim, oppressor and oppressed, students may be led to see aspects of each character that might otherwise remain hidden. These same aspects can then become lenses for looking into the souls of Macbeth, Lady Macbeth, Duncan, and Malcolm.

A third theme that will inform students' encounter with *Macbeth* is that of good versus evil. While maintaining character roundness, both Cormier and Shakespeare construct some characters who appear entirely good (Jerry and Malcolm) and others who appear wholly evil (Archie and Lady Macbeth). If students begin by considering the relative moral stature of various characters (e.g., If Goober is "good," how does his "goodness" compare to Jerry's? Or, what does Carter do or say that suggests he could never arrive at the degree of evil Archie embodies?), an animated discussion can develop around why some characters deserve the label of "good" while others warrant that of "evil." So engaged, students can more effectively consider in *Macbeth* the limits of such categories and the morally grey area in between.

Exploring Symbolism in *The Chocolate War*

Exploring Cormier's use of symbolism will deepen students' initial encounter with themes. This is an important step, not only for understanding the different levels of meaning at work in *The Chocolate War,* but also for creating a vocabulary and a process with which to explore the symbolic dimension of *Macbeth.* In small groups, students can focus on an object representing one of the symbols Cormier employs, perhaps a model football goalpost, a black box, a box of chocolates, or a poster inscribed with "Do I Dare Disturb the Universe?" By tracing the appearance of an object through the novel, noting what happens immediately before, during, and after each appearance, each group can determine what their object represents beyond its literal value. Groups can then share their information, drawing on references from the text to support their observations and conclusions. This "hands-on" treatment of symbolism provides a concrete experience out of which to explore symbolism in *Macbeth.*

Examining the Conclusion of *The Chocolate War*

The last step in examining *The Chocolate War* brings students' attention to one of the novel's more controversial aspects. As such, it offers students an opportunity to sharpen their critical perceptions of Cormier's intent and its fulfillment. For us, this last step involves a reader's theater approach to a group reading of the last chapter. Such an approach serves not only to transform this text into the genre of *Macbeth*, but also to dramatize the various shifts in character that occur over the course of the novel, shifts such as the reversal of control between Archie and Brother Leon. The teacher's role is to facilitate students' examination of these changes: How credible are they? Did Cormier carefully motivate each change? How do these changes affect the ending? Was any other outcome an option? If so, where in the text does a different ending appear possible? Would this ending have accomplished Cormier's purpose as well? These questions can become a vital reference point when students evaluate *Macbeth*'s conclusion.

To anchor this literary bridge solidly in *Macbeth*, discussion must finally turn toward the underlying theme of individual powerlessness and the issue of personal responsibility for social institutions. Has Jerry been "broken"? Who has "won" and who has "lost"? What has been won and lost, and at what price? Does Goober represent the only realistic response to institutionalized authority? What does the conclusion indicate about Cormier's view of the human condition? Do students share his view? Tentative answers to such questions will prepare students for a more sensitive and critical reading of *Macbeth*, its outcome, and the way in which its themes and symbols work.

Introducing *Macbeth*

For the purpose of this illustration, we will assume that by their senior year, students will be at least minimally familiar with the social, political, and cultural background out of which Shakespeare was writing. Thus, we include here only details most relevant for the sake of pairing the two works.

A "black box drawing" offers a playful transition strategy. The teacher shapes relevant background information in the form of questions written on small pieces of paper, which are then folded and placed in a black box. Each student draws a question that then becomes an "assignment," information that the student must find and report on to the class. Including an "X" in the box, of course, heightens the drama of this exercise. If the teacher chooses to include an "X" in the box, the student drawing it receives a "special" assignment.

Following the black box transition, students can consider the play's beginning. Like *The Chocolate War*'s opening scene on the football field, *Macbeth* immediately draws the reader into the action. Showing a film, videotape, or dramatic version of the opening witches' scene (which could be productively juxtaposed with the opening scene in the film based on Cormier's novel) captures this immediacy for students and facilitates a comparison of the two authors' strategies for engaging their audience. Having performed a portion of the Cormier text as well, students will have a stronger basis for considering the difference in *Macbeth*'s diction level. The teacher can move to diffuse the anxiety these language differences often create by reminding students that *The Chocolate War*, now quite familiar to them, will be used as a constant frame of reference in grappling with *Macbeth*.

Considering Shared Themes

While power structures are different in *Macbeth*, students' knowledge of *The Chocolate War* can provide a helpful context for discovering similarities and differences in the way that characters in the two novels deal with them. If students consider how, for instance, Archie, Jerry, and Brother Leon might react in the positions of Macbeth, Duncan, and Lady Macbeth, they will begin to see that the dramatic differences in the eras and institutional systems portrayed by the two works do not fundamentally alter human behavior, in this case, the desire for power. Juxtaposed, *The Chocolate War* and *Macbeth* demonstrate that ambition is a human characteristic that transcends time.

Students have already seen the desire for power embodied in Archie and Brother Leon, and those characters can now serve to inform the observation of Macbeth and Lady Macbeth. Prior to Duncan's murder, students' perceptions will be enhanced by considering how Macbeth and his wife resemble these two characters. As Macbeth and Lady Macbeth change, students can track those changes in relationship to Archie and Brother Leon. As a useful writing exercise stemming from these comparisons, students might develop dialogues between characters from each work, between, for example, Jerry and Lady Macbeth or Goober and Malcolm. Creating a credible encounter between characters across the time and space boundaries of these works requires that the students attend closely to both texts, and particularly to the subtleties of character differentiation.

The gradual shifts in character that take place in Macbeth and Lady Macbeth can be more clearly perceived through such comparisons. As the play ends, Macbeth and his wife essentially have exchanged roles; Macbeth more closely resembles Archie, and Lady Macbeth, Brother Leon. Macbeth's growing disgust for the masses parallels

Archie's disdain for his classmates. Similarly, Lady Macbeth's indifference to the changing course of events is akin to Brother Leon's increasing capitulation to Archie.

Lady Macbeth's manipulation of Macbeth offers another striking link between the two works. In observing Brother Leon's and Lady Macbeth's manipulative strategies, students can expand their grasp of the complex human motives and power struggles being enacted in both works.

Such comparisons point students toward the recurring issue of good versus evil. Students will need to wrestle first with the question of moral responsibility, that is, who is most responsible for Duncan's death: Macbeth, who commits the murder, or Lady Macbeth, who engineers the deed? Once decided, students can again scrutinize Archie as "evil incarnate."

It is interesting to note that in *Beyond the Chocolate War* (Cormier 1985), Archie states that it is not he himself who is evil, but rather everyone else who allows what he does to happen. The "special" assignment for the student drawing the black box "X" might be to read this sequel and discuss this statement of Archie's in relationship to the conclusions students draw from their comparative study.

Considering Malcolm and Jerry as embodiments of goodness will further inform the evil/good dichotomy. An expressive writing exercise in which students write a letter to Malcolm in the persona of Jerry explaining why he believes Malcolm is fighting a losing battle or, conversely, a letter from Malcolm to Jerry detailing a rationale and plan for defeating Archie would push students toward a greater clarification of "goodness" as it exists in each of these characters.

Exploring Symbolism in *Macbeth*

Macbeth provides students with another concrete experience of symbolism. This time, however, the students themselves can create the important symbols. For instance, acting as members of the artistic staff for Roman Polanski's film version of *Macbeth*, students can collaborate in small groups to create a representation of one of the many apparitions (an armed head, a crowned child holding a tree, etc.) that shape the play's symbolic structure. The groups' task is to decide on the best medium—sculpture, collage, mural, mixed media—assemble the materials needed, and together render the image. The very strangeness of the symbols gives students considerable latitude in their visual interpretations, a chance for them to indulge their sense of the macabre.

This is, of course, an excellent anticipation of the film itself, if showing it is a part of the instructional plan.

The groups' next task is to present their rendition of the symbol and review, for the rest of the "staff," how Macbeth interpreted it. By exploring what his interpretation reveals about his state of mind, students will discover how Macbeth's growing moral corruption affects the sense he is able to make of these symbols. Related to this is Obie in *The Chocolate War,* who, by the end of the novel, is unable to remember what the goalposts resemble. Cormier uses this scene to illustrate the blinding influence of Obie's association with the Vigils. This can be compared with Shakespeare's portrayal of Macbeth as unable to interpret and heed the signs emanating from the witches' prophecies, a result of his corrupted faith in his kingdom's invincibility. Having made these connections, students are prepared to look at the two worlds created by Archie and Macbeth, determine the values represented by the symbols, and discern the likenesses in symbols that would otherwise appear disparate.

Comparing Conclusions

In concluding this pairing process, some reflection on Cormier's and Shakespeare's choices is appropriate. Shakespeare leaves his audience with quite a different world than does Cormier. In *Macbeth,* evil is ultimately defeated, good reasserts itself, and faith in the power of right acts is restored. In examining how this ending differs from *The Chocolate War,* students will confront two distinct world views. The question they must finally confront is, Can I believe in either one?

To assist in this reflection, students can be asked which work they consider more "realistic." Moreover, does its realism make the author's world view somehow more tenable? If students are encouraged to look at the ideas of world order shaping both works, it will be possible for them to see more clearly that the chaos of nihilism and despair frequent to the modern age is only one choice. In Shakespeare's world order, governed by the chain of being, human action is an ordering principle. In a universe where all things are connected, when one acts wrongly, that act affects everything. Yet the opposite is also true; right acts have their resounding consequences as well. Finally, this pairing process leads students to consider two fundamental questions: In what ordering principle do I believe? And, what difference does it make?

Summary

The pairing process we have illustrated serves to unify two competing voices. One, growing out of the 1966 Dartmouth Conference, increasingly invokes the importance of beginning instruction with students' interests, knowledge, and experience and including more expressive writing as a way to bring the student voice into course content. The other, growing out of the call for a cultural literacy, calls for more attention to the canon. Pairing strong adolescent literature with works from our literary tradition provides for instruction centered in the students' world. In this way, much of students' apprehension and distrust of more traditional literature can be mediated by their growing confidence (1) that they can gain access to this literary tradition, (2) that the tradition is not unrelated to their own experience, and (3) that developing a critical mind allows them the choice to participate in or reject that tradition.

We do not advocate making the canon the agenda for teaching adolescent literature. Adolescent literature is a genre containing many fine works that can stand on their own as literature. What we do suggest is recognizing adolescent literature as a powerful bridge into the canon and, where strong parallels exist (as in the case of *Macbeth* and *The Chocolate War*), developing an instructional plan that crystallizes the connections. Doing this will further the cause of both literatures. The road to further literary explorations will be more clearly illuminated, and students will find future journeys not only less intimidating, but also increasingly meaningful.

References

Cormier, Robert. 1985. *Beyond the Chocolate War: A Novel.* New York: Knopf.

Cormier, Robert. 1974. *The Chocolate War: A Novel.* New York: Pantheon Books.

Farrell, Edmund J. 1966. "Listen, My Children and You Shall Read . . ." *English Journal* 55: 39–45, 68.

Gildner, Gary. 1983. "First Practice." In *Poetspeak: In Their Work, About Their Work,* edited by Paul B. Janeczko, 38–39. Scarsdale, NY: Bradbury Press.

28 Three Writing Activities to Use with *Macbeth*

Ken Spurlock
Covington Independent Public Schools, Covington, Kentucky

Macbeth is a rich source for student writing. I would like to suggest three activities that might challenge students and help increase their understanding and appreciation of the tragedy.

The Biopoem

The eleven-line biopoem provides a concrete way of getting students to think about a play's characters. The prewriting step requires that students use analytical skills to gather specific facts about a character, while the actual writing of the first draft requires synthesis—drawing together the separate details discovered about the character to form a coherent whole.

Students may not be able to get all the information they need straight from the text or a videotaped version of the play. Instead, they must make intelligent decisions to fill in the gaps that reading and viewing may leave open. Thus, writing a biopoem often involves some creative thinking as well, especially if the character written about does not have a major role in the play.

A biopoem on the character Macbeth is given below, followed by the pattern for the form. This pattern is adapted from Ann Ruggles Gere, ed., *Roots in the Sawdust: Writing to Learn across the Disciplines* (Urbana, IL: NCTE, 1985), 222.

MACBETH, KING OF SCOTLAND

Macbeth
Brave, generous, evil, heroic
Son of Sinel
Lover of honor, power, and his wife
Who feels guilty, overly confident, and, in the end, deceived
Who needs Lady Macbeth's help, more sleep, and the witches' prophecies
Who fears Banquo until he is dead, the forest coming to Dunsinane, and one not of woman born

Who gives much thought to the murder of Duncan, little thought
   to the killing of Macduff's family, and his complete trust to
   the weird sisters
Who would like to see himself King of Scotland, Malcolm and
   Donalbain blamed for the death of their father, and Fleance
   dead
Resident of Glamis and Forres
King of Scotland

Form for the Biopoem

Title	Person's first and last name in capital letters
Line 1	First name of the person
Line 2	Four traits (characteristics) that best describe him or her
Line 3	Relative (brother, wife, daughter, son, etc.) of . . .
Line 4	Lover of . . . (list three objects, people, or places)
Line 5	Who feels . . . (three items)
Line 6	Who needs . . . (three items)
Line 7	Who fears . . . (three items)
Line 8	Who gives . . . (three items)
Line 9	Who would like to see . . . (three items)
Line 10	Resident of . . . (city, state, region, or country)
Line 11	Last name of the person (or perhaps a title, alias, or nickname if no last name is given)

It is probably best to have the students do a biopoem on
themselves before reading *Macbeth*. Writing a personal biopoem will
help students learn the form so that they can more easily use it for
the dramatic characters. If the biopoem is taught prior to reading the
play, students could randomly draw characters' names from an envelope the teacher prepares before assigning Act I. Each character's
name should be repeated several times in the envelope. That way
students might be grouped for collaboration later according to whose
name they draw.

As the students read the play, they can begin to analyze and
take notes on their character's traits, relatives, loves, feelings, needs,
and fears, all of which will be needed to write the biopoem. Macbeth,
Lady Macbeth, Duncan, Banquo, and Macduff are obvious subjects;
however, Malcolm, Fleance, and the witches (as a group), though more
challenging, could also be included in the envelope.

When the play is finished, students can use their notes to
complete a draft of a biopoem. Then they can meet in small groups

with other students who worked on the same character, sharing and comparing drafts and perhaps coming up with a group biopoem combining the best of the individual efforts. The group biopoems may be presented to the class as a form of review before the unit test.

Missing Soliloquies

A second writing activity, for use after the play is finished, is to ask students to become one of the characters in order to write a soliloquy that *could* be in the play but is not. Of course, a big part of this assignment is predicated upon students' knowing the characters and play well enough to figure out where a "missing" soliloquy might be added. The analysis and synthesis needed to write the biopoem should make this process easier.

A good way to introduce this writing activity is to ask the class to brainstorm on places in the play where they would like more information or where they would like to know what a character is thinking. A soliloquy could then be written to fill in such puzzling gaps. Consider these possibilities as starters:

- One of the witches' thoughts after Duncan is killed
- Fleance's thoughts after he escapes the knives of the three murderers
- The Third Murderer's detailed thoughts after Banquo is killed and Fleance escapes
- Lady Macbeth's final thoughts moments before her death
- Malcolm's or Donalbain's thoughts upon fleeing the court after Duncan's death
- Lady Macduff's thoughts as she hides after being chased offstage by Macbeth's hired murderers

New Scenes

Closely connected to writing a missing soliloquy is the idea of writing whole new scenes. Indeed, some of the soliloquies suggested above would really have to become new scenes in order to fit into the play. One good approach that fosters creative thinking is to have students write a scene that might occur after Macbeth's death. Think of the possibilities here:

- The witches meeting with Hecate to plan their next move for Scotland after Malcolm is crowned (more toil and trouble?)

- Malcolm, the new King of Scotland, meeting with Donalbain, who did not return to fight by his side
- Fleance visiting the witches to discover his future (remember, Banquo was to be the father of kings)
- Macduff returning to his empty castle at Fife after Malcolm is crowned
- Macduff and Malcolm reminiscing as old men about the days of Macbeth's reign
- Fleance talking to the Third Murderer, whom he has tracked down

Students should not be limited only to future scenes, however; they may wish to add new scenes between the ones Shakespeare wrote to explain some of the happenings that occur in the play—a scene that explains who the Third Murderer is or a death scene for Lady Macbeth, for instance. Scenes that might happen before the play begins are another possibility. Of course, any new scene should be based upon what happens in the play as Shakespeare wrote it.

These three activities offer students creative options to show what they have learned in their study of *Macbeth*. Perhaps by using writing in these ways, young readers will come to enjoy Shakespeare more and better appreciate his skill as a writer.

29 The Centrality of *A Midsummer Night's Dream*

Hugh M. Richmond
University of California, Berkeley

Students coming to know Shakespeare in the United States still do so primarily through two texts: *Julius Caesar* and *Macbeth*. Recently, my daughter suffered through the first play three times in junior high and high school. From my point of view, the problem is not that these are bad plays, but that they are certainly not inviting, nor very typical of their author; that is, they lack his characteristic humor, charm, and kindliness. I am not impressed by the usual defenses that I encounter for the choice of such harsh texts: the political correctness of Brutus, on the one hand, with his rejection of tyranny, and the ghoulish appeal of witchcraft and murder on the other. For me, both plays require more sophisticated expositions than these to validate their status, such as discussion of the political inadequacies of good intentions in *Julius Caesar* or of the dangers of overvaluing primitive virility in *Macbeth*. Nor does there seem to be adequate awareness of the true challenge in teaching the third strong candidate for required Shakespearean reading, for the classic approach to *Romeo and Juliet* invites total approval of the suicidal extremism and murderous violence of its hero. Even Hamlet seems to me to be seriously misrepresented pedagogically in his familiar guise as a sophisticated but dilatory hero, one who supposedly should hasten on his way to assassination of the head of state, even if he personally remains to the end of the play without a shred of legally acceptable evidence that Claudius killed his father. The killing of Polonius, not to mention that of Rosencrantz and Guildenstern, hardly seems the handiwork of someone hesitant to act.

Of course, all of these are fine plays against which to test the wits of students already refined by exposure to less complex, more accessible Shakespeare scripts—some of the comedies perhaps. Yet I suspect that there is some anxiety among teachers that comedy is too frivolous and too entertaining for serious instruction, however central it may be to the revelation of Shakespeare's artistry and temperament. Perhaps we need to recall what Samuel Johnson (no intellectual lightweight) said about Shakespeare in his provocative Preface to his edition of the plays:

> In tragedy he often writes, with great appearance of toil and study, what is written at last with little felicity; but in his comic scenes, he seems to produce without labour, what no labour can improve. In tragedy he is always struggling after some occasion to be comick; but in comedy he seems to repose, or luxuriate, as in a mode of thinking congenial to his nature. (1949, 18)

Moreover, some of the more seriously challenging plays are now held to be unacceptable to the Politically Correct Teacher. *The Merchant of Venice* is supposed to be anti-Semitic (not about anti-Semitism), so the Santa Cruz Shakespeare Festival was forced to abandon a proposed production in such a progressive community. *Othello* contains racist views (though not necessarily those held by the author), so Olivier's film has been censured by my black students, who object to it being shown. Recently, one of my deaf students advised me that her group feels that *Richard III* defames the physically handicapped. Few feminists (except Germaine Greer) can stomach *The Taming of the Shrew*, though they usually tolerate the negative female role models in *Hedda Gabler* and *Miss Julie*, which similarly raise proper issues about gender through heroines just as disturbing as Katerina. With my Scots ancestry, I sometimes wonder whether I could work up a comparably fashionable critique of *Macbeth*'s fictional misrepresentation of its historical Scottish hero, who was actually a very effective and moral king, and even went on a pilgrimage to Rome.

In asserting the superiority of *A Midsummer Night's Dream* as an introduction to Shakespeare over any of these more ominous and imposing texts, I may seem to invite the charge of frivolity. Yet the play permits a serious investigation of most of the issues raised more bewilderingly in the great tragedies, and does so without abandoning the wit and grace that are among Shakespeare's most endearing and persistent traits. Indeed, only after experiencing this classic comedy is one adquately prepared to evaluate the concerns and achievements of later, more "serious" plays. For example, *A Dream* does not sentimentalize love; the idiocies of its young lovers invite us to be skeptical about endorsing the solipsism of those in *Romeo and Juliet*. In *Shakespeare, Our Contemporary*, Jan Kott (1966) even argues that Titania's relationship with Bottom epitomizes the perverse human tendency to love that which is unsuitable. As Kott sees it,

> The *Dream* is the most erotic of Shakespeare's plays. . . . Starting with Helena's soliloquy (I.i.226) Shakespeare introduces more and more obtrusive animal erotic symbolism. He does it consistently, stubbornly, almost obsessively. The changes in imagery are in this case only an outward expression of a violent departure from the Petrarchan idealization of love. (224)

This view of the bestial effects of intense feeling is hardly Kott's discovery. Indeed, humans reduced to lower lifeforms by their passion provide for the principal themes of Ovid's *Metamorphoses,* which is in fact Shakespeare's principal source for the "Pyramus and Thisbe" play-within. An amusing comparison can thus be drawn from reading Ovid's brief and innocent account of the lovers' misfortunes (IV:55–166), which heightens the ridiculousness of Shakespeare's dramatic treatment by its lyric charm. Nevertheless, the more sinister element in Ovid lies in his sense of how debasing compulsive attitudes may be, as when Daphne is made catatonic by Apollo's desperate pursuit of her (I:452–552), an incident to which Shakespeare's distraught Helena directly alludes (II.i.231). Helena's allusion, however, comes only after she has revealed how her own love for Demetrius evokes an even more degraded metamorphosis than that of Daphne:

> I am your spaniel; and, Demetrius,
> The more you beat me, I will fawn on you.
> Use me but as your spaniel; spurn me, strike me,
> Neglect me, lose me; only give me leave,
> Unworthy as I am, to follow you.
> What worser place can I beg in your love
> (And yet a place of high respect with me)
> Than to be used as you use your dog?
>
> (II.i.203–10)

This perverse aspect of Helena's character matches Theseus's preference for a wife who has only recently attempted to kill him (I.i.16). It also parallels the persistence of the other young lovers in seeking precisely those amatory relationships not currently available to them (whether against the will of parents in Athens or when Lysander and Demetrius try to force themselves on the alienated Helena in the forest).

This is the first educational issue that intense study of the play raises: the invalidity of the sentimental Mendelssohnian vision of cute fairies and puppetlike lovers, as illustrated in Max Reinhardt's film.

That film is now available on inexpensive videocassette; running the first fifteen minutes after the title and credits, up to and including the Busby-Berkeley-style production number of the arrival of the fairy hordes, effectively illustrates Reinhardt's sentimental approach. As a contrast to this cute view of the play, it is salutary to have students excerpt and perform the single plot line of the adolescent obtuseness of the four young Athenians in order to show its modernity (I.i.127–251; II.i.188–244; II.ii.34–65, 84–156; III.ii.43–87, 122–344, 401, 404–5, 413–20, 425–35, 442–47; IV.i.187–94). My students have often staged these passages in a twenty-minute mini-play costumed in ordinary modern dress before audiences varying from hundreds of undergraduates to even larger groups of schoolchildren of all ages. The resulting effect is one of total naturalism, devoid of any fairy intervention to provide an "explanation" for the willful gyrations and unstable affections of the adolescents other than the volatility of the characters themselves. In many cases, such a performance illustrates the advantages of typecasting and elicits quite impassioned discussion of whether the behavior remains fully representative of modern attitudes. This skeptical view of adolescent sexuality is provocatively illustrated in Peter Hall's "New Wave" film of *A Midsummer Night's Dream* (1969, with Diana Rigg, Helen Mirren, Judi Dench, Ian Richardson, David Warner, and Ian Holm), also now available on inexpensive videocassette. This film casually ridicules customary efforts at picturesque and sentimental interpretation, as it is willfully shot during a wet November in the woods near Stratford-upon-Avon, which rapidly reduces everyone to shivering alienation, not to mention literally muddy complexions. The effect is grotesque, amusing, and thought-provoking.

This revelation of the lovers' realistic psychologies in turn permits consideration of the fairies as archetypes of perverse human emotions, in other words, whether what we call "the supernatural" is not simply an abstraction of universal human traits. For example, many husbands' jealousy of their wives' involvement with a child newly added to their relationship is reflected in the role of the changeling boy, who provides the key issue in the initial tensions between Oberon and Titania. They fight to possess him until Oberon manages to deflect her emotional attention elsewhere, only to foster his own jealousy thereby and thus finally seek her recovery as his lover and wife. This episode itself offers an amusing challenge for students to provide a plausible interpretation of a problem in the plot that Shakespeare has skillfully avoided. For I often invite my students to write the missing speech in which Oberon answers Titania's request for an explanation of her recent misadventures:

> Tell me how it came this night
> That I sleeping here was found,
> With these mortals on the ground.
>
>   (IV.i.100–103)

Any explanation offered by modern Oberons must be one that will plausibly permit the pair's sustained reconciliation as seen in the play's conclusion. If students attempt to write this missing piece of sophistry in blank verse (as they should), this exercise provides an opportunity for discussing the function and value of traditional metrics. This in turn provides a convenient starting point for comparable exercises, such as the writing of a Shakespearean sonnet by the Dark Lady in response to Shakespeare's censures of her (or some other theme apt for the sonnet form). I should warn those not familiar with this kind of activity that once its affinities to crossword puzzles are explained to students, the ease of writing sonnets may become addictive. I often receive whole sonnet cycles running to a hundred poems, for it is the rare student who, having successfully written one metrically regular sonnet, can refrain from writing another.

Furthermore, in the investigation of Elizabethan artistic practices, the modern procedure of doubling Oberon and Theseus on the one hand, and Titania and Hippolyta on the other, invites us to explore the allegorical relationship between the two types of characters illustrated by this quartet. This idea of deliberately stressing the artificiality of stage personae by insisting that the audience recognize the actor's function leads directly into one of the play's most stimulating topics: the nature of staged performance and its relationship to the offstage reality of the audience. This seems to me to be a central question that must be addressed before any adequate analysis of Shakespeare's works can be completed. In *Macbeth*, for instance, at the height of the tragedy, Shakespeare seems to insist on the artificiality of the theatrical experience when Macbeth asserts,

> Life's but a walking shadow, a poor player,
> That struts and frets his hour upon the stage,
> And then is heard no more.
>
>   (V.v.24–26)

Even Cleopatra anticipates the style of Elizabethan performances in foreseeing "Some squeaking Cleopatra boy my greatness / I' th' posture of a whore" (V.ii.220–21). Despite such provocative disillusioning of audiences, nowhere else does Shakespeare discuss and illustrate so fully his ideas on theatrical conventions and practice or handle them so dextrously as he does in *A Dream*. Far from being mere farcical interludes, the gyrations of the workmen in the play are central to our understanding of its concerns, and of Elizabethan stage practice in general (not to mention modern acting conventions). Their clumsy explorations in I.ii and III.i of the difference between stage reality and that of the audience, especially in their comments on the lion's role, on mimicry of death, and on artificial versus natural lighting, are pertinent to Shakespeare's own practice, including the implausible impenetrability of his numerous uses of disguise throughout the plays and the careful description of nonexistent settings or weather conditions established by "prologues" to the relevant scenes—Duncan's description of Macbeth's castle (I.vi.1–9), for instance.

Of course, the climactic exploration of stage reality's relationship to audience actuality lies in the performance of "Pyramus and Thisbe," which is no mere farce, but a virtuoso exploration of the ways in which the artist's imitation of life (however clumsy) bears directly on our own impressions of historical experience. It is not just the fact that from the very instant Bottom begins to imagine himself as a romantic lover, he loses himself in a fantasy world in which he turns into an ass, a sensualist, a buffoon, and a suicidal incompetent (thus matching closely to the experience of other more realistic Shakespearean lovers, such as Romeo, Antony, and Othello). Rather, it is that the very clumsiness of the performance as a whole comments on human ineptitude when attempting some role beyond routine behavior. The young lovers on the stage fail to recognize the analogues to their own amatory ineptitude when they judge the workmen's involuntary parody of sentimental tragedy to be merely the behavior of "many Asses" (V.i.154). "Pyramus and Thisbe" reads like a send-up of *Romeo and Juliet* (on which Shakespeare must also have been working at about this time in his career). Indeed, some effects are identical, such as Bottom's confusion of day and night (V.i.272), which duplicates a similar confusion by Juliet (III.v.1–5, 26–35). Surely Shakespeare expects the actual audience offstage to perceive the discrepancy between the young lovers' contemptuous comments about the universal sexual incompetence on stage and their failure to apply the recognition of this obtuseness to their own behavior in the "wood near Athens." Our perception of this lack of self-awareness forces on us the conclusion that Shakespeare is illustrating the pathological incompetence induced by intense sexual feelings. Only Providence (in the form of Oberon) prevents an outcome for the young lovers in *A Dream* as grotesquely tragic as that of the workmen's comical tragedy—or of *Romeo and Juliet*, with its less than effective prince.

In order to pursue this interpretation, our full-length, open-air performance of *A Dream* stressed its contemporary realism by a completely modern-dress approach. What we found was that this concept worked perfectly in the context of the naive idealism of the epoch of the flower children of the sixties. Their naive conviction that their own instable feelings were an adequate guide to behavior matched the young lovers' naive egotism perfectly, while the fairies epitomized all the ecological whimsy that went along with this cult of naive sincerity. By contrast, Theseus became the expression of law and order as the local police chief of some rural municipality enamored of his political prisoner, Hippolyta—a Patty Hearst kind of ambivalent rebel. Far from being an exercise in archaic charm, our production of the play proved a deft parody of the persistent self-delusions of lovers, and, to my surprise, it was welcomed by audiences at every level, from jaded senior professors to young children who had never even seen a play before. At my daughter's primary school, the children were so smitten with the production that they initiated their own ten-minute production of *A Midsummer Night's Dream* without any direct initiative by their English teacher. I was also struck last year when, ten years after our production, the Regent's Park Open Air Theatre in London picked up the concept with a Beatnik interpretation of the play set in San Francisco. An equally mixed British audience responded just as favorably as ours. The playful eccentricity of the script makes it very suited to a Californian setting.

Nonetheless, while the play lends itself to vital, provocative approaches, it also permits a far more sophisticated level of discussion in the exploration of Shakespeare's achievement as a whole, fitting more advanced classes. For example, it is not always adequately recognized that Shakespeare's scripts are deeply interdependent. Of course, everyone knows that there are two parts to *Henry IV* and three parts to *Henry VI*, to which *Richard III* provides a powerful coda. Less explored are the relationships of *Richard II* and *Henry V* to the *Henry IV* plays in the later historical tetralogy. Even less recognized is the fact that *Julius Caesar* provides only the first phase of a trilogy detailing the rise and decline of the Emperor Augustus; in *Antony and Cleopatra*, of course, Augustus triumphs at the eastern end of the Roman world, only to be defeated (to the discredit of the values of Rome) at the western edge of the empire in *Cymbeline*. And even less perceived is that in bringing the historical sequence down to the time of Queen Elizabeth, *Henry VIII* becomes a sequel to *Richard III*, with which it explicitly invites linkage by numerous cross-references.

All of this is by way of preface and confirmation of Glen Wickam's (1980) argument in *"The Two Noble Kinsmen* or *A Midsummer Night's Dream, Part II?"* Wickam sees the full elucidation of the themes of *A Midsummer Night's Dream* in *The Two Noble Kinsmen,* where the author's harsh view of sexuality provides a startling foil to the usual sentimental, trivializing approach to *A Dream.* For both are "Theseus plays" dealing with amatory and marital complexities, as this hero often does in legends such as that of Phaedra. Indeed, this Shakespearean play actually starts within the earlier plot of *A Dream* by breaking off the marriage ceremony that provides its climax. And the *Kinsmen's* quartet of frustrated lovers introduces new levels of amatory and marital complexity, ending in a tragedy intrinsic to the final achievement of Emilia's marriage and thus confirming the ominous undertones of serious meaning that govern *A Dream,* as I have argued following Kott's suggestions. In providing high school English teachers with fresh approaches to both *A Dream* and *Romeo and Juliet,* Professor Richard Adams of the California State University at Sacramento has developed a presentation based on the harsh view of sexuality that Shakespeare borrows from Chaucer's Knight's Tale as the core of *The Two Noble Kinsmen.* Despite controversies over its authorship, this later play matches the themes of *A Dream* too well for it not to be an intrinsic part of Shakepeare's career, whether or not it was finished by his successor as playwright to the King's Men, John Fletcher.

Thus, *A Dream* provides some important clues to scholarly discussion of the contents of the whole Shakespearean canon, clues worthy of discussion in advanced seminars of Shakespeare scholars, critics, and teachers. Still, despite its conspicuous versatility as a source of understanding of Shakespeare, not the least of its virtues is its direct relevance to the experience of adolescents, in ways that one hopes the sinister tone of *Macbeth* is not. In this, *A Dream* affords a corrective prelude to the fatal model provided by too empathetic an approach to *Romeo and Juliet,* of which a false reading is all too likely before experiencing the corrective knowledge of *A Dream.* In stressing such points, I hope I may have provided some indication of both the radical unsuitability of *Julius Caesar* and *Macbeth* as introductions to Shakespeare and the grounds for using the more attractive and more relevant text of *A Midsummer Night's Dream.*

References

Johnson, Samuel. 1949. *Johnson on Shakespeare*. Edited by Sir Walter Alexander Raleigh. London: Oxford University Press.

Kott, Jan. 1966. *Shakespeare, Our Contemporary*. Garden City, NY: Anchor Books. Doubleday edition published 1964.

Shakespeare, William. 1974. *The Riverside Shakespeare*. Edited by G. Blakemore Evans. Boston: Houghton Mifflin.

Wickam, Glen. 1980. "*The Two Noble Kinsmen* or *A Midsummer Night's Dream, Part II?*" In *The Elizabethan Theatre VII: Papers Given at the Seventh International Conference on Elizabethan Theatre held at the University of Waterloo, Ontario, in July 1977*, edited by G. R. Hibbard. Hamden, CN: Archon Books.

30 If Only One, Then *Henry IV, Part 1* for the General Education Course

Sherry Bevins Darrell
University of Southern Indiana

In general education courses, we teach Shakespeare to students of biology and business, history and dental hygiene, economics and elementary education. In such courses, we often feel a special mission, both ambassadorial and religious, to win these students over to Shakespeare. Unfortunately, general ed courses—like Introduction to Literature, Survey of English Literature, and Survey of World Literature—often must cover several centuries and several genres; our syllabi, then, allow only a week or so for Shakespeare, time perhaps for two or three sonnets and one play. Given such time constraints and our mission to save the un-Shakespeared, we must choose carefully the Shakespeare they will read. I contend that one play, more than any other, will teach general ed students to appreciate drama and dramatic technique; to understand genre, structure, theme, and character; to read and comprehend poetry; to love Shakespeare. That play is *Henry IV, Part 1.*

Genre

Three genres conjoin in *Henry IV, Part 1:* history, tragedy, and comedy. *History:* Although not in accurate detail and not in exact chronological order, the action depicts events shortly after Henry IV's usurpation of the throne in 1399. The main plot focuses on Henry's resolve to keep his ill-gotten crown despite a rebellion led by the king-making Percys from the north. *Tragedy:* In Hotspur we have the makings of a tragic hero. He believes the king has wronged him; he sets out to correct this wrong by unmaking the king his family made; he demonstrates energy, idealism, chivalric prowess, and leadership; he fights on despite the abandonment of his cowardly father and other allies; he dies on the battlefield (strains of *The Iliad* here) concerned more for the loss of glory than for the loss of life. Hotspur believes in his cause—usurping the ungrateful usurper— fights for it, and dies for it. When he dies, we reflect on what might have been had Hotspur fought with Hal rather than against him, and we cannot help but conclude that England is the poorer for his passing. *Comedy:* Within *Henry IV, Part 1* are Falstaff, the Gadshill robbery and its consequent tavern scene, the liberal and sometimes hilarious education of Hal, the raucous humor of the Hotspur-Glendower-Mortimer scene, the distrust and then reconciliation between father and wayward son, and the victory in battle concluding the play.

Structure

Structurally, this play is a comedy. After exposition in I.i and I.ii, the inciting event (Hotspur, Northumberland, and Worcester conspire to rebel) commences a downward turn in the plot. Complication comprises the success of the rebels in gaining allies and Henry IV's continued separation from his son, both signs that Henry will not hold his crown long. But the crisis (turning point) in III.ii—a reconciliation between Henry IV and Hal—begins moving the plot upward through the denouement. In this denouement, the conspiracy unravels as ally after ally fails to appear at Shrewsbury to fight with Hotspur. At the climax, Hal slays Hotspur to end the rebellion. And the play reaches comic resolution when Hal allows Falstaff to pretend that he slew Hotspur and then sets Douglas free.

Characters for General Education

Henry IV, Part 1 treats many themes important for general ed students to encounter and examine. And as is typical of him, Shakespeare treats these themes with complexity, avoiding the extremes of black and white. Shakespeare never offers a play that we can sum up with "And the moral of this story is . . ." Shakespeare's characters and themes demand careful reading for their complexities and broad treatment. For example, if at first we succumb to Falstaff, as inevitably we do—for his foibles, for his ignorant pomposity, for his pragmatism, for his fun—ultimately we must perceive the danger in Falstaff: he represents misrule. The same holds for Hotspur. At first we delight in his pacing and racing, his huffy-puffy conversations full of honor-talk, his play with Lady Percy, his bravado. Indeed, neither we nor our students want Hotspur to die. Can't Henry IV or Hal create a safe place in this kingdom for Hotspur? But when it comes down to Hotspur or Hal, we see that Hotspur must go, though we feel immensely sad for it. Such complexities as those of Falstaff and Hotspur, with their widely divergent threats to rule and order, disallow facile readings.

Nor does Shakespeare let us retreat into comfortable relativism. Hal doesn't. Early in the play (I.ii and II.iv), Hal indicates his judgment on Falstaff and Hotspur. He sums up Falstaff and his cohorts in his soliloquy at the end of I.ii: they are men of "Unyok'd humors"; they lack discipline and direction. Then, in II.iv, at the beginning and at the end, Hal ridicules Hotspur. First, he describes Hotspur as killing some dozen Scots before breakfast and then complaining about the quiet life. Later, he mocks both Falstaff and Hotspur by responding to Falstaff's question about fearing Hotspur with a comment about lacking Falstaff's instinct for running away. All of Hal's judgments—on Falstaff, Hotspur, and others—signify that Hal does assess and judge others. And he knows what he must eventually do with them.

Themes to Hook Students

In general ed courses, naturally we want to bait the hook with ideas both interesting and accessible to students, often students both ambitious and undisciplined, eager to succeed if not to a throne, at least to a decent career and a place in the community. *Henry IV, Part 1* raises many ideas that all of us, but particularly general education students, will benefit from reflecting on:

- The stewardship of England—by Henry IV, Hal, the conspirators
- Duty—Henry's, Hal's, Northumberland's, Worcester's
- The education of the ideal Christian king—at court, in battle, in Eastcheap
- Relations between fathers and sons—Henry IV and Hal, Northumberland and Hotspur
- Relations between surrogate fathers and sons—Falstaff and Hal, Worcester and Hotspur, Mortimer and Glendower
- Failed communication between women and men—the Hostess and Falstaff, Hotspur and Lady Percy, Mortimer and his Welsh wife
- Holiday (Saturnalia) versus everyday—the high spirits and hijinks of the Eastcheap set, the worries and responsibilities of court and king, Hal's ability to bridge the two worlds
- Cynicism versus idealism—Falstaff and Hotspur

- Parallels between robbery and usurpation—the Gadshill gang, Hotspur and the conspirators

In addition, general education students will find the following particularly interesting and worthy of discussion:

- A king who stole his crown and who must now face his own would-be usurpers
- A son who ought to display more interest in taking over the family business but seems to prefer wasting his life in taverns
- A dashing, young, would-be hero who wants to fight everyone and fears not the king, not the king's wastrel son, not even an aging wizard
- A hilarious but foolish old man who recounts a great battle with robbers, exaggerating his tale until finally confronted with the truth—and yet continues to deny that truth
- A "let's-put-on-a-play scene" in a tavern that leads a delightful but foolish old man to play first a king and then a prince
- A dashing, young, would-be hero with energy, courage, humor, and leadership who fails to achieve his ambitions
- A perilous battle that leads a wastrel son to save his doubting father and then slay the warrior reputed to be his superior
- A victorious prince who lets one lord of misrule claim credit for slaying the other lord of misrule

Henry IV, Part 1 is such a rich play that these two lists comprise only the most obvious concerns. And these themes can serve as the basis for both discussion and writing assignments.

Techniques of the Playwright

Better than any other Shakespearean play I know, *Henry IV, Part 1* lends itself to teaching dramatic structure, juxtaposition of scenes to illuminate themes, revelation of character through dialogue, importance of soliloquies, imagery, and varieties of language among classes.

Progress and Juxtaposition of Scenes

Since Shakespeare's basic structural unit is the scene, both the progress and juxtaposition of scenes illuminate key issues. The progress of scenes indicates both plot (sequence of events) and structure (significance of individual events to the whole). By juxtaposing scenes, we can observe how Shakespeare creates parallel and contrasting scenes to emphasize themes. For instance, in I.ii, Hal and Poins conspire to rob Falstaff of the gold he steals from the pilgrims at Gadshill; in the next scene, Worcester, Northumberland, and Hotspur conspire to rob Henry IV of the crown he stole from Richard II; both scenes address the issue of usurpation. Moreover, III.i depicts the conspirators wrangling over land and power, not an omen of victory; the next scene, however, portrays the reconciliation of Henry IV and Hal, a reunion that certainly suggests victory to come. Such juxtapositions occur throughout this play, allowing us to teach students how great drama works.

Dialogue and Character

Obviously, dialogue reveals character. We learn about Hotspur's passion and daring and chivalric ideals when we hear him interrupt his uncle Worcester's plot, when he expresses his longing to "pluck bright honor from the pale-faced moon," when he ridicules Glendower's wizardry, when he teases his wife, when he longs to fight despite the failure of many allies to appear with their armies. We learn about Falstaff when he calls again and again for sack, when he complains about walking, when he lies about Gadshill, when he offers his homily about honor, when he dares Hal to claim Hotspur's death as his own victory. We learn about Hal's aims when he assesses Falstaff and Hotspur, when he speaks of his plan for "redeeming time when men think least [he] will," when he vows that his father has mistaken his purposes, when he courageously offers to fight Hotspur alone in order to save innocent soldiers' lives, when he speaks compassionately of the slain Hotspur. For understanding character, only close reading of Shakespeare's dialogue will suffice.

Soliloquies and Imagery

In this play, Hal, Hotspur, and Falstaff speak soliloquies. Hal's soliloquy at the end of I.ii is perhaps the most important. First, that soliloquy suggests that we cannot trust Henry IV's judgment (see I.i) in wishing to exchange his Hal for Northumberland's Hotspur. Second, the soliloquy reveals, early in the play, Hal's maturity and wisdom, both in assessing Falstaff and his cohorts and in planning to reveal himself as only he knows himself to be—a man willing to "pay the debt" of ruling England, a debt he "never promised." Third, the speech introduces important images—the sun (son, Son) hidden by ugly clouds (Falstaff, Hotspur) but capable of glittering (gold, not gilt) when he chooses to redeem the time (save England, legitimize the Lancaster throne). These images, especially those paralleling Hal and Christ, recur in III.ii, IV.i, V.i, V.ii, and V.iv.

Language and Social Class

In addition, *Henry IV, Part 1* distinguishes social classes through language, particularly through the use of poetry and prose. For the most part, the court world uses poetry, and the Eastcheap world uses prose. Hal, however, the only character comfortable in both worlds, speaks both prose and poetry, depending on his audience. To Falstaff, Hal speaks in terms Falstaff will understand; for instance, Hal uses food imagery with Falstaff, who often speaks in terms of food images and metaphors, and swears at Falstaff in the very terms Falstaff swears in. But in the world of court, with his father and with Hotspur, Hal speaks in poetry, the elevated language of the aristocracy.

Production

General education students need to see Shakespearean plays in performance. They benefit most, of course, from live productions because they can listen to language and watch stage business. Those of us in the hinterlands feel lucky if even once a year a school or theater within a hundred-mile radius offers a Shakespearean production. Sometimes we go even farther; at USI we take students annually to Montgomery for the Alabama Shakespeare Festival and to Stratford, Ontario, for the Stratford Festival.

In the meantime, we rely on records, films, and videotapes. Students often check out records and cassettes of plays from the library. With records, students focus on the language, the tone and pace of the lines. Since I always require one to two hundred lines of memorized recitation, recordings help students directly with spoken language. Films and videotapes (from Hollywood, London, Japan) help students begin imagining possibilities for productions. Seeing performances—live or on film—enables students to read both text and subtext more carefully and to comprehend the significance of costumes and lighting and props, of speech and silence, of relationships revealed by how characters move together and apart. In general ed courses, we work in class at staging scenes; we talk about what happens on stage at a given moment; how characters get on and off; what stage business is appropriate and possible for the characters; how costumes and props function; how characters turn, whisper, shout, and so on.

For *Henry IV, Part 1*, I strongly recommend the BBC production starring Jon Finch as Henry IV, Anthony Quayle as Falstaff, Tim Piggot-Smith as Hotspur, and, best of all, David Gwillim as Hal. Even if we can't show the entire videotape (it runs more than three hours), showing three or four individual scenes from this production teaches more about Shakespeare's text and subtext than hours of lecture can.

Conclusions and Recommendations

Henry IV, Part 1 will teach your general ed students more about Shakespearean drama than will any other single play. It will engage and challenge and delight them. If you can teach only one play, choose this one.

31 Teaching *The Taming of the Shrew:* Kate, Closure, and Eighteenth-Century Editions

Loreen L. Giese
Ohio University

Shakespeare's *The Taming of the Shrew* continues to provoke intense debate over the sincerity of Kate in her final speech, a speech exhorting women to submit to male supremacy. How we interpret her sincerity will affect both how we view gender definitions in the play and how we view the position of Kate. If sincere, then Kate accepts Petruchio's superiority, and women are to be submissive and subservient. A wink at the other women on stage indicates that she is not tamed and that women feign submission in order to let men think they dominate, yet nonetheless retain control. A wink at the audience, excluding the other dramatic figures on stage, suggests that Kate retains her spiritual independence while existing within her society's definitions of gender. Finally, involvement in a game with Petruchio indicates that she is not tamed and that men and women can have some sort of mutual affection and compatibility in marriage. While a film, videotaped, or theater performance can interpret Kate's position by manipulating her tone, characterization, gestures, and the like, the lack of closure in the First Folio only complicates the question of her sincerity.

According to the First Folio, *The Taming of the Shrew* has an induction, but no epilogue.[1] Although the anonymous contemporary play *The Taming of a Shrew*—which has a somewhat different beginning from Shakespeare's *The Shrew*—does supply an epilogue in keeping with its induction, Shakespeare does not complete the Sly story. As readers such as Ernest Kuhl (1921) andg Thelma Nelson Greenfield (1954) point out, Shakespeare "did not intend that *The Shrew* should point a lesson" (Kuhl 1921, 327). Without an epilogue, Shakespeare does not offer a frame of reference for what is illusion and what is reality. Greenfield maintains, for example, that with inductions that "create a distinct imaginative realm," the audience "out front" considers that "the frame is 'reality'; the main play is 'pretense' " (1954, 37).[2] Without the completing frame, then, *The Shrew* ends on the pretense of the play proper. In this context, the sincerity of Kate's final speech urging women's submission is part of an illusion.

Eighteenth-century editions have not been fully probed as sources that encourage students to consider the effects of closure on the sincerity of Kate. Eighteenth-century editors, following Pope's edition in 1723, radically emended the First Folio by adding the epilogue from *A Shrew* to provide a more definite ending, thereby imposing their own readings and, in the process, providing their own definitions of gender.[3] In classroom practice, examination of parallel passages from the First Folio and Pope's edition (see appendix) can provoke significant discussion of how the closure of the epilogue affects the position of women, of what could have been possible motives for refashioning the play to have closure, and of the history of Shakespeare criticism, editing, and interpretation. This discussion will encourage students to consider the text as a cultural product, rather than as an ahistorical text.

In this essay, I intend to provide an overview of the textual changes that eighteenth-century editors made in handling the epilogue. I shall then offer an interpretation of the effect of the epilogue on Kate's speech and her position at the close of the play proper.[4] For whether on the stage or on the page, the epilogue makes several readings possible. One interpretation indicates that Kate is a submissive wife and that Sly has learned a lesson on how to tame his wife. Nevertheless, on the stage, Sly's tone of voice and physical stature and presence can manipulate the irony or didactic quality of the lesson. On the page, editorial notes and emendations suggest that the lesson is not ironic, but didactic. Still, in Pope's text, the effect is more ambiguous, since the epilogue can be seen to point to both the sincerity *and* the irony of the lesson.

Convinced that the quartos and folios were corrupt, Pope introduced radical emendations and made substantive changes in the final lines of *The Shrew*. In particular, he cut lines from Kate's speech that he felt were "excessively bad" (1725, 1:xxii), and he was the first editor to supply an epilogue to Shakespeare's *The Shrew*, which he took from *A Shrew*:

> *Enter two servants bearing* Sly *in his own apparel, and leave him on the stage. Then enter a* Tapster.

> Sly awaking. Sim, *give's some more wine*————*what, all the player's gone? am not I a lord?*
>
> Tap. *A lord with a murrain! come, art thou drunk still?*
>
> Sly. *Who's this? Tapster! oh I have had the bravest dream that ever thou heardst in all thy life.*
>
> Tap. *Yea marry, but thou hadst best get thee home, for your wife will course you for dreaming here all night.*
>
> Sly. *Will she? I know how to tame a shrew. I dreamt upon it all this night, and thou has wak'd me out of the best dream that ever I had. But I'll to my wife, and tame her too, if she anger me.*
> (1723, 2:363)

Despite the censure of Pope's editing techniques by some subsequent Shakespeare editors—Johnson, echoing the opinions of Lewis Theobald, for instance, comments that Pope "rejected whatever he disliked, and thought more of amputation than of cure" (1765, 1:x1viii)[5]— Theobald, Sir Thomas Hanmer, William Warburton, Johnson, and John Bell include the epilogue added by Pope in their texts. While Pope introduced the epilogue in 1723, it was not until the Johnson-Steevens edition of 1773 that George Steevens finally sinks it into a footnote. That he does not omit it altogether may indicate his discomfort with the play's open-endedness. Indeed, it was not until the end of the eighteenth century that Issac Reed (1785), Joseph Rann (1786), and Edmond Malone (1790) restored the Folio reading in their respective editions, thereby leaving the play without a completed frame of reality and reviving the indeterminacy of Kate's speech.

At any rate, Pope's edition provides strong evidence that the epilogue makes the play a school for would-be shrew tamers. Nevertheless, it also seems to indicate that the submission of women is only a dream. In the former case, Pope's additions and omissions can be seen as serving a didactic purpose, that is, by adding the epilogue, Pope provides a moral for Shakespeare's play. Indeed, in the closing lines of the epilogue, Sly states what he learned: "*I know how to tame a shrew.*" Now, if Sly *has* learned how to make a woman submissive, Kate's speech appears to be sincere. Pope's emendation then encourages the reader to believe that the lesson of the reality-frame penetrates the pretense frame. If read thus, Pope limits the reader's interpretation, so that one sees Kate as conforming to the male-prescribed cultural location of woman as subservient.

Yet, as mentioned, the epilogue may alternatively be seen to suggest the irony of Kate's speech. In the induction, Sly assumes the role of a lord, which is, of course, an illusion, for he is not a lord but a drunken tinker. In the epilogue, then, he awakens to reality; he comes out of his role. Therefore, since the epilogue stresses acting, Kate too may be playing a role. Like Sly's, Kate's metamorphosis may be momentary; Coppelia Kahn (1981) comments, for instance, that "the transformation of Christopher Sly from drunken lout to noble lord, a transformation only temporary and skin-deep, suggests that Kate's switch from independence to subjection may also be deceptive and prepares us for the irony of the denouement" (104). Moreover, the tapster's reference to a cursing, presumably dominant, wife who awaits Sly at home suggests that the lesson is ironic.

The lines Pope cut and sank into a footnote complicate both interpretations. Pope concludes Kate's speech and the play proper with a line that strongly suggests she plays a role: "our weakness [is] past compare, / That seeming to be most, which we indeed least are" (1723, 2:363).[6] Pope's emendation thus suggests that Kate *pretends* to be submissive. In the reality frame, then, a tame, submissive wife is only a dream; in reality, the shrew prevails. Nevertheless, Pope "degrade[s] to the bottom of the page" (1725, 1:xxii)—puts into a footnote—the very lines whose hyperbolic quality suggest that Kate's speech is ironic:

> Then vale your stomachs, for it is no boot,
> And place your hands below your husband's foot:
> In token of which duty, if he please,
> My hand is ready, may it do him ease.

(1723, 2:363)

Moreover, Pope omits another possible suggestion that Kate is not tamed: " 'Tis a wonder, by your leave, she will be tam'd so" (1723, 2:363). Yet Pope also omits the discussion of the wager among Petruchio, Lucentio, and Vincentio and the command Petruchio gives Kate to go to bed. If Pope hopes to provide a moral, it appears ironic that he omits both lines in which the male, while surrounded by admiring males, revels in his glory over taming the female and lines in which the female makes a gesture of submission.

The presence of the epilogue in subsequent eighteenth-century editions does not provide such richly conflicting evidence. On one hand, Theobald, Warburton, Johnson, Steevens, and Bell appear to allow for the irony of Kate's speech by restoring the hyperbolic lines that Pope put into a footnote. Yet the comments and emendations in the texts of these editors strongly suggest that they include the epilogue for didactic purposes. In fact, Theobald's major textual variant within the epilogue stresses its didactic quality: he (followed by Hanmer,

Warburton, Johnson, and Steevens) emphasizes the lesson by setting the phrase "tame a Shrew" in different type. While this emphasis could be seen to underscore the irony of the line, the case of Theobald in particular, who is seemingly the first to make this emendation, suggests otherwise. He comments that Kate in her speech reveals that she is a "Convert" to the "Doctrine of Conjugal Obedience" and serves as an "Instructer" to the widow and Bianca of their "Duty" (1733, 2:354). The emphasis here is thus on a reformed Kate teaching women their place of subservience.

Johnson's adoption of the epilogue may seem surprising, since his greatest contribution to Shakespearean textual scholarship is his conviction that the First Folio is the authoritative text for Shakespeare's plays. He may have included the epilogue because he believed the indeterminacy of Kate's speech was part of what he calls Shakespeare's "first defect": the lack of a "moral purpose" (1765, 1:xix). He maintains that Shakespeare "sacrifices virtue to convenience, and is so much more careful to please than to instruct, that he seems to write without any moral purpose" (1765, 1:xix). The epilogue would supply just such a purpose.

A few years later, Bell produced a theatrical edition that took up the issue of instruction. His edition advertises that it will render "the essence of SHAKESPEARE, more instructive and intelligible; especially to the ladies and to youth" (1774, 1:9). Because the editor, Francis Gentleman, specifically points to the didactic quality of Kate's speech, it would seem that he too incorporated the epilogue for its moral: in this speech "is a fine display of relative knowledge . . . and we wish that, not only every unmarried, but also married lady, were perfect in the words and practice" (1774, 6:150). Gentleman attached this note to Kate's line ". . . [women] are bound to serve, love, and obey" (1774, 6:150), at which point he thought the play "should undoubtedly end" (1774, 6:151). He thought all subsequent lines, including the epilogue, were "monstrously insipid" (1774, 6:151).[7] Nonetheless, the point at which he wants the play to stop emphasizes a lesson.

The revisions of these editors are particularly significant, since they did not include the epilogue to echo stage performances. The theater records for London from 1701 to 1800 indicate that eighteenth-century performances usually omitted the induction (Hogan 1952 and 1957), a practice that is telling, since eighteenth-century directors catered to audience tastes and practiced wholesale adaptations. Even Garrick's (1786) version of the play ignored the emendations in these editions, though he added other lines to the ending. Kate, for instance, responds to Petruchio's penultimate speech with "Nay, then I'm all unworthy of thy love, / And look with blushes on my former self" (1786, 33). Garrick's omission particularly emphasizes that the editors who incorporated the epilogue were not adhering to production practice. Indeed, Garrick's adaptation was the sixth most performed Shakespeare play between 1751 and 1800 and accounted for 234 of the total 235 performances of *The Shrew* (Hogan 1957, 2:716–19).

Such theater records emphasize the unique position of the editions of *The Shrew* within the eighteenth century. Differences between textual editions and theater performances might suggest that directors and editors catered to the different tastes of a reading audience and a playgoing audience. Nevertheless, the audiences do not appear to be that different. As Gary Taylor (1990) comments, "By the eighteenth century, booksellers had begun acquiring rights in plays even before they were performed—the better to exploit the large but usually temporary readerly interest that the theatre could generate" (68). Even though "the stage sank as the bookshop rose" in the eighteenth century (Taylor 1990, 53), theatergoers were readers and vice versa; they still fed off each other.

The differences between editing and performance practices thus seem to result from other considerations. In terms of the page, Pope's addition of the epilogue might have satisfied his literary neoclassical preference for closure. On the stage, productions omitted not only the newly emended epilogue, but the induction from the First Folio as well. These omissions by eighteenth-century directors—as by some twentieth-century directors—might have been due to the logistics of staging. By leaving off the frame, they avoided staging problems such as where Sly sits during the play proper and when he is carried off. In addition, the omission of the frame may reflect a larger pattern occurring within eighteenth-century theaters. As Taylor points out, popular plays "pitted a strong female lead against a strong male, and audiences took an active interest in which of the two popular performers would dominate the other" (1990, 117). Garrick's shrinking of *The Shrew* to three acts and renaming it *Catharine and Petruchio* may have been influenced by this pattern of focusing attention on the star roles.

After examining these editions, students can see that, even with closure, Pope's edition of Shakespeare's *Shrew* still retains the ambiguity that allows a reader to decide what is reality and what is illusion in Kate's position at the end of the play. The presence of the epilogue in other editions, however, indicates that she is tamed and subservient to male dominance. Students may conclude that because of the wider range of interpretation that the First Folio allows, the addition of the epilogue to *The Taming of the Shrew* was fortunately for an age, and not for all time.

Notes

1. For discussions of whether or not Shakespeare included an epilogue in an earlier version of *The Shrew* than that of the First Folio and his possible pragmatic and artistic reasons for omitting it, see, in addition to Kuhl (1921) and Greenfield (1954), Richard Hosley (1961), Peter Alexander (1969), Karl P. Wentersdorf (1978), and Brian Morris (1981).

2. Greenfield concludes that in the induction to *The Shrew* "Shakespeare sharpened the contrast between the frame and the play proper, and . . . had at least begun to develop a theme concerning an experiment in human nature" (1954, 38).

3. The editors who add the epilogue from *A Shrew* omit its opening and closing lines. See Bullough (1957, 1:108).

4. I base this discussion on the first editions of Nicholas Rowe (1709), Alexander Pope (1723–25), Lewis Theobald (1733), Sir Thomas Hanmer (1743), William Warburton (1747), Samuel Johnson (1765), Samuel Johnson and George Steevens (1773), John Bell (1774), Issac Reed (1785), Joseph Rann (1786), and Edmond Malone (1790).

5. The censure of Theobald is evident in the title of his 1726 review of Pope's edition: *Shakespeare restored: or a specimen of the many errors, as well committed, as unamended, by Mr. Pope in his late edition of this poet.*

6. Kahn also sees this line as a hint that Kate is "dissembling" (1981, 116).

7. Bell's inclusion of the epilogue in his theatrical edition is puzzling; more evidence exists as to why he would not want to include it. Theater records indicate that it was not part of performances, and the editor specifies that his edition is for theatergoers, so that they "will not be so puzzled themselves to accompany the speaker" (1774, 1:7). He also applauds Garrick's version in his introduction to the play and comments that *"the drunken tinker rather appears an absurd intrusion; an excrescence on the general design"* (1774, 6:71). It appears that the didactic quality of the epilogue was important enough to ignore all these considerations for excluding it.

References

Editions, Adaptations, and Sources

Bullough, Geoffrey, ed. 1957. *Narrative and Dramatic Sources of Shakespeare.* Vol. 1. London: Routledge and Kegan Paul; New York: Columbia University Press.

Garrick, David. 1786. *The Taming of the Shrew; or, Catharine and Petruchio.* London: C. Bathurst. Originally published in 1756.

Gentleman, Francis, ed. 1774. *Bell's Edition of Shakespeare's Plays, As they were performed at the Theatres Royal in London; Regulated from the Prompt Books of each House.* Vols. 1 and 6. Facsimile. London: Cornmarket Press, 1969.

Hanmer, Sir Thomas, ed. 1743. *The Works of Shakespear.* Vol. 2. Oxford: Theater.

Hinman, Charlton, preparer. 1968. *The First Folio of Shakespeare.* The Norton Facsimile. London, New York, Sydney, and Toronto: Paul Hamlyn.

Johnson, Samuel, ed. 1765. *The Plays of William Shakespeare.* Vols. 1 and 3. London: J. and R. Tonson.

Johnson, Samuel, and George Steevens, eds. 1773. *The Plays of William Shakespeare.* Vol. 3. London: C. Bathurst.

Malone, Edmond, ed. 1790. *The Plays and Poems of William Shakspeare.* Vol. 3. London: J. Rivington and Sons.

Pope, Alexander, ed. 1723–25. *The Works of Shakespear.* Vols. 1 and 2. London: J. Tonson.

Rann, Joseph. 1786. *The Dramatic Works of Shakspeare.* Vol. 2. Oxford: Clarendon Press.

Reed, Issac, ed. 1785. *The Plays of William Shakspeare.* Vol. 3. London: C. Bathurst.

Rowe, Nicholas, ed. 1709. *The Works of Mr. William Shakespear.* Vol. 2. London: J. Tonson.

Theobald, Lewis, ed. 1733. *The Works of Shakespeare.* Vol. 2. London: A. Bettesworth and C. Hitch.

Warburton, William, ed. 1747. *The Works of Shakespear.* Vol. 2. London: J. and P. Knapton.

Secondary Sources

Alexander, Peter. 1969. "The Original Ending of *The Taming of the Shrew.*" *Shakespeare Quaterly* 20: 111–16.

Greenfield, Thelma Nelson. 1954. "The Transformation of Christopher Sly." *Philological Quaterly* 33: 34–42.

Hogan, Charles Beecher. 1952 and 1957. *Shakespeare in the Theatre, 1701–1800.* 2 Vols. Oxford: Clarendon Press.

Hosley, Richard. 1961. "Was There a 'Dramatic Epilogue' to *The Taming of the Shrew?*" *Studies in English Literature* 1: 17–34.

Kahn, Coppelia. 1981. *Man's Estate: Masculine Identity in Shakespeare.* Berkeley: University of California Press.

Kuhl, Ernest P. 1921. "Shakespeare's Purpose in Dropping Sly." *Modern Language Notes* 36: 321–29.

Morris, Brian, ed. 1981. Introduction. *The Taming of the Shrew.* Arden Edition. London and New York: Methuen.

Taylor, Gary. 1990. *Reinventing Shakespeare: A Cultural History, from the Restoration to the Present.* London: Hogarth Press. Weidenfeld and Nicolson edition published 1989.

Wentersdorf, Karl P. 1978. ''The Original Ending of *The Taming of the Shrew:* A Reconsideration.'' *Studies in English Literature* 18: 201–15.

Appendix

First Folio

Kate. Fie, fie, vnknit that
   threatening vnkinde brow,
And dart not scornefull
   glances from those eies,
To wound thy Lord, thy King,
   thy Gouernour.
It blots thy beautie, as frosts
   doe bite the Meads,
Confounds thy fame, as whirle-
   winds shake faire budds,
And in no sence is meete or
   amiable.
A woman mou'd, is like a
   fountaine troubled.
Muddie, ill seeming, thicke,
   bereft of beautie,
And while it is so, none so
   dry or thirstie
Will daigne to sip, or touch
   one drop of it.
Thy husband is thy Lord, thy
   life, thy keeper,
Thy head, thy soueraigne: One
   that cares for thee,
And for thy maintenance. Commits his body
To painfull labour, both by
   sea and land:
To watch the night in stormes,
   the day in cold,

Pope's Edition

Kath. Fie, fie, unknit that
   threatning unkind brow,
And dart not scornful glances
   from those eyes,
To wound thy lord, thy king,
   thy governor.
It blots thy beauty, as frosts
   bite the meads,
Confounds thy fame, as whirl-
   winds shake fair buds,
And in no sense is meet or
   amiable.
A woman mov'd is like a foun-
   tain troubled,
Muddy, ill seeming, thick,
   bereft of beauty;
And while it is so, none so
   dry or thirsty
Will dain to sip, or touch a
   drop of it.
Thy husband is thy lord, thy
   life, thy keeper,
Thy head, thy soveraign; one
   that cares for thee
And for thy maintenance: commits his body
To painful labour, both by sea
   and land;
To watch the night in storms,
   the day in cold,

First Folio (*cont.*)	**Pope's Edition** (*cont.*)
Whil'st thou ly'st warme at home, secure and safe,	While thou ly'st warm at home, secure and safe,
And craues no other tribute at thy hands,	And craves no other tribute at thy hands,
But loue, faire lookes, and true obedience;	But love, fair looks, and true obedience;
Too little payment for so great a debt.	Too little payment for so great a debt.
Such dutie as the subiect owes the Prince,	Such duty as the subject owes the prince,
Euen such a woman oweth to her husband:	Even such a woman oweth to her husband:
And when she is froward, peeuish, sullen, sowre,	And when she's froward, peevish, sullen, sower,
And not obedient to his honest will,	And not obedient to his honest will;
What is she but a foule contending Rebell,	What is she but a foul contending rebel,
And gracelesse Traitor to her louing Lord?	And graceless traitor to her loving lord?
I am asham'd that women are so simple,	I am asham'd that women are so simple,
To offer warre, where they should kneele for peace:	To offer war where they should kneel for peace;
Or seeke for rule, supremacie, and sway,	Or seek for rule, supremacy, and sway,
When they are bound to serue, loue, and obay.	When they are bound to serve, love, and obey.
Why are our bodies soft, and weak, and smooth,	Why are our bodies soft, and weak and smooth,
Vnapt to toyle and trouble in the world,	Unapt to toil and trouble in the world,
But that our soft conditions, and our harts,	But that our soft conditions and our hearts
Should well agree with our externall parts?	Should well agree with our external parts?
Come, come, you froward and vnable wormes,	Come, come, you're froward and unable worms;
My minde hath bin as bigge as one of yours,	My mind hath been as big as one of yours,

First Folio (*cont.*)	**Pope's Edition** (*cont.*)
My heart as great, my reason haplie more,	My heart is great, my reason haply more,
To bandie word for word, and frowne for frowne;	To bandy word for word, and frown for frown;
But now I see our Launces are but strawes:	But now I see our launces are but straws.
Our strength as weake, our weakenesse past compare,	Our strength is weak, our weakness past compare,
That seeming to be most, which we indeed least are.	That seeming to be most, which we indeed least are.
Then vale your stomackes, for it is no boote,	*Enter two servants bearing* Sly *in his own apparel, and leave him on the stage. Then enter a* Tapster.
And place your hands below your husbands foote:	
In token of which dutie, if he please,	Sly awaking.] Sim, *give's some more wine———what, all the players gone? am not I a lord?*
My hand is readie, may it do him ease.	
Pet. Why there's a wench: Come on, and kisse mee *Kate.*	Tap. *A lord with a murrain! come, art thou drunk still?*
Luc. Well go thy waies olde Lad for thou shalt ha't.	Sly. *Who's this?* Tapster! *oh I have had the bravest dream that ever thou heardst in all thy life.*
Vin. Tis a good hearing, when children ae toward.	
Luc. But a harsh hearing, when women are froward.	Tap. *Yea marry, but thou hadst best get thee home for your wife will course you for dreaming here all night.*
Pet. Come *Kate,* weee'le to bed.	
We three are married, but you two are sped.	Sly. *Will she? I know how to tame a shrew. I dreampt upon it all this night, and thou hast wak'd me out of the best dream that ever I had. But I'll to my wife, and tame her too, if she anger me.*
'Twas I wonne the wager, though you hit the white,	
And being a winner, God giue you good night.	
Exit Petruchio	(1723, 2:362–63)
Horten. Now goe thy wayes, thou hast tam'd a curst Shrow.	
Luc. Tis a wonder, by your leaue, she will be tam'd so.	
(1623, 229)	

32 *Measure for Measure:* Links to Our Time

John S. Simmons
Florida State University

Measure for Measure certainly does not rank with *Macbeth, Julius Caesar,* or *A Midsummer Night's Dream* as a play widely popular with high school English teachers. Having taught it on two different occasions to later adolescents, however, and having had time to reflect on its effect on them, I would propose that it be considered a play worth sharing with students in senior high school classes. In my opinion, at least, *Measure for Measure* contains a number of thematic concerns and studies in personality that give it such stature. Its action, its suspense, its humor, its sober reflection—all provide ample reason for suggesting its use with secondary students, despite its relative obscurity in the current canon of "high school" Shakespearean plays.

My first suggestion for approaching this play is that it not be treated as a comedy. For those who want to use a Shakespeare play to illustrate this mode, *A Midsummer Night's Dream* or *The Taming of the Shrew* would be far better choices. *Measure for Measure,* however, is best presented as a reflection of social conflict and political crisis management. At best, it is a dark comedy, as could be said of *Troilus and Cressida;* nevertheless, the social and political issues are far more absorbing, and thus more potentially attractive to a late adolescent audience. Indeed, it has long been my belief that presenting comedy through *any* Shakespeare play presents a pretty stiff challenge for a teacher of high school students.

My next suggestion to those who would teach *Measure for Measure* is to assign the reading of the play and then presume that the readers are familiar with the plot. This allows teachers to proceed immediately to a review of those themes found within the play, themes that would be meaningful to any audience, high school students included. There are four themes that I will identify and briefly discuss. The intensely dramatic events in the work provide more than adequate media for their consideration once the plot line has been established and the ubiquitous Elizabethan language barrier has been dealt with.

In no particular order, the significant themes to be examined in *Measure* are discussed below.

Sexism. For those interested in feminist issues, this play is dynamite. The fact is that women in *Measure* are treated shabbily, to say the least. In the joust for political power among the male contestants, women are pawns and sex objects. That treatment extends to those of both low and high status. The main female character, Isabella, is faced with an awful moral decision, but the men who have created her dilemma all display, in varying degrees, a certain disdain for her humanity. Her choice between personal honor and her brother's life is an excruciatingly painful one, yet to the involved males, it is viewed only as it affects them. (If Molly Yard or Betty Friedan were teaching this play . . .) The more conventional character, Mistress Overdone, is also treated without regard to her fate as a person in the drama. She is little more than the butt of crude jokes as she attempts to work out her own problems. A concerned teacher may well be able to do a considerable amount of consciousness-raising with this one.

Insofar as the theme of sexism is concerned, Isabella's choice may suggest an intriguing, divergent discussion centering on the nature of goodness; that is, what if a person (in this case, Isabella) *does* sacrifice his or her deepest beliefs (and possibly immortal soul) for another's well-being? (See the Biblical verse John 15:13: "Greater love hath no man than this, that a man lay down his life . . .") Could her sacrifice, albeit to the whims of cruel and insensitive males, be viewed as part of a greater good? And would the play be thus transformed from comedy into tragedy?

Political Corruption. For young people brought up in the era of Watergate, Iran-Contra, and the savings and loan scandal, this theme should hardly be difficult to grasp. From the opening scene, readers learn that Vienna is in rough shape. Morality is scoffed at and abused in high places, offices are for sale, and keepers of the laws often look the other way. Because the Duke wants to find out how bad things really are, he goes underground and leaves the city in the hands of his ablest and most trusted subject, Angelo. It is Angelo's megalomania, abuse of power, and disdain for morality that are really the crux of the play. His rigid enforcement of the laws, in sharp contrast with his own lawless pursuit of personal goals, demonstrates intensively the political theme of the play. Although the happy ending puts all things—quite superficially—to right, the misuse of political prerogative really constitutes the issue that stands above all others. It is the effect that temporary authority can have on erstwhile ethical individuals which can be most decisively exploited in the reading of and response to this play. And the signals are *not* mixed; their lack of subtlety should make the corruption issue quite evident to a wide range of students.

The Law versus Fairness and Reason. Portia, the main female character in another of Shakespeare's plays, *The Merchant of Venice*, at one point asserts, "The quality of mercy is not strain'd; / It droppeth as the gentle rain from heaven / Upon the place beneath." Such a statement applies eloquently to another major conflict in *Measure*. To prove himself a worthy and forceful leader, Angelo applies the law to its limit. He administers justice in its most severe form in order to establish himself as the hardnosed stand-in ruler he wishes to appear to be. But, as noted in the discussion of political corruption, he does not apply the law in any consistent manner. In *his* application of the laws, people suffer unequally depending on his arbitrary, biased perceptions of them. Unlike Gilbert and Sullivan's Mikado, he does not seem to care whether or not the punishment fits the crime. He is also totally indifferent to pleas for mercy or reason. The temperate or sensible application of the law seems to be beyond his understanding or sentiments. Only when he infers that there is some personal gain to be realized does he adjust any judicial decision. Thus, in addition to condemning political corruption, *Measure for Measure* vividly illustrates the eternal need to reconcile the letter of the law to its spirit.

Commitment to Principle. While most of the main characters in *Measure* compromise themselves at one point or another, Isabella stands throughout as a person who is totally unwilling to bend on commitment. Her vow of chastity is sacred to the point that she is willing to forsake her own beloved brother's life rather than yield to Angelo, who, in modern argot, is only too willing to deal. Her unshakable resolution is reminiscent of Socrates' categorical willingness—as articulated in the *Apology*—to give his life for his philosophical precept. Though Isabella may, and probably will, impress the more pragmatic members of a high school class as one who goes overboard in her resolve, the distinctness of contrast between her stance and that of virtually all the other characters should provide the teacher with an excellent opportunity to exploit the issue of what one's sworn word means, especially in times of duress.

In addition to these themes, *Measure* contains a number of characters that can be used to illustrate significant and engrossing human postures, motives, and idiosyncrasies, all of which are most pertinent to highly visible public figures of the contemporary period. I have provided succinct analyses of the play's major characters, but I leave it to each teacher to identify and exploit their correlates in today's milieu. This decision does not reflect indolence, I simply wish to ensure that teachers have the utmost flexibility in choosing parallels in modern life. In any event, here are my analyses of the play's major characters.

Angelo. A good representative villain, although, unlike the Iagos and the Edmunds of the tragedies, he is not destroyed by the evil he perpetrates during the play. A power seeker, unable to curb the very libidinous desires he so severely judges in others, Angelo serves as a classic example of hypocritical behavior for young readers. Yet his soliloquies in II.ii and II.iv reveal a man who is torn by conscience, and one who admires the moral resolve of the very person, Isabella, whose principles he seeks to compromise. It is Angelo's excessive appetites—for power, for sexual conquest, for vindictive enforcement of the law—that constitute the driving force of the play. He is one character whom no one in the class can possibly overlook.

Isabella. Young people of today, when they come across someone who takes extreme, uncompromising positions, may well ask, "Is this person for real?" Such a question fits nicely with the perceptions that many readers of *Measure* have of Isabella. Isabella remains fanatically committed to her vows of chastity throughout the drama, even when they imperil both her and those dear to her. Given the current attitude toward sex, Isabella's rigid defense of her virginity may seem unrealistic or excessively self-righteous, but her courage in the face of immediate, dire consequences cannot be denied. Her unbending honesty also stands out in contrast with the equivocal, manipulative, deceitful behavior of those around her. A skillful teacher can provoke a good deal of animated discussion about the validity as well as the appropriateness of her character. In addition, some fertile discussions might result in comparing Isabella with the title character in Sophocles' *Antigone,* who sacrifices her life in order to secure her brother's immortality.

Claudio. Claudio's cavalier behavior may well be sympathetically perceived by high school students. The image of the "swinger" seems to appeal to male and female students alike. What may cause concern or disagreement is his overall unwillingness to live with and accept the consequences of his actions—a stance that many adolescents condemn in the abstract but are reluctant or even unwilling to accept in relation to their own behavior. That Claudio is perfectly willing to see his sister sacrifice whatever it takes to save his skin could bring about some pronounced debate between male and female members of the class. Although not as reprehensible as Angelo, he may be classified as a "male chauvinist pig" by students who embrace feminist ideology. At any rate, it is Claudio's actions that bring about the confrontation between Angelo and Isabella. For that reason alone, he is worth discussing. But his attitudes toward hanging onto life, toward women, and toward moral principle make him much more than that.

Vincentio. The Duke of Vienna, although physically absent most of the time, is a character who can spur further debate as a representative of certain human values and motives. After all, it is his laxness and indifference as a ruler that lead to the state of moral deterioration in which Vienna finds itself at the outset. Then, when he finally decides to find out the extent of the problem in order to deal with it, his methods will probably seem unduly clandestine to those class members who pride themselves on being "upfront." Clearly, his tactics can be seen as an example of the kind of philosophy in which "the end justifies the means," a philosophy that has been the subject of debate for centuries. His manner of solving problems, exploiting conflicts, and dispensing justice may seem a bit on the expedient side to those students who want to see justice (as *they* perceive it) carried out. And his conduct of the leader's role could be the cause of some rousing differences of opinion.

Lucio. A supporting character who supplies a significant comic element, but who stands apart from the pimps and madams of Vienna, a city whose way of life is greatly undermined by Angelo's determined moral crusade. Not only does the rakish Lucio come from a higher class than the group just mentioned, but he also represents, to a lesser degree, an upwardly mobile, amoral individual who seeks to use the trends of the times to benefit his own selfish ends. In a sense, he comes off as a minor-league Angelo in his attempt to become a "big man." In his clumsy attempts to assert himself, Lucio will probably evoke laughter and a certain amount of contempt from the readers of the play. Indeed, he is yet another example of the excessive posturing found throughout.

In its themes and characters, *Measure for Measure* provides an incisively drawn social/political commentary, a commentary whose relevance extends far beyond the times in which it was written. Its tone, however, is not as somber as the tragedies, nor is it as pessimistic as *Troilus and Cressida,* also labeled by many scholars as a "dark comedy." The humorous elements of the play elevate it from that darkness and offer high school readers some chuckles even as they examine its serious messages. One major example of comedy is found in the use of the "bed trick," wherein Angelo unknowingly makes love to Marianna (whom he has in fact married earlier) instead of his "conquest," Isabella. This bit of slapstick is in keeping with the behavior of the lowlifes in the cast, all employees or customers of the city's brothels, who, with the madam Mistress Overdone, struggle to cope with the new order imposed early on by the vindictive, power-seeking Angelo. This behavior is best exemplified by Lucio, whose posturing evokes laughter, especially when he vilifies the Duke to a monk who is in reality the Duke himself. A minor character, Barnadine, also contributes a caricature of the self-righteous hypocrite, who, as a murderer condemned to death, pompously defends his right to choose the time of his execution. In general, the exaggerated posturing of such characters provides a number of scenes and dialogues that, in their incongruity, provide the stuff of humor.

So there is an abundance of comic relief from the gravity of the themes already described. Such comic elements add to the entertainment value of the play and make it more attractive to a young audience (as contrasted, say, with Ibsen's "problem" plays). What makes *Measure,* along with all Shakespearean drama, hard to read, however, is the language. Having taught the Bard in high school and observed countless student teachers valiantly doing the same, I offer one piece of advice to those who will continue to feature Shakespeare's plays in their programs of study: use recordings—records, cassette tapes, CDs, whatever delivers the language effectively. These, in my opinion, are vastly superior to oral readings by students. No matter how much time and concentration these students devote to their oral presentations, they are *all* uncomfortable with the language. Their lack of fluency, especially as they struggle with the syntactic complexities that abound in the plays, will invariably produce readings that are largely devoid of dramatic intensity. So find some professionally done stuff. It will help to clarify meaning as well as reduce wear and tear on the student body.

With effective recorded reading and carefully structured discussions, *Measure for Measure* can emerge as a meaningful literary experience for a range of high school students. Most importantly, it can aid them in understanding *realpolitik*. Many of them are already getting a taste of this as they participate in student councils, school-sponsored clubs, athletic teams, and groups outside the school such as church clubs, volunteer community organizations, YMCA groups, and the like. *Measure for Measure*, along with the organizations just named, offers the thoughtful observer provocative examples of the dynamics of leadership, both great and small.

Editors

James E. Davis, professor of English at Ohio University in Athens, is a past president of the National Council of Teachers of English. He spent several years as a high school teacher and has been chair of his department. He reviews regularly for *The Alan Review* and is a member of its editorial board. In addition to chapters in many books, he has contributed over one hundred and fifty articles to journals of NCTE and its affiliates. He has edited the *Ohio English Bulletin, Focus: Teaching English Language Arts,* and the book *Dealing with Censorship* and has co-edited the 1988 edition of *Your Reading,* the junior high/middle school booklist for NCTE. Most recently he has co-authored the book, *Presenting William Sleator.*

Ronald E. Salomone is professor of English and chair of the Division of Humanities at the Chillicothe campus of Ohio University. He has served as president of the Southeastern Ohio Council of Teachers of English and as editor of *Focus.* He has published in the areas of modern British fiction and faculty evaluation and administration, was selected Outstanding Faculty Member at OU–C in 1987, and is currently completing a book on the novels of Charles Williams.

Contributors

Philip M. Anderson is associate professor in the Department of Secondary Education and Youth Services at Queens College of the City University of New York. He began his career as a language arts and reading teacher at Parkview High School in Orfordville, Wisconsin, supervised student teachers at the University of Wisconsin–Madison, and taught in the English department at Ohio University and the education department at Brown University. He is the author or co-author of over thirty articles and chapters. In 1989 he was presented the Charles Swain Thomas Distinguished Service Award by the New England Association of Teachers of English.

Sharon A. Beehler, assistant professor of English at Montana State University in Bozeman, is director of the English education program at MSU. She spent several years as a secondary teacher and department chair in Austin, Texas, before moving to Montana in 1986. She has served as editor of the *Montana English Journal* and is a member of the executive board of the Montana Association of Teachers of English Language Arts. She has contributed articles to *Shakespeare Quarterly, English Journal,* and the *Nebraska English Journal* and is currently working on a book about teaching Shakespeare through an emphasis on Bakhtin's theories of communication.

Harry Brent is professor of English and former chair of the Department of English at Baruch College of the City University of New York. He has served on the Executive Committee of NCTE and twice has been elected chair of the NCTE College Section. He has co-edited seven books dealing with the teaching of writing, chief among them *Rhetorical Considerations* and *The Critical Reader.* His latest co-edited work is *The Saint Martin's Horizon Reader.* He has also published extensively on medieval, Renaissance, and modern literature.

Mary T. Christel is an English teacher at Adlai E. Stevenson High School in Prairie View, Illinois. She teaches courses in world literature, creative writing, and film analysis. She has participated in both an NEH institute at Illinois State University, which resulted in the publication of an article concerning the revision process used for T. S. Eliot's "The Hollow Men," and an NEH seminar at the University of Wisconsin–Parkside focusing on the study of Shakespeare's

Henriad. She also co-edits a professional magazine for teachers at Stevenson called *The Scriptor* and cosponsors the school's literary magazine.

Leila Christenbury, associate professor of English education at Virginia Commonwealth University, Richmond, is a former high school English teacher. She is a member of the executive committee of NCTE's Conference on English Education, co-editor of *The Alan Review,* and co-author of *Questioning: A Path to Critical Thinking.* She also wrote a regular column for *English Journal* for four years. At VCU she teaches graduates and undergraduates, supervises student teachers, and is director of the Capital Writing Project.

Ann Legore Christiansen teaches Major British Writers, College English Skills, and American Literature/Composition at Adlai E. Stevenson High School in Prairie View, Illinois. She is a member of the State Advisory Board for Reading Assessment in Illinois and a member of NCTE, IATE, IRA, and the Illinois Reading Council. She attended the National Endowment for Humanities seminar on Shakespeare's Henriad at the University of Wisconsin–Parkside.

Michael J. Collins is dean of the School for Summer and Continuing Education and teaches in the Department of English at Georgetown University.

Samuel Crowl is professor of English and dean of the University College at Ohio University, where he has taught since 1970. He has published articles on stage and film productions of Shakespeare in *Shakespeare Quarterly, The Shakespeare Survey,* and *The Literature/Film Quarterly* and has delivered papers at the Modern Language Association, the Shakespeare Association of America, the World Shakespeare Congress, and the Ohio Shakespeare Conference. His book *Shakespeare Observed* was recently published by the Ohio University Press. He is a fellow of the Royal Society for the Arts and held an observership with the Royal Shakespeare Company in 1980.

Sherry Bevins Darrell, associate professor of English at the University of Southern Indiana in Evansville, teaches various composition and literature survey courses, Greek tragedy, and Shakespeare. A native Texan, she earned a B.A. in philosophy and English at McMurry College in Abilene, Texas, and her M.A. and Ph.D. from George Peabody College for Teachers in Nashville, Tennessee. This summer she will complete a book of monologues by ancient Greek women.

Annette Drew-Bear, associate professor of English at Washington and Jefferson College in Washington, Pennsylvania, regularly teaches a two-semester course on Shakespeare in which she uses a variety of performance approaches. She has also directed three of Shakespeare's plays for W & J: *Twelfth Night, The Taming of the Shrew,* and *Much Ado about Nothing.* She is currently completing a book to be entitled "Painted Faces on the Renaissance Stage: The Moral Significance of a Convention."

Margo A. Figgins is assistant professor of English education at the University of Virginia's Curry School of Education. She also founded and directs the UVA Writers Workshop, a program that brings together aspiring teenage writers and professional poets, novelists, playwrights, and song and freelance writers. She taught high school English, humanities, and the performing arts for eleven years, both overseas and in the United States. Her work has been published in *Language Arts, Innovative Education, Iris: A Journal About Women,* and *Artemis.*

Michael Flachmann is professor of English at California State University, Bakersfield. He has written six books, the latest of which, *Beware the Cat: The First English Novel* (co-edited with William A. Ringler, Jr.), was published in 1989 by the Huntington Library Press. In addition to his scholarly work, Flachmann has served as dramaturg for over fifty professional Shakespeare productions at such West Coast theaters as the Oregon Shakespearean Festival, the La Jolla Playhouse, and the Utah Festival, where some of the teaching techniques in his article were developed. Flachmann is currently completing a book on teaching Shakespeare in the English classroom.

Roy Flannagan, professor of English at Ohio University, is best known for being long-time editor of *Milton Quarterly.* He has published approximately three hundred reviews, articles, or books, many of them about Milton, but some about such esoteric subjects as country stores or cows, since for many years he owned and operated a farm. At present, he is working on an edition of the *Complete Poetry and Selected Prose of John Milton* for Macmillan; a separate *Paradise Lost* volume came out in 1992. He is also assembling the one hundred megabytes of information necessary to begin filling the memory of a CD-ROM complete reference library for Milton, including all the texts, all the best-respected commentaries and annotations, and all the best-known bibliographies.

Charles H. Frey teaches Shakespeare at the University of Washington in Seattle. He is the author of *Shakespeare's Vast Romance: A Study of* The Winter's Tale and *Experiencing Shakespeare: Essays on Text, Classroom, and Performance,* and he is the editor of *Shakespeare, Fletcher, and* The Two Noble Kinsmen. He has led workshops and summer seminars on the teaching of Shakespeare, and he is currently working on connections of mind/body theory and therapy to the teaching of drama.

Ruth Ann Gerrard, high school English instructor and secondary gifted coordinator in the Austintown Local Schools, Youngstown, Ohio, wrote her master's thesis on Shakespeare's histories and has published several articles on the Bard, including ones in *Ohio English Bulletin* and *Focus.* She has also published numerous other articles on gifted education and literary subjects and has written over forty book reviews. Other special interests include speaking, curriculum design, and teaching, especially on composition and Shakespeare.

Loreen L. Giese is assistant professor of English at Ohio University in Athens. She has an article forthcoming in *The Bodleian Library Record* on a seventeenth-century Anglo-Saxon dictionary manuscript. She is currently at work on a book on social rituals in Shakespeare.

David B. Gleaves is chairperson of the English department at Seneca High School in Louisville, Kentucky. He has taught English for twenty-two years and is a member of the National Council of Teachers of English and the Greater Louisville English Council. He was a presenter at NCTE's Spring Conference in Indianapolis. He is also a recent recipient of a grant from the Student and Teacher Achievement Recognition Program sponsored by the General Electric Foundation.

James Hirsh, associate professor English at Georgia State University, is the author of *The Structure of Shakespearean Scenes* (Yale, 1981) and of articles and reviews in *Modern Language Quarterly, Shakespeare Quarterly, Essays in Theatre,* and elsewhere. He taught at the University of Hawaii for ten years and was the visiting scholar at the Oregon Shakespearean Festival in the summer of 1986. His earlier publications on teaching Shakespeare include an essay in the anthology *Teaching Shakespeare's* King Lear, published by the Modern Language Association, and an article in *Shakespeare Quarterly* on teaching paradoxes.

Joan Ozark Holmer, associate professor of English at Georgetown University in Washington, D.C., teaches first-year through graduate English courses on a variety of subjects, chiefly the short story and the novel, medieval and Renaissance dramatic and nondramatic literature, and Shakespeare. Before pursuing her graduate work, she taught high school and designed a creative dramatics program, which was adopted by the Minneapolis Public School System. She has published articles on William Browne, Robert Herrick, Thomas Nashe, and John Milton, as well as on Shakespeare's *Romeo and Juliet, Othello,* and *The Merchant of Venice.* She is currently writing a book on *The Merchant of Venice* for Macmillan.

Delmar C. Homan, Mountcastle Professor in Humanities and professor of English at Bethany College in Lindsborg, Kansas, has taught Shakespeare for thirty years at Bethany. Earlier experiences included teaching at Iowa State University and in the Red Oak, Iowa, and Farmington, New Mexico, public school systems. He has reviewed regularly for *Choice* magazine since its beginning in 1964. His other scholarly work has ranged from reviews for other magazines and a note in the *Shakespeare Newsletter* to articles on teaching medieval literature and on Kansas theater and Shakespearean festivals.

Larry R. Johannessen, assistant professor of English at Saint Xavier University in Chicago, Illinois, is author of *Illumination Rounds: Teaching the Literature of the Vietnam War* (NCTE, 1992) and co-author of *Writing about Literature* (NCTE, 1984) and *Designing and Sequencing Prewriting Activities* (NCTE, 1982). He taught high school English and sometimes history and social studies for twelve years. In addition to chapters in books, he has contributed several articles to journals of NCTE and its affiliates.

Linda Johnson is chairperson of the English department at Highlands High School in Fort Thomas, Kentucky, where she also advises both the yearbook and newspaper. She was the general co-chair of the 1992 NCTE Convention and has been on the executive committee of Recognize Excellence in Literary Magazines. She is a past president of the Kentucky Council of Teachers of English/Language Arts and of the Publications Advisers of Kentucky. She was also guest editor for an issue of *The Bulletin,* published by KCTE/LA, which focused on literary magazines. She has had articles published in the *English Journal, Quill and Scroll, CSPA Bulletin,* and *C:JET* and edits *School Facts,* a yearly publication of the Fort Thomas School District.

Robert Carl Johnson is professor of English and acting associate provost at Miami University at Oxford, Ohio, where he teaches an undergraduate Shakespeare course and a course in sports literature. A former chair of the department, he has recently completed a three-year term as a member of the board of directors of the College English Association. He is the author or editor of five books and has contributed articles to such journals as *College English, University Review,* and *The Journal of Sports Literature.*

Elizabeth Oakes is assistant professor of English at Western Kentucky University in Bowling Green. She has published on Shakespeare in the *Shakespeare Quarterly* and read papers on Shakespeare and John Webster at the Southeastern Renaissance Conference and the International Patristic, Medieval, and Renaissance Conference. Also interested in performance and pedagogy, she conducts a workshop for high school teachers on Horse Cave Theater's annual Shakespearean production. She has also led a session on *Romeo and Juliet* at a Kentucky Council of Teachers of English meeting.

Daniel J. Pinti is assistant professor of English at New Mexico State University, where he teaches classical, medieval, and Renaissance literature. He has published and presented papers on Old and Middle English poetry and is currently working on an edition of Gavin Douglas's Middle Scots translation of Virgil's *Aeneid,* the *Eneados.*

Hugh M. Richmond is professor of English at the University of California, Berkeley, where he directs the Shakespeare Program. He has produced many live and televised performances of Shakespeare, such as the educational video documentary *Shakespeare and the Globe* (distributed by Films for the Humanities). His books include *Shakespeare's Sexual Comedy, Shakespeare's Political Plays,* and *Shakespeare in Performance:* King Richard III. He received the UC Berkeley award for distinguished teaching and heads the advisory council for the rebuilding of Shakespeare's Globe Theatre in London.

Martha Tuck Rozett is associate professor of English at The State University of New York at Albany. She is the author of *The Doctrine of Election and the Emergence of Elizabethan Tragedy* (Princeton, 1984) and articles on Shakespeare and Renaissance drama that have appeared in *Studies in Philology, Shakespeare Quarterly, Bulletin of Research in the Humanities,* and *Renaissance Drama.* Her current project is a book to be entitled "Talking Back to Shakespeare."

Gregory L. Rubano teaches English at Toll Gate High School in Warwick, Rhode Island. From 1978 to 1985, he was also a methods associate in the Master of Arts in Teaching program at Brown University. He received a B.A. from William and Mary, an M.A.T. from Brown, and is currently completing a Ph.D. in Curriculum and Instruction at the University of Connecticut. In 1986 he was selected as an NEH Fellow for Independent Study in the Humanities, and from 1987 to 1991 he was a member of the Test of Standard Written English Committee for Educational Testing Service.

John S. Simmons is professor of English education and reading at Florida State University. He is currently the chairperson of NCTE's Standing Committee against Censorship. He began his teaching career in 1957 and has been a teacher educator since 1962. He has been program chair of NCTE's Conference on English Education and has served on that group's executive committee. He has also chaired NCTE's International Assembly on the Teaching of English. He is the author or co-author of ten books and over eighty articles. His books include *Decisions about the Teaching of English* (Allyn Bacon, 1976) and *Teaching Literature in Middle and Secondary Grades* (Allyn Bacon, 1991).

Patricia A. Slagle, a member of the Seneca High School English department, has taught high school English for twenty years. Within NCTE she has served as associate chair of the Secondary Section, on the Executive Committee, and on the Strategic Planning Committee. She currently serves on the advisory committee for the Louisville Writing Project and the executive committee of the Kentucky Shakespeare Festival.

Alan Smiley is a graduate of Middlebury College and of the University of Virginia, where he received an M.Ed. in English education from the Curry School of Education. He currently coaches and teaches English at the middle and high school level at Kent Denver School in Englewood, Colorado, where he has used the teaching strategies presented here with great success.

Ken Spurlock, writing supervisor for the Covington Independent Public Schools in Covington, Kentucky, has served as president of the Kentucky Council of Teachers of English/Language Arts. Prior to his current position as supervisor, he taught *Macbeth* for twenty years to high school seniors and AP juniors as a teacher at Holmes High School. He has had articles published in *The Writing Notebook*, NCTE's *Ideas Plus* series, and the *Kentucky English Bulletin*. His special interest is in publishing student writing. As a consultant, he has presented workshops on how to start literary magazines to local, state, and national audiences. Mr. Spurlock supervises nine different magazines in the Covington district—one for each school.

Ronald Strickland is assistant professor of English at Illinois State University. His essays and reviews on topics relating to early modern England, critical pedagogy, and critical theory have appeared in journals such as *ELH (English Literary History)*, *College English*, *Shakespeare Quarterly*, *Novel: A Forum on Fiction*, *Poetics Today*, and *Textual Practice*.

J. L. Styan is the Franklyn Bliss Snyder Professor of English Literature and professor of theater at Northwestern University (Emeritus); before that he was the Andrew Mellon Professor of English at the University of Pittsburgh. He has held an NEH Research Fellowship (1978–79) and a Guggenheim Fellowship (1983–84). He has published some one hundred articles and fifteen books on the theory and practice of drama, the most recent being *Restoration Comedy in Performance* (1986) for Cambridge University Press.

John Wilson Swope is assistant professor of English education at the University of Northern Iowa. Before this position, he spent eleven years teaching middle and high school English, speech, and drama. In addition to being a presenter at regional and state language arts conferences, he appears frequently on NCTE programs. His articles and reviews have appeared in *English Journal*, *Focus*, *The Virginia English Bulletin*, and *The Leaflet*. He has also co-authored, with Edgar H. Thompson, "Three R's to Promote Critical Thinking" in NCTE's *Activities to Promote Critical Thinking*.

Kay E. Twaryonas teaches English and humanities at Seneca High School. A teacher for twenty-three years, she serves on the advisory committee for the Louisville Writing Project. She has presented at NCTE conferences and has participated in the Kentucky Shakespeare Festival's Teachers' Institute.

Gladys V. Veidemanis is past chair of the English department at North High School in Oshkosh, Wisconsin. She has held numerous offices in NCTE; served as director of NCTE's Secondary Section and NCTE's Commission on Literature; published some forty articles and reviews in *English Journal*, *Wisconsin English Journal*, *Media and Methods*, and *College Board Review*; and contributed to five books. Currently, she is serving as a consultant to a volume of Shakespearean literary criticism for high school students to be issued next year by Gale Publishers.

Robert F. Willson, Jr., professor of English at the University of Missouri–
Kansas City, has taught Shakespeare courses to undergraduates and
graduates for twenty-six years. His scholarly books on Shakespeare's
dramatic structure are *Shakespeare's Opening Scenes* (1977) and *Shakespeare's Reflexive Endings* (1990). He has published essays in the
Shakespeare Quarterly, Shakespeare Studies, Shakespeare Jahrbuch (East
and West), the *Shakespeare Bulletin,* and the *Shakespeare on Film
Newsletter.* For several years he edited the "Landmarks of Criticism"
column for the *Shakespeare Newsletter* and published a collection of
those columns, *Landmarks of Shakespeare Criticism,* in 1978. He is also
series editor for *Studies in Shakespeare,* a monograph series published
by Peter Lang Publishers. At the moment, he is working on a study
of Hollywood versions of Shakespearean plays.